A CULTURAL HISTORY OF MONEY

VOLUME 4

A Cultural History of Money
General Editor: Bill Maurer

Volume 1
A Cultural History of Money in Antiquity
Edited by Stefan Krmnicek

Volume 2
A Cultural History of Money in the Medieval Age
Edited by Rory Naismith

Volume 3
A Cultural History of Money in the Renaissance
Edited by Stephen Deng

Volume 4
A Cultural History of Money in the Age of Enlightenment
Edited by Christine Desan

Volume 5
A Cultural History of Money in the Age of Empire
Edited by Federico Neiburg and Nigel Dodd

Volume 6
A Cultural History of Money in the Modern Age
Edited by Taylor C. Nelms and David Pedersen

A CULTURAL HISTORY OF MONEY

IN THE AGE OF ENLIGHTENMENT

Edited by Christine Desan

BLOOMSBURY ACADEMIC
LONDON • NEW YORK • OXFORD • NEW DELHI • SYDNEY

BLOOMSBURY ACADEMIC
Bloomsbury Publishing Plc
50 Bedford Square, London, WC1B 3DP, UK
1385 Broadway, New York, NY 10018, USA
29 Earlsfort Terrace, Dublin 2, Ireland

BLOOMSBURY, BLOOMSBURY ACADEMIC and the Diana logo are trademarks of
Bloomsbury Publishing Plc

First published in Great Britain 2019
Paperback edition published in 2023

Copyright © Bloomsbury Publishing, 2019

Christine Desan has asserted her right under the Copyright, Designs and Patents Act, 1988, to be identified as Author of this work.

For legal purposes the Acknowledgments on p. xvii constitute an extension of this copyright page.

Series design: Raven Design
Cover image: *Midas, Transmuting all into [Gold] Paper*, pub. 1797 (hand-coloured engraving), Gillray, James (1757–1815) (© Private Collection/The Stapleton Collection/Bridgeman Images)

All rights reserved. No part of this publication may be reproduced or transmitted in any form or by any means, electronic or mechanical, including photocopying, recording, or any information storage or retrieval system, without prior permission in writing from the publishers.

Bloomsbury Publishing Plc does not have any control over, or responsibility for, any third-party websites referred to or in this book. All internet addresses given in this book were correct at the time of going to press. The author and publisher regret any inconvenience caused if addresses have changed or sites have ceased to exist, but can accept no responsibility for any such changes.

A catalogue record for this book is available from the British Library.

A catalog record for this book is available from the Library of Congress.

ISBN: PB Set: 978-1-3503-6718-0
HB: 978-1-4742-3707-9
PB: 978-1-3503-6567-4
ePDF: 978-1-3502-5352-0
eBook: 978-1-3502-5351-3

Series: The Cultural Histories Series

Typeset by RefineCatch Limited, Bungay, Suffolk
Printed and bound in Great Britain

To find out more about our authors and books visit www.bloomsbury.com and sign up for our newsletters.

CONTENTS

LIST OF ILLUSTRATIONS	vii
NOTES ON CONTRIBUTORS	xii
SERIES PREFACE	xiv
ACKNOWLEDGMENTS	xvii
Introduction: Strange New Music—The Monetary Composition Made by the Enlightenment Quartet *Christine Desan*	1
1 Money and its Technologies: Industrial Opposition and the Problem of Trust *Mara Caden*	25
2 Money and its Ideas: Enlightenment Debates about the Morality of Money *Carl Wennerlind*	53
3 Money, Ritual, and Religion: A Secularization Story *Dwight Codr*	75
4 Money and the Everyday: New Practices in the Enlightenment *Craig Muldrew*	95
5 Money, Art, and Representation: The Look and Sound of Money *Rebecca L. Spang*	121

6 Money and its Interpretation: Paper Currency in Early America   143
   Jennifer J. Baker

7 Money and the Issues of the Age: Thinking about Money in
   the Eighteenth Century   163
   Daniel Carey

NOTES   187
BIBLIOGRAPHY   203
INDEX   225

LIST OF ILLUSTRATIONS

INTRODUCTION

0.1	One of the first printed public bonds, an Order of Repayment issued by the English government in 1667.	10
0.2	1708 Bank of England bank note. Part-printed note, with date and inscription written by hand, for the amount of £150; showing a first payment of £100 and a final payment of £50. Signed by Joseph Newell. Countersigned by Barth Manning. I/016.	14
0.3	*New Three Per Cent Office, Bank of England*, 1808, London.	15
0.4	*The bubblers bubbl'd, or the devil take the hindmost*. Portrayal of the Stock Exchange by James Cole, 1720.	19
0.5a	Bank note issued by the Berwick Bank.	21
0.5b	Bank note issued by the Durham Bank, with coat of arms at top left.	21
0.6	*Le Diable d'Argent*.	22

CHAPTER ONE

1.1	Screw press, engraving originally printed in Diderot and d'Alembert's *Encylopédie*.	30
1.2	Silver penny, Elizabeth I, clipped and worn.	34

1.3	Mathew Boulton's Coining Press, printed in Challis.	44
1.4	Cartwheel penny, produced by steam-powered coining press at the Soho mint, 1797.	45
1.5	Pennsylvania paper 20s note, 1739, printed by Benjamin Franklin.	49

CHAPTER TWO

2.1	*Thomas Hobbes* by John Michael Wright.	56
2.2	*John Locke* by Michael Dahl, oil on canvas, *c.* 1693.	61
2.3	*Charles de Secondat, baron de Montesquieu (1689–1755)*.	63
2.4	*David Hume* by Allan Ramsay.	65
2.5	*Jean-Jacques Rousseau* by Allan Ramsay.	72

CHAPTER THREE

3.1	*St. Christopher's Church, The Bank of England, & St. Bartholomew's Church*, etching (1770). South front of the bank, with one additional wing to the right; Illustration to Chamberlain's *New and Compleat History and Survey of the Cities of London and Westminster*.	81
3.2	1864 US two-cent piece. The first coin to display "In God We Trust" was the 1862 two-cent piece.	84
3.3	Frontispiece ("Dutch Weight") to *A History of New York, From the Beginning of the World to the End of the Dutch Dynasty* by Diedrich Knickerbocker [Washington Irving].	87

CHAPTER FOUR

4.1	Total number of theft offences of all kinds in the Old Bailey Proceedings (1678–1820).	109
4.2	Total mentions of different types of currency in trial reports from the Old Bailey Criminal Court (1680–1820).	117
4.3	Number of mentions of shillings (est.), guineas, and paper notes (1680–1820).	118
4.4	Percentage of cases mentioning shillings (est.), guineas, and paper notes (1680–1820).	118

LIST OF ILLUSTRATIONS

4.5 Percentage of cases mentioning shillings (est.), guineas, and paper notes (1680–1820). 120

CHAPTER FIVE

5.1 Jean-Antoine Watteau, *L'Enseigne de Gersaint* (1721), oil on canvas. Watteau's *L'Enseigne de Gersaint* shows an enticing assortment of luxury goods but depicts no money: aristocratic consumers almost always bought on credit. 123

5.2 William Hogarth, "The Rake Taking Possession of his Estate," scene one of *The Rake's Progress* (1734), engraving. As his inherited wealth is chiseled from the wall behind him, Hogarth's "Rake" tries to buy off his one-time affianced with a handful of coins. 124

5.3 Anne-Louis Girodet de Roussy-Trioson, *Portrait of Mlle. Lange as Danae* (1799), oil on canvas. Portraying an actress as the mythological Danaë, Girodet implied she could be easily seduced with money. 126

5.4 "Valeur des assignats" (c. 1796–7), engraving. French Revolution era paper moneys lost value with the collapse of political legitimacy; *trompe l'oeil* prints like this one suggested the bills had never had substance. 128

5.5 Jacques-Louis David, *La Mort de Marat* (1793), oil on canvas. The *assignat* on Marat's bath-side table signifies both his faith in the Revolution and his generosity. 129

5.6a Louis XV écu (1765), obverse. Louis XV, "By the grace of God, King of France and Navarre." 132

5.6b Louis XV écu (1765), reverse. "Blessed be the Name of God." 132

5.7 Maria Theresa thaler (1780). Minted for more than 150 years after her death, the Maria Theresa thaler may have been the first global currency. 134

5.8 Spanish imperial dollar, or "piece of eight" (1739). The pillars wrapped in banners are said to be the origin of the dollar sign ($). 135

5.9 Bank of England banknote (1725). Though partially printed, early banknotes belonged visually to the manuscript culture of bills of exchange. 137

5.10 John Smith, *The Prince of Wales* (George II) (1716), mezzotint. When the Royal Bank of Scotland reproduced this portrait of

George II on its notes, it implied that they derived their value
from his sovereign authority. 138

5.11 John Singleton Copley, *John Hancock* (1765), oil on canvas.
Copley's painting depicts a man with nothing to distract him
from his ledgers. 139

5.12 Delaware note for 2s. 6d. (January 1776), obverse, ink on paper.
"This indented bill . . . " 141

5.13 Pennsylvania note for 15s. (April 1759), reverse, ink on paper.
Benjamin Franklin's ingenious anti-counterfeiting technique
involved imprinting paper money with actual leaves. 142

CHAPTER SIX

6.1 A two-pound bill, issued by New York on February 16, 1771,
bears images of transatlantic trade. 147

6.2 A one-dollar bill, issued in 1775 by New York, bears the
image of a bundle of wheat and the words *E PARVIS GRANDIS
ACERVUS* (A Massive Stack from Small Things). 149

6.3 A Massachusetts four-shilling "Sword in Hand" bill, issued
on December 7, 1775, bears the image of a soldier and the words
"Issued in defence of American Liberty." 150

6.4 A South Carolina thirty-dollar bill, issued on February 14,
1777, bears the words *SERVITUS OMNIS MISERA* (All Forms
of Slavery Are Wretched). 151

6.5 A South Carolina twenty-dollar bill, issued on February 14,
1777, bears the image of a bird escaping from a cage and
the words *UBI LIBERTAS IBI PATRIA* (Where There is Liberty,
There is Homeland). 151

6.6 A six-dollar Continental bill, issued on November 29,
1775, bears the image of a beaver and the word
PERSEVERANDO (By Perseverance). 158

6.7 A two-dollar Continental bill, issued on May 20, 1777,
bears the image of a hand threshing wheat and the words
TRIBULATIO DITAT (Tribulation Improves). 158

6.8 A one-third-dollar Continental bill, issued in 1776, bears
the image of thirteen interlocking rings—each representing
a colony—and the words *WE ARE ONE*. 159

CHAPTER SEVEN

7.1 and 7.2	William III crown, 1696, obverse and reverse.	168
7.3	Examples of William Wood's halfpence and farthings.	171
7.4 and 7.5	George I South Sea Company shilling of 1723, obverse and reverse.	175
7.6	Portrait of Sir James Steuart by Wolfgang Dietrich Mayer (1761).	179
7.7	Engraved portrait of Adam Smith by Robert Graves.	181
7.8	Title page, Henry Thornton, *An Enquiry into the Nature and Effects of the Paper Credit of Great Britain* (1802).	184

NOTES ON CONTRIBUTORS

Jennifer J. Baker is an Associate Professor of English at New York University. She specializes in American literature, culture, and intellectual history, with particular interest in eighteenth- and nineteenth-century writing. Her first book, *Securing the Commonwealth: Debt, Speculation, and Writing in the Making of Early America* (Johns Hopkins University Press, 2005), examined the impact of financial developments, particularly the advent of public debt and paper money, on eighteenth-century American writing. She is currently at work on a study of American Romanticism and the nineteenth-century life sciences.

Mara Caden is an NEH Long-Term Fellow at the Massachusetts Historical Society. She completed her PhD in History at Yale University in 2017 and has held fellowships at the University of Richmond, the Library Company of Philadelphia Program on Early American Economy and Society, and the Huntington Library. Her book manuscript, *Mint Conditions*, is a study of money, manufacturing, and political economy in the early modern British Atlantic world and early America.

Daniel Carey is Director of the Moore Institute for Research in the Humanities and Social Studies at the National University of Ireland, Galway. His publications include the monograph *Locke, Shaftesbury, and Hutcheson: Contesting Diversity in the Enlightenment and Beyond* (Cambridge University Press, 2006), and edited volumes on *Money and Political Economy in the Enlightenment* (Voltaire Foundation, 2014), and *The Empire of Credit: The Financial Revolution in the British Atlantic World, 1688–1815* (Irish Academic Press, 2011). He has published widely on literature, the history of philosophy, history of science, anthropology, and travel in the sixteenth, seventeenth, and eighteenth centuries. He was elected to the Royal Irish Academy in 2014 and serves on the board of the Irish Research Council.

Dwight Codr is Associate Professor of English at the University of Connecticut. He has two primary areas of research. The first is the cultural history of money in the British eighteenth century; the second is the history of disability, with a particular emphasis on disabilities of speech, in the same period. He is the author of *Raving at Usurers: Anti-Finance and the Ethics of Uncertainty in England, 1690–1750* (University of Virginia Press, 2016), which maps literary, theoretical, and historical connections between a Christian ethic of risk and the financial revolution.

Christine Desan, the Leo Gottlieb Professor of Law at Harvard Law School, approaches money as a mode of governing. She argues in *Making Money: Coin, Currency, and the Coming of Capitalism* (Oxford University Press, 2014) that a radical transformation in the way societies produce money ushered in capitalism as a public project. She is co-founder of Harvard's Program on the Study of Capitalism, and teaches about the international monetary system, the constitutional law of money, constitutional history, political economy, and legal theory.

Craig Muldrew is Professor of Social and Economic History and a member of Queens' College, University of Cambridge. His research focuses on two areas. The first is the investigation of the economic and social role of trust in the development of the market economy in England between 1500 and 1700. The second is the living standards and work of agricultural laborers in the early modern English economy. He is the author of *The Economy of Obligation: The Culture of Credit and Social Relations in Early Modern England* (Macmillan, 1998) and *Food, Energy and the Industrious Revolution: Work and Material Culture in Agrarian England, 1550–1780* (Cambridge University Press, 2011).

Rebecca L. Spang is Professor of History at Indiana University, where she also directs the Liberal Arts and Management Program. Her *Stuff and Money in the Time of the French Revolution* (Harvard University Press, 2015) was a *Financial Times* "Book of the Year" and multiple prize winner.

Carl Wennerlind is Professor of History at Barnard College, Columbia University. His work focuses on the history of political economy and the history of monetary thought, and he writes and teaches about the history of capitalism. Professor Wennerlind is author of *Casualties of Credit: The English Financial Revolution, 1620–1720* (Harvard University Press, 2011) and co-author of a forthcoming (Chicago 2019) book on Hume's worldly philosophy; he is also co-editor of *David Hume's Political Economy* (Routledge, 2009) and *Mercantilism Reimagined* (Oxford University Press, 2013).

SERIES PREFACE

When the British Museum decided in 2012 to redesign Room 68, the hall containing objects from its Department of Coins and Medals, its curators made a bold departure from how numismatic material had conventionally been displayed. Rather than cases filled with rows upon rows of gold, silver, and bronze coins of European antiquity, the new gallery design featured all manner of objects, not limited to coin or paper currency, capturing the history of transactional artifacts and infrastructures from shells to mobile phones. Each case had a theme: cases on one side of the gallery spotlighted money's institutional supports and issuing authorities, while cases on the other underscored all the myriad ways people use money, not just for exchange or payment but for ritual or religious observance, political contestation, adornment, and storytelling.

The intention in preparing these six volumes was to provide readers with a similar experience, inviting them into the wonder-cabinets of money in all its variegation, multiplicity, and complexity. What emerges is money's irreducible plurality, the multiple stories it tells. Money opens windows into plural economic and moral worlds, too, worlds of value and evaluation, wealth and worth. Never merely coin, cash, or credit rendered in strictly economic terms, money is so much more than the old couplet would have it: "Money is a matter of functions four: a medium, a measure, a standard, a store." Instead, money is always also a medium of communication, a set of instruments with which people exchange messages with one another—about price, to be sure, but also about political conviction and authority, fealty, desire, or disdain. And money is a method of memorializing the past so that relations established among people, institutions, the gods, and the ancestors can be carried forward through the present and into near, distant, and imaginary futures.

Money is in this sense both irredeemably "cultural" and "historical," and so it is apt that this six-volume *A Cultural History of Money* should spotlight money's relation to religion, technology, the arts and literature, everyday life, metaphysical interpretation, and a wide variety of issues of the age. While many contributors to the first several volumes are numismatists and archaeologists, trucking in the material evidence of coin and bullion, the volumes also contain contributions from scholars of digital infrastructures, literary and legal historians and science fiction scholars, sociologists and anthropologists, economists and artists.

Archaeologists have long bemoaned the fact that the great majority of ancient coins in museums and private collections today were unearthed without any data having been collected on their surrounding context, rendering much of the ancient and even more recent past a mystery. Even where the context for a particular find is present, its interpretation is always ambiguous. In the contemporary period, money is surrounded by context—cables and wireless signals, data protocols and computer servers, lobbying groups' and legislators' voluminous writings, television soap operas and online social media. Yet just as with ancient hoards, we have difficulty escaping our own assumptions about what money is, what people do with it, and the style with which they do so.

Take a basic plastic credit card transaction at a physical till. How many users of this everyday payment device would be able to explain how it works? How would a museum curate this technological assemblage? Moving from the simple act of paying to more involved interactions with money, how might an archaeologist of the future deduce, for example, the practice in some central Asian Muslim immigrant communities known as the "Imam Zamin," which consists of the wrapping of a coin in a piece of cloth tied about the upper arm to protect a traveler? Or the practice from around 2005–9 of what people called "doing tuning" (튜닝하다) to a transit card in Seoul, Korea—dissolving the plastic payment card with acetone so as to remove the radio-frequency identification (RFID) antenna and chip, and creatively stitching it into one's pocketbook, bracelet, or the elbow patches of one's blazer, so you can breeze through the turnstile, with style?

Trapped in our own "coin consciousness," we assume money has to be, or that its value should be found in, a tangible thing, despite the fact that our own interactions with it are increasingly dematerialized in digital networks. We hold on to bullionist conceptions of money's worth, despite our bearing continual witness to its fluctuations based on prevailing political whims. We think of money as abstract, even as we use it in the most concrete and interpersonal relations. We believe money equilibrates values, rendering goods and services commensurable with one another measured on one scale of value, even as we use money to demarcate difference—national difference, religious difference, intergenerational difference, differences in class, race, and gender.

The periodization of these volumes is somewhat arbitrary but still Eurocentric. The selection of authors and themes is intended to help disturb this Western-oriented history by globalizing it and insisting on bringing into the frame its political, imperial, and often racial dynamics.

The chapters in these volumes capture money's complexities in both substance and form. In substance, insofar as they attempt a cross-cultural, transhistorical survey of money technologies and cultures that will illuminate its variability and complexity. In form, in that each volume takes up the same thematic areas, but in reading across the volumes one will discover that these themes are themselves complicated by having different eras' understandings of said theme juxtaposed with other eras' often incompatible understandings. Like a ledger book, then—one of the most basic manifestations of money's record-keeping devices—the volume can be read "down," reading the chapters within one historical period, and "across," reading the affiliated thematic chapters from volume to volume. What emerges is an affirmation that money itself is a cultural history.

Bill Maurer
University of California, Irvine

ACKNOWLEDGMENTS

This work owes much to our colleagues and students, individuals who teach us every day about the Enlightenment, money, and the way those subjects come together. We would also like to thank Bill Maurer, an astute and wise editor. We appreciated Farah Qureshi's help on illustrations, and are particularly grateful for assistance from Ellie Paton (Bank of England Museum), Kristen McDonald (Lewis Walpole Library, Yale University), Melissa Murphy (Baker Library, Harvard Business School), Sara B. Weber (Hesburgh Libraries, University of Notre Dame), and Lisa Olrichs (National Portrait Gallery). The team at Bloomsbury Press was extraordinary throughout, especially Geraldine Billingham, Kakul Butt, Lara Covill, and Ronnie Hanna. At Harvard Law School, Susan Smith coordinated all aspects of the project with unparalleled grace, intelligence, and, happily for all of us, patience.

Introduction

*Strange New Music—The Monetary Composition
Made by the Enlightenment Quartet*

CHRISTINE DESAN

At the very start of the eighteenth century, the Bank of England asked the government to extend its young charter. It seemed a simple request—except to those who understood that the Bank represented a novel experiment in making money. If Parliament prolonged the Bank's operation, it would expand that experiment in ways no one could quite anticipate. The debate that followed was rather like the history that unfolded: it put money at the heart of a profound project to reorchestrate exchange, holding the very character of public authority and private agency in the balance.

Innovation in England was illustrative of a wider shift. Across Europe and the Americas, the Enlightenment brought intellectual and institutional tumult over that most basic attribute of the political economy—its medium. By the time the age was over, money operated according to a new design. It enabled a set of financial practices that were unprecedented: modern money worked synergistically with circulating public debt, capital markets, and commercial banking. Together, that quartet of innovations transformed the political economies of the West. They would later spread across the globe.

* * *

The small contest over the Bank's extension, represented here by a pair of dueling pamphlets, suggests the themes of change. That microcosm captures the way protagonists embraced conceptual change, made real their monetary experiments, and understood the profound stakes of the argument.

Partners in the debate began from common ground. They agreed that England ran on credit. "[B]y credit alone we subsist," wrote John Broughton as he prepared to attack the Bank, "without it [we] should make as mean a figure in the world, as our country does in the map of it." Both the government and individuals were credit-hungry. The government often had to respond quickly to meet a sudden demand; it needed loans while it waited for its taxes to bring in revenue. Likewise, England's traders moved "three parts in four" on the basis of credit rather than specie.[1] Broughton's opponents could not agree more; the Bank was indispensable to both government and people in private business (e.g., "A Vindication" 1707: 7–8, 20–1).

But if everyone considered credit essential, they also understood that it was not adequate. The government could empty the accounts of lenders, but that would starve traders of money. Or the government could buy all goods on the promise of future payment, but that would drive up costs for the public (Broughton 1705: 5–6). Individuals were in the same predicament; credit came at too high a cost. What England needed was a way to make the abstraction of credit into an instrument of everyday use. It needed money.

Broughton advocated the public option. In his view, the answer lay in the government's ability to make currency out of its own credit. He proposed the method in a parable. Imagine, he suggested, the owner of a "large estate, consisting of the most secure and valuable rents, with a great number of tenants." The landlord broke even most of the time, using the rent revenues to cover his operating expenses. But at one point, an exigency occurred—perhaps a dam broke on the property or a well needed repair. The landlord could rebuild the waterworks with materials on the estate if he could purchase "considerable supplies of stores" from his tenants—sand, for example, or bricks and labor. But he ran into a money shortfall: the estate was self-sufficient and the landlord was solvent, but he was not "before-hand in cash." If he borrowed from some tenants to pay the others, he would have to pay a high rate because money was so scarce on the estate (Broughton 1705: 7).

At last the landlord "lit upon" an ingenious idea. He would use his own paper promises-to-pay for the supplies—IOUs denominated in money amounts. At the same time, he would commit to take the IOUs back in satisfaction of rent due. The strategy would create a supply of circulating credit when the landlord issued the IOUs—and demand for the IOUs when he took them back for value. For good measure, the landlord even agreed to redeem his IOUs for money at the request of holders (Broughton 1705: 7).

Lo and behold, the solution worked. People sold supplies to the landlord for IOUs and "soon understood how secure and how convenient these bills were." They did "all the business of money with everyone and with much greater dispatch." The influx of cash-like credit eased the scarcity of money within the estate and did so in a light, easily transferable instrument. In fact, very few people ever asked to change their IOUs for money—and why should they, when the landlord's IOUs worked just as well and were far more convenient? Broughton closed his pamphlet with this moral:

> And thus this wise Governour (for so I will venture to call him) by a dexterous management of his own good credit, bought as cheap, and was as well supply'd in all respects as he could have been by so much ready money; and thereby kept his estate clear; at the same time promoting trade, and causing plenty among his tenants.
>
> —Broughton 1705: 8

Broughton's parable may have promised harmony, but it met with fierce resistance in the real world. Proponents of the Bank countered with the private option they had refined over the last decade. The Bank of England began life as a lender to the English government; it made a £1.2 million loan in 1694. But then as well as later, the parties to the deal recognized that the English needed more than an advance of the existing money stock—they needed to expand that supply of money. So the Bank lent in the form of its own *promises-to-pay*: it gave Bank of England notes to the government, which the government spent and, eventually, accepted back in taxes and other payments.[2] To the extent that people took the notes and used them without demanding coin at the Bank, Bank notes could operate as "a credit equal to money . . . ready money" ("A Vindication" 1707: 15; see also 22). Analogous to the public option, the arrangement created a supply of credit notes—and demand for them when the government accepted them back for value.

The Bank's success in circulating its notes on "a par with money" during its first decade struck some as unfair. It followed from privilege, opponents pointed out. The Bank, unlike other lenders, extended "their credit," that is, issued Bank notes, "upon so good a foundation as the security of an Act of Parliament" ("A Vindication" 1707: 15, 13). In other words, the Bank had an unparalleled advantage: the nation itself provided the fund that was pledged to pay the Bank. The Bank could not fail, then, "but with the nation" (Paterson 1694: 12).

In response to the charge of privilege, the Bank's defenders emphasized as its distinctive advantage the business acumen of those running it. "Parliament have not power to extend their own credit farther than the opinion which the people will entertain of the security which they give . . . much less can they give this power of extending credit to others." The Bank had *earned* its "extended credit"—its ability to circulate its notes. That capacity was, a defender wrote, "the natural result of its own indubitable fund in the hands of the government, its large and well-employ'd stock, its just and punctual dealing, and its prudent and thriving managements," not "the power given them by the Parliament to borrow money." Proponents of the Bank underscored how carefully it managed its specie reserve, using it "tenderly, and with great discretion" ("A Vindication" 1707: 13–15, 17).

With great deliberation, the Bank's defenders here returned to the public. They acknowledged that "extending credit" by way of Bank notes was "one of the principal branches of the Bankers' profit." But it was the Bank's method of expanding the effective stock of money that "'tis the very thing that enabled them to work so cheap." Making "a lesser sum of money circulate a larger sum of credit" allowed the Bank to "do so much good to the public." "For every penny they get" at the Bank, pronounced a pamphleteer, "the public gets a pound" in credit made less costly. The Bank was, then, "an assistant so helpful to the Government, and so useful in trade" ("A Vindication" 1707: 20–1, 6–7).

* * *

The debate touched off by the Bank of England evokes the larger Enlightenment drama over exchange and how to enable it. The debate showcases, first, a novel orientation toward theorizing money, one that was startling in its inventiveness. Second, contemporaries in the period moved beyond theorizing to transform money's design—the Bank of England was the fulcrum of a real, indeed revolutionary, redesign of financial institutions. Third, the debate had an existential quality: it threw deeply held values, like the role of the state, into question and it raised novel ideas, notably the utility of the profit motive, to prominence. A closer look at these themes follows. They inform a short tour of four new financial practices that, together, transformed the modern political economy. Much more happened in the history: the essays collected here populate the drama with other actors, events, and interpretations. The volume as a whole aims to make the case that we must understand Money in the Enlightenment in order to understand the modern world.

THE THEMES OF THE ENLIGHTENMENT COMPOSITION

Long before the Enlightenment, money was an object of political debate, even obsession. Across Europe in the medieval world, authority over money was sovereign power, closely held. Both civilian and common law officials agreed that the right to mint "inheres in the bones of princes," while political elites negotiated their power relative to monarchical control over the mint.[3] Those engineering commodity money worked out its dynamics over centuries, with a sophistication that often eluded their successors. Commodity money demanded constant attention because it was ever a fragile medium, susceptible to recurring destabilization as it lost commodity content and to erratic shifts as bullion supplies to the mint ebbed and flowed.[4]

By the seventeenth century, money had become the focus of early mercantilists in England. Again, their approach was more astute than later commentators granted. Balance of trade theorists argued that England had to maximize its acquisition of metal from the sale of exports while minimizing the loss of coin due to the purchase of imports. The goal was to secure a flow of metal to domestic mints. Later scholars would charge mercantilists with the naive belief that a commodity like silver or gold, rather than productivity, represented wealth. In fact, the early theorists were struggling to save the commodity money system. If they could bring the raw material of money to the mints, they could nourish the local economy with a medium of exchange. Money was "the vital spirit of trade, and if the spirits faile, needs must the body faint," wrote Edward Misselden about the kingdom of England.[5]

At some point in the seventeenth century, the tenor of monetary discussions changed. For all their attention and erudition, medieval and mercantilist thinkers had labored within the traditional bounds of the monetary system they inherited. In a departure resonant with Enlightenment optimism, political commentators after mid-century began to retheorize money and its role. Most conspicuously, they argued that polities could re-engineer money, producing alternatives to coin that would better support the economic development of their communities. Thus John Broughton's parable, sparkling with simplicity of design and hopefulness of purpose. With only a pact among themselves, participants could construct their own money-like instruments; that medium would keep "the estate clear, promot[e] trade, and caus[e] plenty amongst [the] tenants." Likewise the Bank of England's notes or "extended credit." Engineered this time by a partnership between public and private, it could effectively expand the money supply. A "pound" for every "penny" would benefit public and private alike. The Enlightenment approach to money begins, then, with a striking turn toward theorizing money as an institution that could be designed and redesigned.

The new orientation sprang from several sources. At the broadest level, it followed from the gathering argument in political philosophy that the social order had contractual roots. According to this view, human beings had the ability, indeed the responsibility, to shape their surroundings. Rather than assume a divine ordering or await providential intervention, they should act to support productive enterprise, alleviate poverty, or improve the political order. Another set of reformers, the scholars and natural philosophers associated with Samuel Hartlib, asserted that progress toward the inherent development of humankind was possible "through the continuous pursuit of knowledge, innovation, and industry." They attended particularly to money's capacity to enable productive exchange, arguing that it could unlock resources otherwise unattainable. Alchemy offered one way to expand the money supply, an effort they undertook with Baconian commitment to scientific technique. When that failed, they turned their experimental efforts toward reconfiguring credit into a monetary form.[6]

The efforts of social reformers converged with the initiatives of political officials desperate to improvise financial expedients in the recurring fiscal crises of the late seventeenth century. Tasked with collecting funds in an era of rising military costs, political authorities recognized the limited and fragile money stock as a central problem. In response, they explored a wide repertoire of ideas, including everything from home-grown devices like tallies (a public credit instrument that had circulated with money-like qualities since the fourteenth century in England) to foreign innovations pioneered by the Dutch and others. In the last decade of the century, Whig political leaders promoted the active sensibility that enterprise in manufacturing, commerce, and labor practices could break England out of old scarcities. With an adequate medium, trade could become a source of mutual benefit rather than a zero-sum struggle for resources. Political strategists matched social reformers, then, as they brainstormed new ways to construct money as a tool for human productivity.[7]

The dueling pamphlets of the early eighteenth century illuminate a second quality characteristic of the Enlightenment approach to money. The debate they represent went beyond mere theorizing; the government actively engaged in testing out design alternatives. Broughton's parable sketched the logic of an expedient actually adopted by Parliament in 1696. Exchequer bills were IOUs issued by the government in relatively small denominations. Swap Broughton's "landlord" for the English sovereign, and you had the plan: the government spent its IOUs as needed, inhabitants of England (the "estate") could use them to pay their taxes and other fees ("rents") or could redeem them.[8] As for the private option—the proposal by the Bank of England that the government use its notes as cash—that was a strategy accepted and put into effect by the government in 1694. From that year on, the Bank negotiated ceaselessly with its government patron to extend the bills' circulation by improving the way they operated.[9]

The radical experimentalism of the English government reached beyond money to construct a new array of institutions. In fact, Enlightenment actors redesigned money in concert with complementary institutions that were themselves novel. The enterprise was improvisational and erratic, experimental at best and punctuated with unintended consequences. But by the end of the eighteenth century, a quartet of institutions operated together, compounding the effects of each innovation.

We have already met the *modern money* that would become central to the new order. The Bank of England did indeed obtain its charter, which was successively renewed in the centuries that followed. Its notes become central bank money, called "high-powered money" in the next centuries.[10] The Bank's notes depended on *public debt*, an instrument remade in the Enlightenment era and itself fueled by the expanding money stock the Bank made possible. Modern (high-powered) money and public debt together created and stabilized new *capital markets* in securities, both public and private. Finally, *commercial banks* organized on a modern model took off in the late eighteenth century, amplifying the high-powered money supply to an unprecedented extent. In short, institutional experimentation accompanied the intellectual ferment of the Enlightenment—attempts and ideas about new designs fed each other.

The contest over the Bank's charter illustrates a last feature that typifies the Enlightenment foray into monetary innovation. That process was enormously contentious. The way a society created money, issued public debt, circulated capital, and amplified credit—those practices implicated essential values. As they debated what to do, participants asserted particular claims about human agency and motivation. Each initiative controverted traditional understandings, troubled many participants, and confused those unable to anticipate how change would proceed, even as it excited others to extend the innovations further.

The debate over the Bank's charter reflected the depth of divergence. Most obviously, proponents of a public option maintained that creating money should remain a sovereign prerogative. In Broughton's world, the sovereign/landlord was an actor both responsible and insightful. Public authority properly coordinated the contributions of a community. That coordinating activity promoted individual wellbeing within the estate.

The Bank's defenders advocated instead a system that put public commitment in the shape of incoming revenues behind a private investment, the Bank's promises-to-pay. In this alternative order, individual enterprise and commercial expertise furnished economic initiative and, indeed, leadership. The Bank succeeded in creating a medium because its directors used business judgment—astute management, constant and judicious diligence—in circulating and supporting its promises-to-pay. As they acted to raise profits for themselves, the Bank's investors benefited the larger community, supplying the enlarged money stock that England needed.

The difference amounted to a clash in approaches to governance. When the British chose to delegate money-making to a group of investors—the Bank of England rather than Broughton's "governour"—they commissioned bankers to manage a process long considered public and political. In a variety of ways, the monetary instruments engineered during the Enlightenment embedded entrepreneurial self-interest as the organizing principle of the economy. Given the power and disruptive impact of that principle, the essay tracks that theme in particular. But the debate over self-interest was one controversy among many. Monetary innovation threw many profound values into doubt, from conceptions of value to theories of sovereignty to the place of risk, calculation, and probability. The contention sampled here is merely suggestive of the general tumult.

The next pages take the themes of change to the four practices that revolutionized money. The Enlightenment was a time of wildly creative theorizing about money, radical institutional innovation, and controversy over a quartet of practices that came to comprise the modern political economy.

FINANCIAL INNOVATION CONSIDERED AS A QUARTET

Public Debt

As the contest over the Bank revealed, turning public borrowing into currency was the breakthrough that sent European polities on a new monetary course in the late seventeenth century. In fact, the public debt as a practice was the place where seismic shifts to the existing order started. They began quietly enough with experimentation across Europe. The Dutch issued interest-bearing annuities in the sixteenth century, the French soon after offered another annuity-based option called "tontines," and the English attached interest to an instrument they had long used to anticipate taxes, wooden Exchequer tallies (Murphy 2009: 46–9; Weir 1989; Desan 2014a: 240–3).[11] Innovation accelerated after the English Restoration when George Downing, an erstwhile soldier of Oliver Cromwell, sometime minister, and up-and-coming advisor to Charles II, offered a new scheme to expand the Crown's borrowing. A colleague called Downing a "perfidious rogue," perhaps for his chameleon-like ability to travel between political factions, but there is little doubt that Downing had an astute understanding of the financial landscape of the day. Born in Dublin but raised in Massachusetts, he apparently convinced the king that although he had "sucked in" republican notions in America, he had since been set straight. More to the point, Downing offered Charles II an idea to relieve the fiscal pressures that mounted in the 1660s.[12]

The proposal exemplified the Enlightenment originality and optimism recommended by the philosophers and social reformers. The Crown had long borrowed from a limited circle of lenders, including customs farmers and large financiers. Downing suggested breaking out of those constraints. If the king could persuade a broad group of investors to lend to him, he would enlarge the funds available and lower interest rates. In effect, Downing advocated popularizing public debt: he would create a form that was more flexible for the state than alternatives like annuities or tontines and safer and more transparent for individuals.[13]

The institutional design, to become commonplace in the modern era, was path-breaking in its era. The Crown would offer interest-bearing public bonds that were backed by a specific revenue stream. That meant that there were funds earmarked in advance for making good the obligation. The bonds would be numbered, registered, and paid off "in course." That meant that the order of repayment was fixed and publicly accountable, not discretionary as was virtually all previous sovereign borrowing. Finally, the bonds could be transferred easily by endorsement, another innovation. Lenders were more likely to opt in if they could easily opt out by retrieving their cash by selling their bonds (see Figure 0.1 (1667).[14]

A pamphlet that Downing published to pitch the initiative fairly brimmed with confidence. The new system, wrote Downing, would be "better both for the lenders and for the King." Lenders would earn money from a safe and liquid investment; the king could raise money quickly, at low cost, and without limit by the existing revenue. Downing next posted the "in course" schedule of payments in the *London Gazette*, broadcasting the opportunity and the government's new orientation toward investors ("A State of the Case" 1666: 1; Roseveare 1973: 125–6). They were acting for "the public service" and "the public safety," the Crown confirmed in another pamphlet. It was a system of mutual benefit (Charles II 1667).

Maybe so, but the invitation that Downing extended contravened traditional understandings on one issue after another. His bond scheme implied a wider engagement between the Crown and the lay public, and a striking transparency of administration. It suggested a greater respect for financial (as opposed to landed) wealth and a new stature for the subject. But most obviously, Downing's public bonds endorsed profit-driven behavior in moneylending, identifying it as a patriotic act. Earlier European initiatives had enlisted self-interest as an incentive in schemes dressed as insurance or lottery-like systems, often at the provincial level. The English system presented the idea cleanly and on a national scale.[15]

The ascendance of self-interest from a matter of grave theological concern in the medieval era to a beneficent motivator in the early modern period drew from many developments. The Reformation arguably elevated reference to individual experience insofar as it legitimated personal experience of the divine. As Protestant sects struggled to sanctify productive activity as a godly use of time, some reconceptualized material incentives as proper within their place. At a political level, theorists from Machiavelli to Grotius had articulated the "interest" of states in defending their boundaries, civil order, and trade. As Albert Hirschman argued, the idea of interest would migrate from the political sphere into the more personal realm as a passion that could counteract other destructive impulses. Developments in England focused the query through the tragic lens of civil war. In the mid-seventeenth century, competitors for political legitimacy strived to articulate the "interest of England" and the way that concept respected the individuated claims of a mobilized people.[16]

In those circumstances, an institutional design that integrated the interest of the nation with the private interests of its citizens was a critical innovation. It made conceivable, indeed it made manifest, the possibility that individuals' pursuit of their own wellbeing might further the public good. Pamphleteers

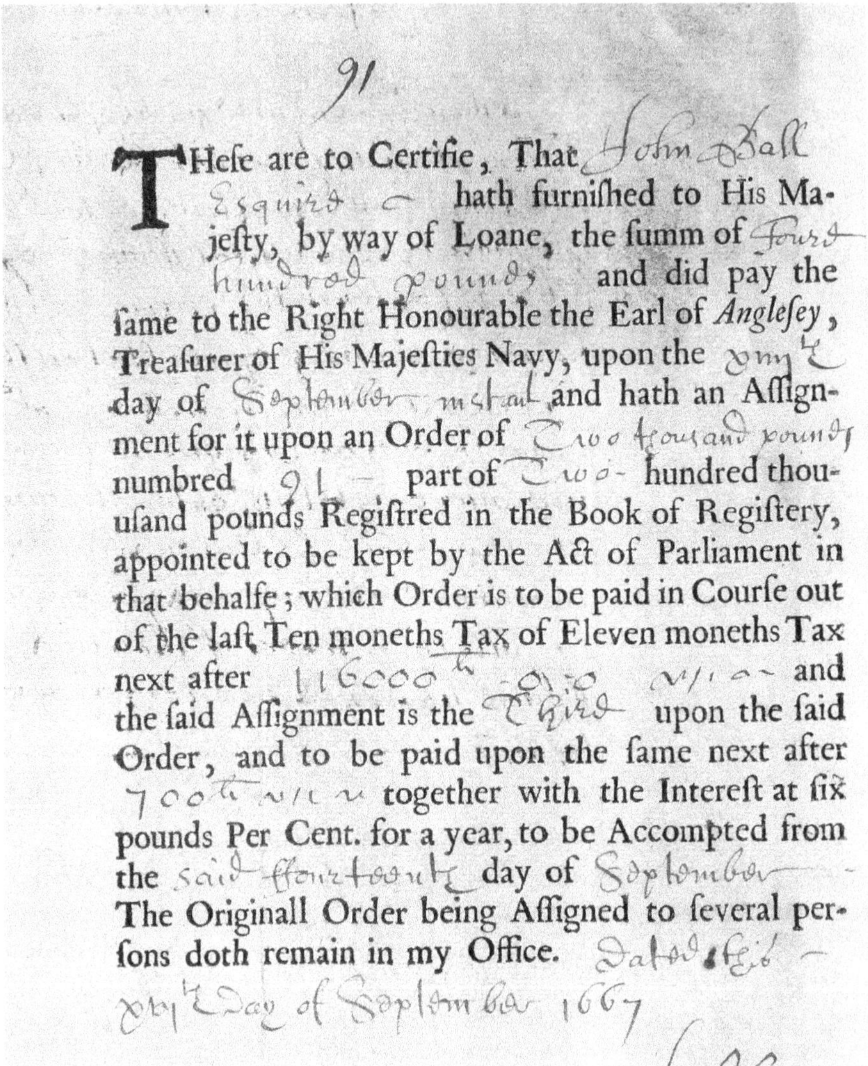

91

THeſe are to Certifie, That John Ball Esquire hath furniſhed to His Majeſty, by way of Loane, the ſumm of Foure hundred pounds and did pay the ſame to the Right Honourable the Earl of *Angleſey*, Treaſurer of His Majeſties Navy, upon the xiiiith day of September instant and hath an Aſſignment for it upon an Order of Two thousand pounds numbred 91 part of Two hundred thouſand pounds Regiſtred in the Book of Regiſtery, appointed to be kept by the Act of Parliament in that behalfe; which Order is to be paid in Courſe out of the laſt Ten moneths Tax of Eleven moneths Tax next after 116000li -0-0 and the ſaid Aſſignment is the Third upon the ſaid Order, and to be paid upon the ſame next after 700li together with the Intereſt at ſix pounds Per Cent. for a year, to be Accompted from the said ffourteenth day of September The Originall Order being Aſſigned to ſeveral perſons doth remain in my Office. Dated the xiiiith Day of September 1667

Rob Long

FIGURE 0.1: One of the first printed public bonds, an Order of Repayment issued by the English government in 1667. The National Archives, Kew—P.R.O. E407/119.

proposing similar schemes publicized the notion. "This unites the King, and people, by the strongest bonds; I mean, *their interest*, to support each other," argued one. Writing about the Bank of England loan later in the century, another commented that the Act "was framed on purpose to convince every man it was his private interest to serve the publick . . . and to encourage the advancing of money, upon the credit and reputation of that Act."[17] A century before Adam Smith, the mundane engineering of public bonds thus institutionalized the argument that rewards for individuals could work to good in the aggregate.

The new arrangement brought along another controversial revision. The creditors who relied on the Crown's pledges would soon reconceive their "interests" as "rights," legally enforceable against the sovereign. As it turned out, Downing had been a little too optimistic in his forecasts. Mired in war against the Dutch, Charles II defaulted on a significant portion of the Downing plan bonds in 1672. The creditors eventually sued, presenting the common law Court of Exchequer with the argument that their claims should trump competing public concerns. Their position also painted sovereign authority, formerly untouchable, as a matter appropriately policed by judicial authority.[18]

The *Bankers' Case*, as it came to be known after the profession of most of the king's creditors, arose in a procedural guise. The issue was whether the bankers could sue the Crown directly or whether they had to petition the sovereign to hear their suit. Precedent suggested that a petition was needed: that route safeguarded the Crown's discretion ultimately to reject any demands inconsistent with the public interest. As one judge explained, "suppose there was only £4,000 in the exchequer, and we were threatened with a foreign invasion, how shall this money be disposed?" If creditors claimed a right to it, the common law judges would order it disbursed, "though at the same time we open the gates, and let in Hannibal to our utter ruin and destruction." By contrast, a petition preserved the Crown's ability to reorder creditors so that it could "pay the army and our fleets, that by their assistance we may prevent the enemy from coming amongst us" ("The Case of the Bankers" 1812 (1696, 1700): 103). Against the baseline of the medieval monarch's ability to define the public good, the sovereign claim to latitude was clear (e.g., Ullman 1966 (repr. 2010): 150–93).[19]

The Crown had, however, itself revised traditional practice. According to its creditors, the real danger was not barbarians at the gates—it was the threat to new modes of finance. Downing's bonds, along with the annuities, lotteries, tontines, and other experimental forms of finance, were too promising to undermine. As a judge sympathetic to the argument observed:

> [I]t would be a hard thing to say that the court of Exchequer can relieve the king against the subject, and not help and relieve that subject when he produces a legal title against the king.
> —"The Case of the Bankers" 1812 (1696, 1700): 109

When the House of Lords agreed on appeal, it restricted the Crown's discretion over that most precious resource of all, the "treasure of the Crown ... that upon which the safety of the king and kingdom must, in all ages, depend" ("The Case of Mixed Money" 1605: 43).

The impact was profound, a shift in the legal order that promoted the rights of creditors as actors essential in the emerging order. Those rights were far from airtight; the decision may have gone against the Crown precisely because Parliament was asserting its own authority over the purse at the same moment. Should it fail to appropriate funds—and it would do just that to those who had come before the court—the creditors would have to reckon with that legislature as well as the courts.[20] But the *Bankers' Case* represented the dawning liberal sensibility. Whig theorists in and out of Parliament honed an emancipatory discourse of private rights and public limitations, clashing with Tory and conservative efforts to defend older understandings. Mercantilists who approached the public as the authority that ordained markets confronted a world in which subjects refashioned themselves as investors in that very (public) authority. Even spokesmen for the new order had doubts: David Hume and others attacked the national debt as a danger to financial integrity and distributive equities. But through it all, those engineering the financial order increasingly identified as a basic tenet the idea that creditors and their interests could and should animate the political economy.

As the turmoil over the *Bankers' Case* suggests, the innovation of circulating, interest-bearing public debt like that Downing pioneered was a change of constitutional dimension. Over the century that followed his initiative, the public debt grew from £1.25 million to £78 million. In 1672, a small circle of twenty-five goldsmith bankers held most of Downing's bonds; by 1750, 60,000 English subjects participated in lending to the government. Debt charges rose from about 30 percent of public expenses in the late seventeenth century to consume almost 60 percent at the end of the eighteenth. Public debt had become an institution elemental to Britain's development in the eighteenth century and the engine of its military machine (Carruthers 1996: 10, 64–7; 't Hart 1991: 41).[21]

Modern Money

Before it became a powerhouse, however, the institution of public debt came up against the obstacle that started off our story. Credit alone could not meet the government's need for funds, nor could it provide the retail cash to ease everyday exchange. According to a series of indicators, including significant deflation over a number of years, the rise of currency substitutes, and the intensive use of credit, the money stock was low in late seventeenth-century England compared with exchange that people sought to service.[22] But if public debt could not go it alone, it could provide the very ingredient necessary to make a new kind of currency. That modern money would be the second essential instrument in the Enlightenment quartet.

Recall the Enlightenment enthusiasm about an alternative to coin. From the Restoration on, commentators and officials in England and elsewhere proposed one design after another to alleviate the money shortage (e.g., Grubb 2016; Desan 2014: 331–41; Wennerlind 2011: 67–79; Horsefield 1960). The alternatives we met at the outset were both built on the foundation of a dedicated public debt. According to the public option advocated by Broughton, the government took loans by issuing its own IOUs: it spent its own promises (known as "Exchequer bills") directly into circulation and took them back for taxes. According to the private option advocated by the Bank of England, the government took loans by borrowing the Bank's IOUs: the government spent the Bank's promises-to-pay (its notes) into circulation, and after some delay, began taking them back for taxes.[23] The public therefore supported each currency through its public borrowing, indeed *as media of public borrowing*. The key to making credit into an official currency was to give out an IOU, either public or private, and then receive the IOU back to cancel out an obligation otherwise owed the state.

Broughton's parable captured the logic perfectly: his landlord assumed public debt when he distributed IOUs and then paid off the public debt when he received the IOUs in rent and canceled them. But once Bank notes became established as a medium that the government spent but took back in taxes, they operated according to the same basic design. The only difference was that public debt played an even larger role in the latter case. When it borrowed from Bank investors, the government gave them long-term public bonds that memorialized the government's liability. Those investors, now public creditors, then had the motive to police the government's fiscal practice. Thus the importance of the *Bankers' Case*: Bank investors had gained the right to sue for repayment of the bonds they held and could pressure the government to impose sufficient taxes to pay them back.

Modern money—Enlightenment money—changed the economic order because it provided retail cash. Banks had existed for centuries, but they generally transferred debts between merchants and other depositors, clearing their credit. Private credit instruments like bills of exchange likewise operated between those with reciprocal commercial relations or within limited circles of trust (Desan 2014: 262–3; Wennerlind 2011: 95, n.74; 't Hart 1991: 39–52; Kerridge 1988: 47–68).[24] By contrast, anyone could accept Exchequer bills or Banknotes because they carried value that the government itself recognized and had committed to accept.

In a way, the constancy of money's new design—the commonality in the way Exchequer bills and Bank notes operated—stoked controversy in the contest between them. Broughton and others argued as they did in part because the fact that a public option existed made the statutory privilege granted to Bank investors seem all the more suspect. The Bank's defenders reacted by emphasizing as distinctive the capacity of private creditors to intermediate the monetary relationship between the government and individuals. In a critical transformation of governance, the government enthroned self-interest as a guiding force when it reached agreement with the Bank of England (see Figure 0.2).

Note that, now, the profit incentive did more than invite lending to the government; it functioned to influence money creation itself. When it began producing the money stock by borrowing from the Bank in the form of its notes,

FIGURE 0.2: 1708 Bank of England banknote. Part-printed note, with date and inscription written by hand, for the amount of £150; showing a first payment of £100 and a final payment of £50. Signed by Joseph Newell. Countersigned by Barth Manning. © The Governor and Company of the Bank of England.

the government was sharing its ancient monopoly over making money. In the future, the Bank of England would influence the pace and availability of the money supply. Its compass was the business acumen that the Bank's advocates emphasized, the commercial judgment it used to gauge earning opportunities. In other words, the government had contracted out production of the money supply, putting a profit-driven actor in charge of calibrating the pattern of expansion.

That development throws the tumult over England's economy and its changing shape into sharper light. For many, the fervor for paper credit was a quest for illusory wealth. Joint-stock companies had boomed and crashed in 1690s, even as the Bank was born. To critics, these new forms of enterprise undermined the anchors of landed wealth and trade. The political system itself seemed at stake. Many feared that investors would endanger parliamentary independence, as they expanded their holdings of public debt and established themselves as indispensable agents in lending to the government (Murphy 2009: 1–38, 66–87; Banner 1998).

By contrast, Whig enthusiasm for the growth of manufacturing, domestic commerce, and international trade projected faith in men of business, their energy and calculation. Confidence of that kind supported a role for financiers at the helm of an important state process; grand architecture would soon reinforce that message (see Figure 0.3).[25] Self-interest reappeared here as a tonic. Bank notes were redeemable, after all. The Bank's directors agreed to convert notes on demand into silver or gold coin and were liable to the extent

FIGURE 0.3: *New Three Per Cent Office, Bank of England*, 1808, London. Engraved by [John?] Roffe, published by J. Stratford. Photo by Hulton Archive/Getty Images.

of their investment if they failed. That stake—what a modern banking theorist calls "skin in the game"—focused their efforts (Ricks 2016: 159–60). So it should, wrote our Bank pamphleteer, "or else they were fitter to bear the title of a *bankrupt* than a *Bank*"("A Vindication" 1707: 20).

Indeed, Bank defenders emphasized the role of the specie reserve as primary to distinguish the notes they issued from Exchequer bills. According to the Bank's projector, only money having "intrinsick value" was real; the rest were "false and counterfeit." The claim was at odds with the law on money confirming the sovereign's authority to define the unit of account ("The Case of Mixed Money" 1605), but it played well to an audience that sought to elevate private initiative over public authority.[26] In that sense, the project was a classically liberal one. It invited arguments that the market flowed from individual exchange and flourished best where the state interfered least, the vision that Adam Smith proposed as the Enlightenment peaked.

Capital Markets

Smith's vision drew on a third monetary innovation, the capital market where both debt (bonds, short-term bills, and other IOUs) and equities traded. The capital market was just as much a matter of Enlightenment engineering as public debt and modern money. In fact, it depended on both those innovations to operate.

We can begin again with public debt. According to a stream of current scholarship, public debt critically anchors securities markets. It appears that "*sovereign* debt markets are effectively prerequisites to the emergence and sustenance of large *private* debt and equity markets" (Hockett and Omarova 2017: 1168; see also Neal 2000: 127). It may be that capital markets need to reach a critical mass before they can operate in a stable way and that public debt provides the necessary stuff of trading. In the 1690s, a market for private securities had formed in England, but it was thin and vulnerable. Shareholders were relatively few, and trading occurred at a slow pace. Investors were quick to abandon private stocks for public funds as those became available, and most joint-stock companies collapsed in the economic stresses of the Great Recoinage in the mid-1690s (Murphy 2009: 24, 31–8).

The growing availability of public debt changed that condition. According to Larry Neal, government debt facilitated risk-sharing for English investors. They could hold government debt as a kind of "insurance against the risks incurred when dealing in less liquid markets for real or private financial assets" (Neal 2000: 127). When the government cleaned up the South Sea Bubble by standardizing the debt that creditors held, it institutionalized that system. For Neal, that public act provided the "big bang" to create financial capitalism in England. Public debt or trading in government instrumentalities also appears to have anchored private securities markets in Amsterdam, Paris, and New York (Neal 2000: 128).[27]

The connection between public debt, the capital market, and cash (or its lack) was closer still. The government in England used public debt as cash on critical occasions, both when it spent and when it orchestrated the expansion of joint-stock companies. Other European polities likely experimented with similar techniques. As in the case of the Bank, the drama had its roots between 1688 and 1714, when a series of wars drove all European combatants deeply into debt. England, like its counterparts, innovated broadly, borrowing by short-term methods like tallies, debentures, and Exchequer bills and by longer-term methods (Carlos et al. 2013: 150–2).[28] But borrowing can be done in goods as well as specie: given the continuing shortage of coin, the English government often paid suppliers, soldiers, and other creditors with short-term instruments. That is, it "spent" short-term debt instruments (including tallies, debentures, and Exchequer bills) as if they were Bank notes. All were different forms of IOU that the government used to pay for materials and services, discounting the amount they bought as necessary to continue the war effort.[29]

Having used short-term debt instruments as cash, the government then allowed individuals to do the same—but only for an approved purchase. That purchase was equity stock in the joint-stock companies willing to support the government. The basic idea was a debt-for-equity swap. Individuals holding government debt could trade those instruments for ownership shares in a particular joint-stock company. The company would hold the government debt and receive an interest payment for it. The arrangement shored up the value of the short-term debt and consolidated it in the hands of one creditor. In 1697, the Bank of England agreed to expand its shares in return for tallies; the New East India Company made a similar deal in 1698; other swaps followed. In 1710, the South Sea Company literally went into business by convincing the government to authorize individuals to purchase its shares with government debt. Licensed to trade African slaves to Spanish ports and British goods along the western coast of the Americas, the company took in nearly £10 million in depreciated public debt at face value and issued inaugural shares to investors in return (Carlos et al. 2013: 152–3; Wennerlind 2011: 197, 200–1; Clapham 1970: 46–50). Thus the English government expanded the largest joint-stock companies in the country by using public debt, now as cash given for company shares.

That experiment returns us to the controversial career of self-interest in the Enlightenment. By the early eighteenth century, the English government had legitimated self-interest as the motive that induced individuals to lend to the public, reinforced it in the hands of creditors with the right to sue, and installed it as the compass for an expanding money supply. Similarly here, supporters proposed the public debt-for-equity swaps as an arrangement of mutual benefit. One pamphlet lauded the official who proposed the swap establishing the South Sea Company as a measure that managed the public debt:

> His capacity's greater by far, than
>   Any statesman that e'er went before him;
> Having paid *a vast debt* to a farthing
>   *Without money*, for which we adore him.[30]

Investors gained as well, as the joint-stock companies flourished and their shares rose in value.

The agency of astute businessmen also reappears here, as agents who supported the public debt by running profitable enterprises (Wennerlind 2011: 202, 207). In a modern echo, recent scholarship attributes Britain's financial revolution to the success of the capital market that developed. If public debt helps anchor capital markets, those markets in turn allow the government to float public debt that will be readily bought in part because it can also be easily unloaded (Carlos et al. 2013: 147–8).

The burgeoning capital market brought discord as well as riches. Europeans had long condemned speculation in food and money as strategies that used dearth against those in need, bred deceit, and motivated people "whose goals ... gave them every incentive towards evil" (Murphy 2009: 17). "Stock-jobbing" seemed similarly to generate profits out of quick dealing. According to Daniel Defoe and a bevy of others, "the villainy of stock-jobbers" would bring down the English economy (Murphy 2009: 27). The government's debt-for-equity swaps attracted particular condemnation. The only way that people could protect their interest payments, complained one pamphleteer, was to participate in trading ventures about as likely to succeed as "a voyage to the world in the moon." Credit had been forced, "the liberties and properties of Englishmen" abused, and sacred obligations undermined (Wennerlind 2011: 208). The South Sea Bubble, a stock market boom followed by a notorious bust in 1720, confirmed skeptics in condemning the infant capital market (see Figure 0.4).

The South Sea Company exposed a last source of discord, one tragically present even so long as the company succeeded, investors gained, and the government carried its debts. As Carl Wennerlind has argued, capital investment turns on the anticipation of profit or "credit fetishism." In the case of the South Sea Company, projectors emphasized how lucrative its trade would be, including its trade in human beings. That portrait succeeded so well that neither supporters nor critics of the company objected to the inhumanity of its enterprise, or even to the risk that traffic in people presented given their own ability to resist (Wennerlind 2011: 197–234). Invited to imagine their own profit, people complied with such creativity that the pursuit of self-interest occupied their vision, obscuring the brutality of slavery, the role of the government in subsidizing that trade, and the contribution of everyday shareholders to the project of transporting enslaved people to the New World.

FIGURE 0.4: *The bubblers bubbl'd, or the devil take the hindmost*. Portrayal of the Stock Exchange by James Cole, 1720. Courtesy of the Lewis Walpole Library, Yale University.

Commercial Banking

Making capital markets out of public debt was praiseworthy, the poet said, because it occurred *"without money."* On a second look, the whole sequence is striking on just that score. When the government paid for goods with public debt, it economized on specie. When the government converted that debt into equity, it serviced its obligation without cash. As the Bank of England matured, it issued more money into circulation. But those innovations still fell short: throughout the Enlightenment period, demand for money outran its reach (see Muldrew in this volume). By the end of the eighteenth century, financial innovation refined a last practice to fill the gap: commercial banks that produced retail cash for individuals.

Banks issuing their own notes proliferated first in the countryside, where small proprietorships could operate without invading the joint-stock monopoly claimed by the Bank of England (see Figures 0.5a and 0.5b).[31] In an echo of the arrangement that the government had with the Bank, an individual who wanted to borrow would give a country bank an IOU, basically a promise of productivity to pay in the future. The country bank would create local notes denominated in the official unit of account (the sterling penny) and give them to the borrower to use immediately. Banks need only maintain a reserve against demands for the notes' redemption in coin or Bank of England notes—and that was less constraining than met the eye. In small communities, banks incurred many reciprocal obligations against each other, as customers cashed the notes of one local bank at another. The banks could offset many notes against each other without any need to access the reserve.

Similarly, banks might lend to a local businessman who used them to pay local wages, taking in return a bill of exchange for funds in London. In turn, the banks would sell the bill of exchange to a tax receiver who needed funds in London but who could pay the bank in local notes he had collected.[32] In time, country banks became adept at using brokers in London for credit in times of need; those intermediaries bought and sold bills of exchange for Bank of England notes and specie, providing an emergency source of funds. Should those brokers go short of funds, they would turn to the Bank of England, asking it to discount bills for ready Bank cash (Pressnell 1956: 75–80, 195–7, 210–12, 217–24; Rogers 1995: 111–14, 121). Commercial banks developed, then, within the support system provided by the government, the Bank of England, and the specialized capital market (the money market in bills of exchange) that surrounded it.

The system expanded during the nineteenth century. Eventually allowed to use the joint-stock form, commercial banks moved into a lucrative niche: in the mid-century alone, they would multiply the money supply almost fivefold, corrected for inflation, by issuing checkable deposits instead of notes. During the same period, the Bank of England worked out its role as a central bank, accommodating its commercial cousins as a lender of last resort (Desan 2014a: 399; Knafo 2013).

INTRODUCTION 21

FIGURE 0.5a: Bank note issued by the Berwick Bank (1983,1109.165). Image CBA881, ncq 1799 © Trustees of the British Museum.

FIGURE 0.5b: Bank note issued by the Durham Bank, with coat of arms at top left (1882,0311.3156). 1798 © Trustees of the British Museum.

Like the other financial innovations of the Enlightenment, commercial banks institutionalized self-interest as an organizing principle. That calculus provided the incentive for lending beyond the specie reserve. Issuing notes was "the grand source of profit" observed one country banker.[33] The business model would become standard; later analyses almost universally assume that money's multiplication is an appropriate source of private profit (Ricks 2016: 203, n. 6).

Here too, however, earlier commentators criticized the innovation. Before the model became entrenched, an official commission of the early nineteenth century objected. Commercial note creation "operat[ed] in the first instance and in their hands, as capital for their own benefit," exploiting the public support that made it possible (Select Committee on the High Price of Gold

Bullion 1810: 71). The committee referred to notes issued during the period when those promises-to-pay were inconvertible to specie. But qualified by the expense of a specie reserve when it was required, the objection applied more widely. During the seventeenth century, many felt that notes issued in excess of specie held one-for-one was "almost a fraud on the subject."[34] But developments over the Age of Enlightenment collided with and eventually undermined that sensibility. The debate over profit enveloped as well an enduring discomfort with money's modern shape—credit without the collateral content of coin.

Finally, the profit calculus deployed by commercial banks disrupted norms about how credit should be allocated. Private banks, operating for profit, loaned money only to those who could make a promise of productivity: borrowers as well as bankers had to be profit-generating to be creditworthy. That contention flipped the moral order associated with the usury prohibition. For all its exceptions, that doctrine long denied that profit should guide moneylending. The religious principle had ancient roots. Aristotle had identified "not profit and desire for gain but the establishment of equality [as] the proper motive and end of exchange" (Kaye 1998: 35). The fear that the profit motive would disrupt both human relations and economic production fueled cultural critique throughout the Enlightenment, and afterwards. See, for example, the sketch by a French artist of *Le Diable d'Argent*, in which the lure of money induced people to drop the instruments of their trade in a single-minded pursuit of profit (Cameron 2012) (see Figure 0.6). The conviction that commercial banks

FIGURE 0.6: *Le Diable d'Argent*. Bleichroeder Print Collection, Kress Collection, Baker Library, Harvard Business School.

should direct money production according to profit was yet more problematic, given its power in channeling the flow of money.[35]

By contrast, the momentum of financial innovation had generated a very different conclusion by the Enlightenment's end. Money loans were always, not exceptionally, made for profit and with the expectation that they would be profit-generating. From a medium designed to ensure commensurability, money had become a medium understood as an instrument of gain.

CONCLUSION

Over the course of the Enlightenment, European polities reordered the way money operated. The contest over the Bank's charter was the small signal of a change that swelled. Experiments abounded throughout the age, and more lasting national (soon to be central) banks followed in the United States (1791), France (1800), Denmark (1813), Norway (1816), Prussia (1846), the Ottoman Empire (1863), Germany (1875), Japan (1882), China (1897), and Switzerland (1905) (Goodhart 1988: 105–60; Eldem 2005: 436–40). Circulating public debt became an indispensable instrument of sovereignty. According to the conventional wisdom, the "financial revolution" fueled Britain's military power and drove its imperial ambition. Its national debt rose dramatically with each war in the eighteenth century, reaching almost 200% of national income in the century that followed. The surge in public debt seemed to stimulate, rather than crowd out, private investment. Capital markets, stabilized by the ballast of public debt, allowed individuals to fund companies that offered shares and bonds. Like central banks, they became a global phenomenon. Finally, during the nineteenth century, commercial banks demolished the age-old ceiling imposed on the money stock by the medieval commitment to make money out of precious metal. Commercial banknotes now abundantly irrigated everyday exchange. In 2009 Britain, for example, the money supply was sixty-five times larger, corrected for inflation, than it had been when the Bank was established (Piketty 2014: 130; Desan 2014: 203; Neal 2000: 125–7).

In the late eighteenth century, liberal theorists excoriated mercantilist-minded policymakers as officials driven by their own interests, ready to confer public power by monopoly and unable to account for a public with aims outside their own. Rather than abandon the power of interest-oriented action, however, the new liberal thinkers identified it with the individual rather than the polity. Drawing on decades of public ferment, they suggested that the secret to managing human productivity lay in organizing material life around individuated decision-making and its effect when aggregated. Exchange occurred as every person chose the goods he or she valued. Propelled by different tastes, divergent interests, and unfathomable preferences, the process proceeded in ways no one could coordinate from the outside. It included accident and illogic, discord and strife. But in the aggregate, it produced an astonishing affect—a self-equilibrating system, a harmonious whole (e.g., Sheehan and Warhman 2015; Hanley and Paganelli 2014).

From this vantage point, the market was largely a "self-organizing" matter, consistent with phenomena in the natural world, from biology to physics. (Indeed, for some thinkers, the emanating order even bespoke divinity.) If so, the market stood apart from or perhaps prior to politics. It operated with autonomy; indeed it generated a logic that eluded even well-intentioned legislators. Their role was to remove the obstacles that "impeded the realization of the beauty and order of the system of natural liberty" (Sheehan and Wahrman 2015: 231–70; Hanley and Paganelli 2014: 198).

It was an alluring vision, and thinkers from Locke to Smith put money at the heart of it. Here, however, the music becomes more mysterious. Those most convinced of the market's natural operation offered an account of money as a product of spontaneous activity. It was, they explained, a trade token that emerged from barter as people naturally settled on a commodity that would facilitate their trade (Desan 2014; Hanley and Paganelli 2014: 188–9). The description comported perfectly with the theory that decentralized activity produced a beneficent solution for the group—but it collided with the innovation that set the Enlightenment apart.

The Enlightenment world took shape by aiming at material strictures as well as conceptual ones. When they began retheorizing money, seventeenth-century strategists advocated engineering a medium rather than passively awaiting the results that might be generated by private activity. Their enterprise created money issued by new national banks. It engendered the complex orchestration of public debt and its relationship to emerging capital markets. Those developments in turn enabled the modern industry of commercial banking. In short, a quartet of radical institutions operated by public authority made possible the very initiatives that later authors celebrated as private. A governing ensemble—far from a "system of natural liberty"—made the monetary composition of the modern world.

In their effort to organize a world so thoroughly upended, Enlightenment theorists heard only the harmony they coveted. Imagining private efflorescence as the essence of their age, they missed the collective orchestration that actually underlay financial innovation. In fact, the more they insisted that modern practices emanated from individuated decision-making, the more they deflected attention to the complicated structure, the intricate design, that produced the modern monetary system.

That discord—the strident incongruity between theory and practice—has haunted the quartet and its music ever since.

CHAPTER ONE

Money and its Technologies

Industrial Opposition and the Problem of Trust

MARA CADEN

The mint, Sir, is a *manufacture*, and it is nothing else; and it ought to be undertaken upon the principles of a manufacture; that is, for the best and cheapest execution, by a contract, upon proper securities, and under proper regulations.

—Edmund Burke, 1780[1]

The concept of technology took on something like its contemporary meaning during the Age of Enlightenment in eighteenth-century Europe. Technology, in this period, began to describe the scientific pursuit of "useful knowledge" about the "mechanical arts" and manufactures.[2] This chapter will explore money and its technologies during that same period: the eighteenth-century Enlightenment. And while the technologies of money now mean many things to us—modes of accounting, the calculation of interest rates, rates of exchange between various currencies, or even the calculation of value for digital currencies such as bitcoin—this chapter will focus on the technologies involved in the physical manufacture of money. There is a wealth of material on credit and banking, especially in early modern Europe, the European Enlightenment, and early America, but historians of money have paid relatively little attention to the manufacture of currencies themselves, outside of the conversations in numismatics journals (Dickson 1967; Murphy 2009).[3] Economic and social historians of the eighteenth century have neglected this topic in part because they have tended to treat currency as merely an instrument in the increasingly complex networks and technologies of credit in this period. But other economic historians have shown that the extension of credit in the early modern period was dependent on and intimately linked to the supply of money (Mayhew 1995).[4] Even as instruments of credit exploded, money continued to matter. Money backed the paper bills that circulated in the early modern and Enlightenment periods. Long-running book credit could be settled in money, and bills of exchange needed the promise of specie to function. Most states in the Enlightenment period maintained a monopoly on the manufacture of money from precious metals, or else they licensed and supervised local or private producers. Either way, money itself was central to the power of states. It was essential for collecting taxes. Monetary policy was one of the primary ways that early modern states regulated trade and economic activity at home and abroad. And it carried the mark of the sovereign, inserting royal power into every transaction.

All over Europe, the Atlantic world, the Indian Ocean world, among empires on the Eurasian land mass, and even across the Pacific Ocean, coins of silver, gold, copper, and tin circulated. In one sense, these coins were commodities, enabling a trade in precious metals between states and continents, and facilitating the trade in other commodities such as cloth, spices, sugar, and enslaved people. As a commodity, the market value of these precious metals gave coins their value. But states also assigned a legal value to the coins they produced, and the difference between what contemporaries considered their "intrinsic value," that is, the exchange value of the metal that coins contained, and their face value was a matter of great debate and constant tinkering (Redish 2000; Desan 2014: 110–20).[5] The seventeenth and eighteenth centuries were a time of significant and expanding global trade, and they also contained many moments of acute political crisis across Europe and the Atlantic world. As monarchs and governments sought to make money work domestically and across oceans, the problem of trust plagued their currencies. Most states passed foreign coins at rates according to their weight and metal content, and coins were judged on their fineness (that is, the ratio of precious metals to alloy), their weight, and other physical properties that signaled their authenticity. For those states and monarchs whose legitimacy was in question or who were weathering domestic upheaval and foreign wars, the quality of the coin they issued could be inseparable from their personal reputations and their legitimacy. The credit of a monarch or a state depended upon the precious metal content of their coins, and that credit could be rapidly undermined by counterfeits. Counterfeiting was both a lucrative industry and a capital crime in Europe and its colonies (Wennerlind 2011: 123–60).[6] Whether at home or abroad, radically debased or counterfeit money made exchange difficult, and in the course of trade, many people refused to accept currency that was vulnerable to counterfeiting or paid a lower price for money that they suspected had reduced metal content. It is in this sense that trust was essential to making money work.

It is tempting to imagine that by the time that Enlightenment thought traversed Europe, thinkers had departed from an attachment to the metallic values of money. It seems intuitive, in other words, to associate an attachment to intrinsic value with ancient and medieval monetary worlds of coin hordes and sovereigns' stamps, while the modern era ushered in a world of flexible credit instruments and a functionalist view of money as an instrument to facilitate trade. But the world of commodity money had not yet disappeared from view. In Denis Diderot and Jean le Rond d'Alembert's classic compilation of Enlightenment thought, the *Encyclopedie*, Louis, chevalier de Jaucourt's contribution, "Money," presented a decidedly commodity-based view of money. Arguing against a Mr. Boizart, who had argued that money was politically constituted—that is, it held value because a public authority assigned it a value to facilitate trade—Jaucourt argued that the public authority that certified the value of the coin only demonstrated and affirmed its value, but did not create it. Rather, for de Jaucourt and many eighteenth-century monetary authorities and philosophers, coins derived value from the metal they contained; in other words, "the matter gives it its value."[7]

It is possible to see the fact that people still cared about intrinsic value as an indication of a problem with trust in states. As the monetary economist Charles Goodhart writes,

> ... the balance between the metallic content and the face value of a coin represented the credible commitment of the issuer. Local confidence that an IOU could and would be honored meant that coins could generally be accepted and used in exchange. The better the credit of the issuer, the wider the circulation, and the less need for intrinsic value of the money object.
>
> —2008: xii–xiii[8]

In this chapter, I will argue that the technological innovations in the minting of money during the Enlightenment period were an answer to the problem of trust. Virtually every new technological innovation was a response to the persistent problems of culling, clipping, and counterfeiting. When coins were irregular, some contained slightly more gold or silver than others, and so people would take the heaviest coins out of circulation to melt, hoard, or export, leaving only the lighter coins in circulation. Standard, mechanical processes of production ensured regularity, so that people could rely on the metal content of the coins they received. Coin clipping plagued currencies throughout Europe and the Atlantic, wherein people would take advantage of the irregularity of coins to cut slivers of silver or gold from the edges, circulating the diminished coins and keeping the precious metal. Techniques that produced perfectly round coins made it more difficult to clip undetected, and novel methods of inscribing letters and patterns around the edges of coins made clipping impossible. Finally, widespread counterfeiting threatened most currencies in Europe and the Atlantic, and this chapter will survey the technologies that minters and engineers invented to make counterfeiting more difficult and costly. When states sought to transform the technologies of minting to address these problems, however, they repeatedly encountered the opposition of guild-like bodies of mint workers who maintained and guarded traditional techniques of making money. After centuries of protracted struggle, when European states finally implemented new coining technologies, these mint workers saw their status depleted and their skill made obsolete.

This chapter will deal first with metal technologies. The process of minting underwent a gradual mechanization throughout Europe from the sixteenth through the eighteenth centuries. At the very end of the eighteenth century, British minting was transformed once again when industrial manufacturers applied steam-powered technology to the manufacture of money. Then, we will look at the ways that the technology of extracting, refining, and minting metals in the Americas changed over the course of our period. Mints in Spanish America adopted mechanical coining technology in the later eighteenth century, and a new amalgamation process in the silver mines there boosted silver production in a waning mining industry, enabling a higher volume of minting and continued trade across the Atlantic and the Pacific. Then we will turn our attention to paper money, which began to gain importance in European economies in the late seventeenth century and took on a central role in North American colonial economies. In each of these cases, novel inventions responded to the pressures of counterfeiting and sought to establish confidence in the value and authenticity of the currencies that circulated.

METAL TECHNOLOGIES: MECHANICAL COINING

Two great transformations in the technology of minting bookend our period. First, the mechanization of the coining process, where mills and presses replaced hand-hammered coinage; and second, the introduction of steam power to British coinage in the industrial mints of Birmingham and later at the new mint on Tower Hill. The move from hammered to milled coins marks the first transition, and its history stretches back beyond the confines of this volume. It is a story of experimentation and invention across Europe, but it is also a story of surprisingly slow implementation. Into the middle of the seventeenth century, most of the coins minted in Europe were made by hand using methods that were virtually unchanged from those of ancient Greek mints. Skilled engravers would create dies and puncheons: heavy stone pieces with engravings to be stamped onto each side of a coin. With the die resting on a pedestal, a moneyer would sit on a low stool, place a blank disk of gold or silver between the die and the puncheon, and strike the puncheon with a hammer to stamp the engravings simultaneously onto each side of the coin (Stewart 1992: 76–82).[9]

While the technology was rudimentary, it took great skill to make coins that were uniform, round, centered, and stamped in sharp relief by this method. In England, the medieval Corporation of Moneyers, which functioned very much as a craft guild, trained its members with long apprenticeships and carefully guarded entry into the Corporation. For many generations, their skill made them indispensable to the operation of the mint. France relied on a similar body to conduct and oversee the technical aspects of minting money for the kingdom: the Cour des Monnaies. In the sixteenth century, the Monnaies acquired a more heavily administrative role than the English Moneyers: France had many disparate mints throughout the kingdom, and the Monnaies, concentrated in Paris, became auditors of those provincial mints and gained the power to conduct criminal trials in cases of suspected corruption (Parsons 2015: 17–59).[10] In both cases, the moneyers were exclusive and tightly controlled bodies of craftsmen who were the guardians of coinage techniques.

But by the seventeenth century, a new method would overtake the moneyers' hammered coinage. The first traces of this technology originate in the Renaissance, at the Papal Mint in Rome. The architect Donato Bramante, who created medals and seals for Pope Julius II, developed and manufactured a novel machine for striking these medals at the beginning of the sixteenth century. His invention employed a screw mechanism, which used rotational torque to drive a press downward with great force. This screw press for striking medals had some advantages over hand-hammering: the strike was more exact, and so engravings could be more intricate; the medals had the gleam that we associate with newly minted coins because the power of the screw press made it possible to strike while the metal was cool; and the resulting medals were more uniform and more perfectly centered. But in order to make the most of this invention, perfectly smooth and round blanks were required, rather than the slightly irregular disks that metalworkers cut out of sheets of metal with shears. The inventions of the great polymath Leonardo da Vinci would eventually solve this problem. Da Vinci's notebooks contain sketches of a machine designed for the Mint at Rome using a hollow cutting punch, which would cut perfectly round and uniform disks out of the strip of metal by forcing them upward into a hollow upper chamber. In his notebook, da Vinci described the benefit of making all coins perfectly round and uniform in size and thickness. Although it was not built in his lifetime, da Vinci's invention would join Bramante's to form the set of machines that would eventually transform European coinage (Hocking 1909: 60–2).

FIGURE 1.1: Screw press, engraving originally printed in Diderot and d'Alembert's *Encylopédie*. Case Number 7362775, the Royal Mint Collection. Bridgeman images.

Not long after, these machines found their way into the Mint at Rome when Benvenuto Cellini, the Italian goldsmith and sculptor, became the stamp-master of the Mint and used Bramante's screw press to make medals there. It seemed a perfect opportunity to begin to use the new technology to make coins, and Cellini actively promoted the screw press as a superior method of coining money. The medals he was able to make with the press were beautiful, but they were more expensive to produce than traditional hammered coins. And so, despite Cellini's skill and enthusiasm, the Mint at Rome maintained its traditional coining methods (Usher 1954–8: 338–9; Redish 2000: 55–6; Hocking 1909: 62–5).

But as the sixteenth century wore on and European kingdoms faced persistent problems of inflation, debasement, and counterfeiting in their currencies, the new technology wound its way through Europe. In 1551, the French ambassador to the Free Imperial City of Augsburg, Charles de Marillac, was awed by the machines that the inventor Marx Schwab was developing in the Augsburg Mint. These machines—a rolling mill to roll smooth sheets of metal of uniform thickness; a cutting press that punched out perfectly round blanks; and a screw press for imprinting the coins—so impressed de Marillac that he wrote to the king, Henry II, and convinced him to invest in such machines for France. De

Marillac returned in a delegation that included his brother, who was master of the Lyon Mint, and the French engineer Aubin Olivier, and they worked for several months with the Augsburg engineer to perfect the machines and import them into France. Back in Paris, they installed the first truly mechanized mint for coinage on the site of a mill on the Île de la Cité that had originally been built to polish precious stones. The new Monnaie du Moulin, or mill-money, used a combination of water power, horse power, and human power to operate the Augsburg machines, and also featured Olivier's own invention: the technology to mark the edges of coins with letters and patterns, which protected the new coins from the most persistent problem: clipping. In order to accomplish this feat, Olivier developed a segmented collar that surrounded the blanks as they were being pressed. This collar, which was slightly larger than the blanks, was engraved, so that when the screw press struck the blank, the coin expanded into the collar, taking on the letters and figures that were engraved into it. The ability to impress letters and patterns around the edges of coins would be one of the most closely guarded trade secrets and the most coveted technology among the mints that mechanized more widely in the seventeenth century. Notoriously difficult to replicate and impossible to clip, the coins with this feature seemed to answer some of the biggest monetary problems for early modern states (Mazerolle 1907; Hocking 1909: 67–72; Parsons 2015: 109–13).

The mechanized mint in Paris was short-lived, however. Plagued by frequent breakdowns and expensive to operate, the machines proved too unwieldy for the regular coinage of the kingdom. By 1586, the new mill was relegated to striking medals and copper tokens, while the gold and silver coinage reverted to the old hammered method (Hocking 1909: 72; Parsons 2015: 112–13). It would be the first of several abortive attempts to mechanize European mints in the sixteenth and seventeenth centuries. In the 1560s, an employee of the Paris Monnaie du Moulin, Eloi Mestrelle, ventured to England, where he offered his services to Queen Elizabeth and to the mint at the Tower of London. There, Mestrelle installed machines that were modeled on the ones in Paris, and minted a small number of gold coins to demonstrate their capabilities. Once again, officers and observers praised the quality of the coins, but did not convert to mechanized coinage: swayed by the opposition of the Corporation of Moneyers, the Royal Mint determined in 1572 that coinage by hammer was the superior method. A similar pattern occurred in 1625, when the French engraver and engineer Nicholas Briot arrived in England after the Cour des Monnaies purportedly drove him out of France when he tried to resume gold and silver coinage at the mechanized Paris Mint. Briot engraved dies for Charles I and set up machines for coining in the Tower of London Mint, where he trained the Moneyers to operate them and struck a small number of coins by methods he had adapted from the technology in the French mint. Briot's methods, too, failed to become standard, though his machines did find their way to the

Scottish Mint when the master of the mint there brought them to Edinburgh after the Tower mint had retired them (Hocking 1909: 72–83; Challis 1992: 300–2, 339; Parsons 2015: 111–12).

The Paris Mint was the first to make the full transition to coinage by machine. In 1639, the new director of the Paris Mint, Jean Varin, convinced King Louis XIII and Cardinal Richelieu of the need to fully mechanize the minting of gold and silver coins. Varin adapted some of the old machines, which he moved to the Louvre Palace, and built some of them anew. At last, the machines worked reliably. In 1645, the king abolished coinage by hammer in Paris, making mechanical coinage the new standard (Hocking 1909: 83–4; Redish 2000: 57).

It would take longer for England to make the transition to mechanically produced money. After the failure of Briot's machines at the Royal Mint, the Commonwealth government invited another French engineer to the Mint in 1649 to introduce new machinery for coining money. Pierre Blondeau promised that his machines could make money that was superior to any that came before it: uniform in weight, perfectly round, lustrous, with intricate engravings in high relief, and lettered around the edges by a new a superior method—in short, secure from clipping and counterfeiting, and safe from hoarding and arbitrage in their uniformity. Blondeau's unique method of marking coins around the edges was shrouded in deep secrecy: he discussed it only in vague terms, and those who did not operate it directly were prohibited from trying to learn the technology. But we now know that it involved a process totally distinct from the segmented collar of Olivier's invention. (The French mints employed a segmented collar with an engraved surface that surrounded the blank as it was pressed, so that the metal expanded into the collar when the screw press struck it, transferring the design to both faces and edge of the coin simultaneously.) Blondeau noted that the heavy segmented collar had a tendency to break the upper engraved die if the die accidentally landed on the edge of the collar as it struck a coin. Instead, he devised a machine that marked the edges of coins before they went into the screw press. This device consisted of two parallel metal strips: one fixed and with an engraved edge, the other moved by a wheel. When a coin was placed between the two strips, the moving surface propelled it forward so that its edge turned against the engraved surface, which marked the coin with letters or patterns. In addition to avoiding the problem of breaking dies upon a collar in a screw press, the new device produced a different effect from the previous "edged" coins: instead of indented letters around the edge of the coin, the letters around the edge of Blondeau's coins were raised, which he claimed made them even more difficult to counterfeit (TNA Mint 1/1: ff. 142–6; Pepys 1663; Hocking 1909: 85–93; Gaspar 1976: 55–63; Challis 1992: 327–31, 346).[11]

Although the Commonwealth government ultimately decided to adopt Blondeau's coining methods, their efforts were interrupted by the death of the

Lord Protector Oliver Cromwell, and then by the restoration of the monarchy in 1660, when Charles II's government seized Blondeau's equipment for fear that it would fall into the hands of counterfeiters and enemies of the state. In their urgency to take the Commonwealth coins out of circulation, produce money that reflected the restored monarchy, and coin bullion as quickly as possible, Charles II's mint initially reverted to coinage by hammer. But in the following year, Charles II ordered that all new coins be produced mechanically, and employed Blondeau to implement mechanical coinage once again. Although the machines worked well, the new coins did not remain in circulation for long. The volume of coinage was too low during the 1660s, 1670s, and 1680s to replace the hammered coins in circulation with new, mechanically produced coins. Most of the silver coin already in circulation was old, badly worn, and degraded. Centuries of coin-clipping and wear had left the old coins irregular and their silver content diminished. Counterfeiters, who melted down coin clippings and "washed" their counterfeit coins in it to give them the appearance of solid silver, had mastered the production of the old hammered money. Those who got their hands on the heavier and more uniform milled coins often melted them down or hoarded them because of their silver content, so that the only coins that remained in circulation were old, light, clipped, or counterfeit (Challis 1992: 335–97). This rapid disappearance of the new milled coins was a prime example of "Gresham's Law" in operation: the tendency of money with a lower metallic value to drive higher-intrinsic-value money out of circulation because people tended to hoard, melt, or export the coins with higher precious metal content and circulate depleted or debased money in their stead.

In response to this crisis, the English state undertook a full silver recoinage by machine in 1696. This massive undertaking involved calling all the hammered and clipped money into the mint, along with plate—silver vessels and tableware—and coining all of it anew by the mechanical process they had adopted several decades earlier. In order to accomplish the Great Recoinage, the Royal Mint commissioned more machines to be built in the Tower of London, and established five new mints in English provincial towns, which they equipped with Blondeau's mechanical coining apparatuses. It was only after the completion of this extensive and disruptive project that mechanically produced money became the standard in England.

There are several patterns that emerge from this story of the gradual spread of mechanical coining technology across Europe. First, virtually all of the attempts to reform the coinage by converting to a mechanical minting process occurred at times of political and economic crisis. When Charles de Marillac led the development and purchase of Marx Schwab's Augsburg machines for the French Mint in 1551, France was plagued by uncontrolled inflation that brought French currency to near collapse, caused by a combination of the

FIGURE 1.2: Clipped and worn penny of Elizabeth I, struck at London
c. 1587–1590. Winchester Museum Service, photographed by Robert Webley. Portable
Antiquities Scheme. HAMP-34135000 © Trustees of the British Museum.

importation of overvalued foreign coin, uncontrolled minting throughout the kingdom, arbitrage based on fluctuating gold and silver prices, counterfeiting, and the influx of specie from mining (Parsons 2015: 104–9). When Elizabeth I hired Eloi Mestrelle shortly after her succession to build coining machines on the French model in the Tower of London Mint, the new monarch faced a desperate monetary situation in England after what has been termed Henry VIII's Great Debasement and a currency awash in clipped and counterfeit coins (Hocking 1909: 72–3; Challis 1978; Challis 1992: 228–44). In France, the regency of Marie de Médicis, when the engineer and engraver Nicholas Briot tried unsuccessfully to resume coining gold and silver money at the mechanized Paris Mint, was marked by intense instability, political intrigue, and revolt (Parsons 2015: 111). Briot was hired in England to build coining machines at the Tower shortly after the accession of Charles I, a monarch whose fiscal policies would lead his kingdoms into the Civil Wars and would end in his execution (Hocking 1909: 82–3; Parsons 2015: 111; Challis 1992: 300–2). The French government's decision to mechanize the Paris Mint in earnest with the minting of gold *louis d'or* in 1640 and then for all silver and gold coinage from 1645 on was also undertaken in the midst of an intense crisis: an expensive war, domestic insurrection, monetary disorder and depletion, and high-profile counterfeiting prosecutions (Hocking 1909: 83–4; Redish 2000: 57; Thomson 2004: 755–66). Blondeau arrived to mechanize the London Mint just after the execution of Charles I, during parliamentary rule and in the middle of the English Civil Wars. The eventual adoption of Blondeau's coining methods began a year after the restoration of the monarchy in England, as Charles II attempted to consolidate his rule after nearly two decades of war and upheaval. And in the 1690s, the English state undertook the Great Recoinage in the aftermath of the Glorious Revolution of 1688 and in a decade marked by acute economic distress and constant suspicion of political conspiracy (Weil 2013; Waddell 2015: 318–51).

For the monarchs and governments of states in this kind of acute crisis, it could be imperative to shore up confidence in the currency of the realm. The mechanical technologies of the sixteenth and seventeenth centuries were invented to solve some of the most urgent and damaging currency problems of the age. Mechanical rolling mills and blank-cutting machines made it possible to make coins of uniform thickness, shape, and weight, so that in theory, each coin would have the same silver content. This technique took aim at the persistent problem of culling, where people hoarded, melted, or exported the heaviest coins for their metal content, and left only the lightest coins in circulation. If all coins were uniform, treasurers and mint-masters reasoned, they would circulate more freely, and those who spent or received them could trust that they each had equal amounts of precious metals.

Second, the novel edge-marking techniques that engineers and engravers developed over these centuries were meant to combat another persistent problem: the clipping of coins. Those who clipped coins would shave or cut silver or gold from the edges of the coins, sending the clipped coins back into circulation and keeping the clipped metal, which they could melt down and sell, or use to coat counterfeit coins of baser metals. Coin clipping was so prevalent among the irregular hammered coins that it was one of the most important sources of their depletion. While a skilled clipper could disguise their handiwork when working with slightly irregular hand-hammered coins, the activity became impossible with milled coins that had lettered edges: only a milled coin with the engravings on its edges intact would pass as current, and the edging technology of the seventeenth century virtually eliminated the clipping of milled coins altogether (Redish 2000: 60–1).

Finally and most importantly, mechanical coining technologies were meant to address the unshakeable problem of counterfeiting, which undermined public confidence in currencies and further depleted the precious metal content of the money in circulation. The more sophisticated the coining technologies and the more intricate the final product, the more difficult the process would be to replicate. Mint officials took great pains to keep mechanical coining technologies secret, and they knew that as soon as knowledge of these technologies spread beyond the walls of the mint, their coins would be less secure. Furthermore, it would be much more difficult for counterfeiters to coin in secret if the process involved heavy and conspicuous machines that took multiple workers to operate. Indeed, as mechanical coining became standard in England, button-makers became suspect because of the similarity of their machines and the suspicion that button-making technologies could be readily adapted to making counterfeit milled coins.[12] It was a prescient suspicion, because the next great transformation in coining technology would take place at the hands of Birmingham button-makers who adapted industrial technology to coining at the end of the eighteenth century (Selgin 2008). And while counterfeiting did not disappear completely with mechanized coinage, it became much more difficult to accomplish and easier to detect.

If the new machines—screw presses, rolling mills, blank-cutting mills, and edging machines—addressed so many persistent monetary problems of early modern European states, why did they take so long to implement? After all, nearly a century and a half passed between the first successful use of Bramante's screw press, and the wholesale adoption of mechanical coining technology in France. England took even longer to make milled coinage standard. Of course, there were initial flaws in the technology itself. Machines broke down or required constant supervision and tinkering by engineers. Mechanical presses required engravers to master new engraving techniques, and they also had a tendency to break the dies that had been so painstakingly engraved in the process of minting. It was also costlier to coin money by machine, sometimes nearly twice as expensive as producing coins by hammer. Not only did building and maintaining machines require a substantial outlay of capital, but mechanized coining could also be a less efficient use of raw materials, and some mint workers noted that the new methods produced more dust and scrap that wasted valuable gold and silver bullion (Challis 1992: 348; Parsons 2015: 112). Although it was difficult for anyone to dispute the quality of the coins that came out of mechanical processes, converting to machine production did require states to commit additional resources to their mints, often at times when their finances were at their most dire.

But the most powerful reason why it took so long to implement mechanical coining technologies and make them standard was the opposition of the Corporation of Moneyers or the Cour des Monnaies, those guild-like organizations composed of the people who maintained and executed coinage by the old, hammered method. In France, the Cour des Monnaies successfully held off the full conversion to mechanized coinage for nearly a century after the mechanical mint was first built in Paris in 1551. Their fierce opposition to the Monnaie de Moulin eventually convinced Henry III to issue a proclamation that prohibited the mechanical minting of gold and silver money in France. Eloi Mestrelle's attempt to mechanize the London Mint during the reign of Elizabeth I was thwarted by the opposition of the Corporation of Moneyers, and it is difficult to disentangle the Warden of the Mint's determination that Mestrelle's machines were defective from the active opposition of those who worked in the Mint. The Monnaies warded off Nicholas Briot's attempt to revive coinage by machine in Paris in the early seventeenth century, and when Briot went instead to England, he met the vigorous opposition of the Corporation of Moneyers at the Tower of London Mint, who ensured that his machines did not supplant their methods. The Cour des Monnaies resisted the edicts that officially mechanized the Paris Mint in 1640 and 1645, but their power waned under Cardinal Richelieu and they eventually had to bend to the will of the king (Hocking 1909: 72, 82–3; Redish 2000: 56–7; Thomson 2004: 761–7).

The drama of mechanization played out in the extended conflict between Pierre Blondeau and the Corporation of Moneyers in England. When Blondeau arrived in London in 1649, the Moneyers fiercely opposed the introduction of his machinery to the Tower Mint. They tried a number of tacks to make their case. Although machine coinage was supposed to protect against counterfeiting, the Corporation argued that it in fact made the Mint more vulnerable to counterfeiters: sooner or later, knowledge of Blondeau's technology and methods was bound to become public, and once counterfeiters learned to replicate it, any advantage would be lost. Even though the machines required large workshops and multiple workers to operate, counterfeiters would be able to coin in secret more easily because they were quieter to run than the noisy hammering that often gave counterfeiters away. The Moneyers declared that they had the ability to create coins that were superior to Blondeau's, and they challenged Blondeau to a trial of skill. The competition, which hinged on whose method of marking the edges of coins was most effective, was carried out between Blondeau and one of the Moneyers, David Rammage, who had worked with Briot and adapted some of his methods, including the segmented collar for marking the edges of coins. Blondeau, who collaborated with the exceptionally skillful Mint engraver Thomas Simon, won the day, and the Council of State and a Committee of the Mint judged his coins to be more beautiful, more perfect, and with more ingeniously lettered edges (TNA Mint 1/1: ff. 142–6; Violet 1650; Corporation of Moneyers 1653; Hocking 1909: 85–94; Craig 1953: 157–9; Challis 1992: 329–31). By the time the Tower Mint mechanized in earnest during the Restoration, the Moneyers found their resistance outmatched by the exigencies of monetary reform, the enthusiasm of the Mint master Henry Slingsby, and the wider public's admiration for the new milled coins.

Moneyers had a number of reasons for opposing the new technologies. As the people closest to the process of making money, they were often quicker to notice the deficiencies and glitches in the machines that so enamored inventors and higher-ranking officers. In France, Monnaies knew that the early machines caused a greater loss of materials in the minting process than the hammered method. In France and England, whether sizing up the inventions of Olivier, Mestrelle, or Briot, they could see that the frequent need for machine repairs slowed down the operation, and they could be shrewd in discerning flaws in the final product.

But moneyers also had personal reasons for opposing mechanization. Their institutional structure, designed to replicate and maintain skill over generations, made them inherently conservative, and their very status depended on their maintenance of existing coinage techniques. When engineers outside their ranks became the new authorities, and expertise in minting technology slipped out of their hands, moneyers became skilled laborers rather than masters of a trade. Coinage by machine would make it more difficult to justify their unique privileges and status, more difficult to justify their long apprenticeships and craft guild structure, more difficult to maintain their income, and easier to hire laborers outside of their ranks to operate the machines, eventually sapping the Corporation of Moneyers of their power to oppose new measures.

Indeed, the status and leverage of the moneyers declined precipitously after mechanization. By the Great Recoinage of 1696, the Mint officers ignored the moneyers' frequent complaints about operations in the provincial mints and about the long hours expected of them (mills were supposed to operate twenty hours a day), and threatened to replace them with other laborers if they would not comply.[13] Although the Cour des Monnaies and the Corporation of Moneyers continued to exist through the eighteenth century (in the case of the Monnaies, until the French Revolution), they no longer had the leverage to impose their vision of monetary production on the mints. By the eighteenth century, the Corporation of Moneyers complained that they could not sustain themselves on the piece rates they received, and by the middle of the next century, their numbers had dwindled to five members and two apprentices.[14]

MINES AND MINTS IN AMERICA

As mechanical coining became the new standard for France and England, merchants trading throughout the Atlantic world recognized milled coins for their regularity and the confidence they bestowed in their metal content. The French *louis d'or*, the first coin produced by machine on a wide scale, was coveted throughout Europe and the Atlantic world for its authenticity and value. And as more European states adopted mechanical coining technology in their own mints, these technologies spread to the overseas empires of the Atlantic world.

Not all European colonies in the Americas had mints, but mints were an important feature of the Spanish American colonies, where silver mining formed the basis of colonial wealth extraction. There were two major silver mining sites in Spanish America: New Spain, in an area north of Mexico City centered on Zacatecas; and Potosí, in the viceroyalty of Peru and within the modern borders of Bolivia. Both of these mining areas had mints to coin the silver they generated: in Mexico City for the New Spain mines, and in Potosí and Lima for the South American silver.

Initially, many of the technological innovations in the production of money in Spanish America were directed toward the extraction of silver rather than the minting of coins. In Potosí, the mountain in the viceroyalty of Peru where Spanish settlers and indigenous and African forced laborers mined huge quantities of silver for nearly 250 years, miners had to engineer a number of unfamiliar technologies to take advantage of the vast deposits of silver. The mines of Potosí were at such a high altitude that European bellows could not operate for heating the ores, so Spanish miners used an indigenous smelting system that harnessed the high winds on the ridges of the mountains to bring the smelting ovens to the proper heat; indeed, Inca servants built and operated these early furnaces (Lockhart and Schwartz 1983: 101). Once the richest ores were exhausted, miners built artificial lakes and installed hydraulic ore-grinding mills to process the silver more efficiently. By 1621, there were thirty-two such lakes that powered the silver mills, which have been recognized as a substantial engineering feat (Hanke 1956: 21). Miners continued to develop mining technology into the eighteenth century, including a major innovation in the Mexican mines which involved the large-scale use of gunpowder to blast mines in order to build larger mine shafts and drainage passageways (Lockhart and Schwartz 1983: 334).

The labor to build and operate these mines, refine the silver ore, and coin money at the mint came in several overlapping forms, but in none of the American cases did mine or mint workers enjoy the protection of the guild-like corporations that the mint workers in Europe labored under. Indeed, many of the workers in Spanish American mines, refineries, and mints were coerced or unfree laborers. While the refineries and mints of New Spain relied on some enslaved people of African descent, at Potosí, where fully half of American silver originated around the turn of the seventeenth century, Spaniards adapted an indigenous labor rotation system, the *mita*, to compel indigenous people from a large catchment area to work in the mines and refineries. Once the Viceroy Francisco de Toledo implemented this system in the 1570s, adult males (and sometimes whole households) would travel to Potosí every seventh year from as far as 600 miles away to fill an annual quota of 13,000 *mitayos*. These workers received wages, but they were often below subsistence levels, and they were always lower than the wages that the free *minga* laborers who supplemented the *mitayos* received. However, *mitayos* often took advantage of their time in Potosí to engage in other activities that could augment their wages. Whether they were allocated to mines or refineries, they labored in three-week rotations, with one week on and two weeks off. During those two weeks of "rest," many of them worked as *minga* laborers for higher wages, or even as self-employed small-scale miners, or *k'ajchas*. Coerced and free labor coexisted in the mines and refineries of Spanish America (Bakewell 1984; Tandeter 1993; Brown 2012; Barragán 2017).

But where mining and refining technology depended so heavily on the operations of unfree laborers, the workers at these sites had little ability to resist the adoption of new technologies as they did in Europe. Indigenous smelting was replaced by a mercury amalgamation process with little overt resistance from workers. American mints converted to milled coinage in the eighteenth century with little fanfare. In the absence of corporations of moneyers, resistance and opposition took other forms. In the 1630s, royal officials discovered that silver merchants had been collaborating with mint workers at Potosí to produce debased coins after hours that contained far less silver than the standard, in order to increase their profits. A late eighteenth-century mission to send European experts to Potosí to improve technological efficiency ended in failure when refiners determined that the new methods were expensive and ineffective. And increasingly, the *k'ajchas* who mined silver ore for themselves refined their ore at small-scale mills, or *trapiches*, away from the mills operated by colonial authorities (Bakewell 1988; Brown 2012; Barragán 2017).

Refining the silver that miners extracted required significant technological expertise. The refinery—called an *ingenio* in Potosí and a *hacienda de minas* in Mexico—was an enclosed compound that housed skilled workers and often the owner of the *hacienda*, and was usually located near running water to power the refining mills. Many of the skilled workers in these refineries were enslaved people of African descent. In order to turn silver ore into refined silver, refiners used an amalgamation process with mercury that drew on the findings of German chemists but was first developed and put to use in Spanish America. Refiners pounded the ore to a fine consistency, mixed it with mercury, and then washed the mercury out after a given period. The process involved stamp mills, pumps, and vats, and technical experts including the mercury man, or *azoguero*, who adjusted the timing and ratios of mercury amalgamation according to the quality of the ore (Brading 1971:137–40).

Once they developed the amalgamation process, mercury became indispensable to the mining industry. It did not take long for the Spanish Crown to make mercury a royal monopoly; indeed, there were only two major mercury sources, one in Spain and one in Peru. Establishing a royal monopoly on mercury made the sale of mercury to miners another important source of Crown revenue, and enabled the Crown to measure silver output for tax collection purposes. Spanish officials obtained figures of mercury sold to various mines from the mercury administration, and using a known ratio between mercury and silver for the amalgamation process, were able to corroborate output figures to prevent fraud and ensure the Crown received its fraction of the silver processed in America (Hanke 1956: 22; Brading 1971: 140–6; Lockhart and Schwartz 1983: 149).

Because silver processing was so tied to the availability of mercury, Spanish silver mines went into decline when mercury became difficult or expensive to maintain, as in the 1630s. But in the three Mexican mines of Zacatecas, Guanajuato, and la Valenziana, the era of the Bourbon Reforms in the later eighteenth century brought about important technological transformations. After Spain's defeat and the end of the Seven Years War, Spanish reformers implemented fiscal and administrative changes to centralize and rationalize the relationship of the mother country to its colonies. Among the changes was a renewed focus on mining, as these reformers sought to make the colonies more profitable to the Spanish economy. Mexico experienced a huge silver boom as a result of important technological transformations in the amalgamation process, as well as a greater availability of mercury. When the Crown increased mercury production from the mine in Almadén in central Spain, it enabled a surge in output from the Mexican mines in Zacatecas in the later eighteenth century, and drastically lowered the price of mercury (Bakewell 1971: 187–9, 194–5; Brading 1971: 140–6).[15] This greater availability of mercury and changes to the amalgamation process allowed Mexican miners to exploit mines with ores that had been more difficult to extract, and Mexican silver output soon eclipsed that of Potosí (Lockhart and Schwartz 1983: 151–2, 334–5).

As refining techniques kept silver production high in the eighteenth century, the mints in Peru and New Spain continued to churn out coin, which went across the Pacific to the Philippines and China, and across the Atlantic into Europe and the Middle East. The process of getting silver from the mine to the colonial mint sometimes involved middlemen. Silver merchants, or *mercaders de plata*, bought unminted silver cheaply from mine owners, and paid for it in coin, which enabled the mine owners to pay wages (Lockhart and Schwartz 1983: 152). Over the course of the eighteenth century, some of these mints, including the ones in Mexico City and Lima, converted from the hand-hammered method to the mechanized coining methods that had overtaken European mints in the seventeenth century. The milled pieces of eight *reales* that they manufactured circulated widely throughout Europe and the Americas, and became the main circulating currency in British American colonies that had little other money in circulation.[16]

But the minting methods in Potosí remained fairly rudimentary, at least according to some outside experts. In 1788, the Spanish state sent a cadre of German scientists to Potosí to study the mining and minting methods there. The scientists were not impressed by what they found. One of the experts described the existing mining and minting processes at Potosí as "slovenly, wasteful, and unscientific" and the "incredible barbarism and ignorance that prevailed in the mint and mining departments there" (Hanke 1956: 23).[17] The arrogance of these scientists may have been unfounded, however: after a long stay and countless lectures and workshops, the European experts failed to make any measurable improvement in the existing mining techniques (Lockhart and Schwartz 1983: 147, 335).

THE PROBLEM OF SMALL CHANGE AND THE ADVENT OF INDUSTRIAL MINTING

The transition to mechanical coining, halting though it may have been, addressed basic problems of trust in currencies and in the states that issued them. It virtually eliminated coin clipping, it made coins of any given denomination more uniform and discouraged culling and hoarding, and it made counterfeiting much easier to detect. But it did not solve the monetary problems of European states, and problems of trust continued to plague monetary authorities. Bimetallic ratios between the face values of gold and silver coins drove one or the other—usually silver—out of circulation. Fluctuations in the rates that the mint paid for those metals confused the situation still further: a problem that was particularly bad in France in the first quarter of the eighteenth century. In France and Spain, depreciations and reratings were a frequent strategy to raise Crown revenue, and the uncertainty that those strategies engendered encouraged hoarding, exporting, or fraudulent overstamping so that people could avoid bringing coins to the mint (Tortella and Comín 2001: 150–5; Rowlands 2012: 90–107). And virtually everywhere, populations faced the persistent problem of a lack of small-denomination coin for change (Redish 2000: 107–35; Sargent and Velde 2002).

Small change carried its own technical and logistical problems. When states minted small change out of silver and kept the same fineness and corresponding silver content as more valuable coins, the coins were often so small as to be inconvenient, and they were expensive and technically difficult to mint. In mint systems where officers and mint workers were paid piece rates—that is, paid according to the amount of gold and silver that was minted—mint workers often resisted making small-denomination coins because it was labor-intensive and expensive: they were paid much less for the same amount of work. In many cases, mints only coined small change when there was a specific decree that required them to do so. Mints could also coin small change out of less valuable metals like copper, tin, or a mix of metals, and many did so. Some minted full-value copper coins: that is, coins that contained an amount of copper equivalent to their face value, as in Sweden, which ran on a copper standard in the seventeenth century (Sargent and Velde 2002). Others, like Spain and France, coined small change—called *billon* or *vellón*—out of a mixture of copper and silver (Tortella and Comín 2001; Sargent and Velde 2002). Whether minted out of base metals or small amounts of precious metals, small change was expensive and cumbersome to create, and European states often neglected to make enough to provide for the daily transactions and wage payments that their populations required.

When states used base metals like copper and tin to mint coins that were tokens—that is, coins that carried a face value above the value of the metal they contained, and had no semblance of having an intrinsic value that corresponded to their stated value—these coins were especially vulnerable to counterfeiting. Since they were a form of fiat money, holding value because the issuing authority guaranteed that value, there was a wide gulf between the cost of materials and the value of the coins, which meant that unofficial coiners could reap large profits by replicating them. Indeed, in eighteenth-century Britain, the meagre stock of copper money was shot through with counterfeits: up to half of the copper coins circulating in England in the 1750s were counterfeit. The high volume of counterfeit copper money further discouraged the Royal Mint from producing more small change, both because they reasoned that any new copper coins would only be copied and exacerbate the problem, and because of a prevailing belief that too much token money in circulation would drive out gold and silver money (Dyer and Gaspar 1992: 434–7; Sargent and Velde 2002: 155–6; Selgin 2008: 20–4).

The next great technological transformation in the manufacture of money was a response to the inadequate supply of small change in Britain, and the vulnerability of copper coins to counterfeiting. And it is a story that is inseparable from a wider transformation of the era: the Industrial Revolution. As industrial operations grew in scale and sophistication in eighteenth-century Britain, the shortage of small change made it extremely difficult to pay workers in mines and factories. When they could not obtain the small change necessary to pay wages, employers resorted to a variety of means: they paid partial wages in kind, they issued notes that workers could use to purchase necessities at a company store, they paid a group of workers with a single large coin and left them to find a way to divide the earnings, they paid workers less frequently and in larger sums at a time, and they arranged with nearby alehouses to keep running tabs for workers, whose drinks would come out of their wages and reduce the cash payments that employers would eventually have to pay them (Selgin 2008: 24–9). These arrangements satisfied no one: neither workers nor their employers. Before long, copper mining and metalworking operations began to mint their own tokens: copper coins impressed with the company name, which they offered to redeem for official coins. Although the legality of minting company tokens was ambiguous, such manufacturers made no effort to hide their operations; instead, the most successful of them tried to parlay their company coining into government contracts to produce public money for the nation. At first, no one obtained such a contract, but the tokens of the mining and manufacturing companies of the West Midlands were skillfully made and enjoyed wide circulation in the region (Selgin 2008: 35–78).

A breakthrough came a few years later, when the prominent manufacturer Matthew Boulton adapted industrial technology to the minting of tokens in his sprawling Soho factory in Birmingham. Boulton was the business partner of James Watt, and together they had developed the rotative steam engine that

FIGURE 1.3: Mathew Boulton's Coining Press. Photo by: Universal History Archive/UIG via Getty Images.

was so central to early industrial development. Boulton's Soho works was already an impressive operation, and specialized in manufacturing "toys," or small metal objects, especially buttons. When Boulton began producing copper coins at his factory, he created a minting operation that was truly industrial. He adapted the technology of industrial button manufacture to the minting of coins, and built a mint that used steam engines to power the machines. The fine-grained division of labor that characterized his factory, along with steam power and a new set of technologies, meant that he could coin much faster than the Royal Mint, and the coins that the Soho mint produced were perfectly uniform and much more difficult to counterfeit (Selgin 2008: 88–93, 129–31).

The steam engine did not power all stages of the coining process. Boulton's mint was equipped with a water-powered rolling mill to roll sheets of copper, which he also used to polish the rough sheets into polished sheets of uniform thickness once they were cool. A rotary motion Lap Engine powered the six blank-cutting presses in an adjoining structure. The main rotative steam engine powered the final two stages of the coining process: the machines that delivered the finished blanks to the coining presses, and the presses themselves. Boulton's coining room consisted of eight coining presses that operated automatically by means of a rotating wheel overhead that was powered by the engine.

FIGURE 1.4: Cartwheel penny, produced by steam-powered coining press at the Soho mint, 1797. Creative Commons.

Boulton sought a mint contract to coin national money at his Soho mint from the outset, and he believed that his methods would be the best safeguard against the rampant counterfeiting that plagued the official copper currency. The restraining collars that held the blanks as they were pressed at a rapid speed made the coins perfectly round. In Birmingham, he had access to some of the best metalworkers in the realm, and the quality of the engravings that he used for dies made the coins difficult to imitate. He also began to mark the edges of his copper coins, as the Royal Mint did with gold and silver coins but had so far neglected to do with copper. Boulton explained that his machines would inscribe the edges of coins at the same time as the press struck the faces of the blanks, and the letters would be in relief, which he maintained was more difficult to replicate. Indeed, the incuse legends around the edges of these coins meant that counterfeiters could not follow the popular method of casting molds out of existing coins and pouring molten copper into molds to make counterfeit ones, because the edge inscriptions would have to appear along the seam between each half of the mold, so anyone seeking to replicate the coins would have to try to do so by hand (Selgin 2008: 65, 96, 137, 280–1).

Over the strident opposition of the officers of the Mint and the much-weakened Corporation of Moneyers, Boulton finally acquired a contract to mint national copper coins at his Soho mint in 1797, and further orders followed in 1798, 1799, 1805, 1807, and 1808, along with large orders of copper coins for Ireland and for the East India Company. In response to the first three orders alone, Boulton effectively doubled the amount of official copper coin circulating in Britain, and also took on a distributional role to ensure that the new coins reached the outer reaches of Britain (Dyer and Gaspar 1992: 446–54; Selgin 2008: 110, 117). There were some drawbacks to the new technology; namely, in order to run at any speed, the coining presses had to use relatively shallow engravings. In shallower relief, the images on the coins would wear down more quickly. In order to prevent the image from wearing away,

Boulton manufactured his coins with a broad raised rim with inscriptions in incuse lettering, which served to protect the images at the center of the coins from wear and tear (Selgin 2008: 165–6).

Even as the British state contracted copper coinage out to Boulton's Soho mint, the Home Secretary and former mint-master Lord Liverpool worked to bring Boulton's technology into the fold. It was clear that in order to adopt Boulton's industrial coining methods, they would have to leave the cramped and ancient Tower. In 1807, the Mint began construction of a new building on a hill overlooking the Tower of London, and contracted Boulton to equip the new mint with the industrial machinery he had used. At the new mint on Tower Hill, the Royal Mint could produce gold, silver, and copper coins by Boulton's steam-powered industrial process. The new machinery transformed a languishing mint, churning out uniform coins at greater speed and a more constant pace. The machinery required constant attention, but the Moneyers found their role once again diminished: as laborers could just as well operate the industrial mint, the members of the Corporation of Moneyers took on a more managerial role and faded further into the background (Dyer and Gaspar 1992: 451–68).

The relationship between minting and the Industrial Revolution was a reciprocal one. To be sure, the technological inventions that accelerated Britain's industrialization, like the rotary motion steam engine, also transformed the technology of coinage; indeed, many of the same figures at the forefront of large-scale industrial manufacturing and technological innovation also produced copper coins during the early industrial era. But these new copper coins, which addressed a long-standing shortage of small change, also enabled industrial growth. Without a sufficient supply of coins in small denominations that were difficult to counterfeit, which enabled industrial managers to reliably pay wages, it is difficult to imagine that industrial growth could have kept the pace that it did (Selgin 2008: 2).

PAPER MONEY AND THE PROBLEM OF TRUST

European colonies in the Americas faced chronic shortages of metallic currency, and became some of the first economies in the early modern era to rely primarily on paper currency.

With paper money, the problem of trust became even more acute. Paper money, a quintessential monetary technology of the eighteenth century, further divorced the face value of money from the intrinsic value of its materials. If the technologies of making money—mechanized production that produced standard weights and difficult-to-counterfeit imprints, milled edges that protected against clipping—helped to reassure people of the intrinsic value of the gold and silver coins they received, paper money used a material that had no relationship at all to the face value of the currency. Without recourse to a valuable metal inside, with only the printed denomination lending any value to the money, it became even more important to trust the institution that issued the money. And just as copper currency that circulated at rates far above the value of its metals was especially vulnerable to counterfeiting, so too was paper money. Perhaps it should not come as a surprise that the principal challenges of the coinage remained similar even when money was no longer based on its silver content. Indeed, whether fiat money or a metallic standard, money needed to be protected from counterfeiting, and issued by a credible authority (Redish 2000: 12, *passim*).

Paper money came to Europe in the later seventeenth century, when Johan Pamstruck received a license from the Swedish Crown to establish the Stockholms Banco, and began issuing paper money in 1661 as a substitute for Sweden's cumbersome copper money (Newman 2008: 9). In the Netherlands, despite the lack of any substantial issuing of banknotes, many kinds of credit instruments circulated, including bank deposit receipts, promissory notes, and bills of exchange, and this paper credit augmented the money supply and supplemented the various foreign currencies that freely circulated, along with the remarkably stable metallic currency, the guilder (de Vries 2001: 115). And while various forms of paper credit, especially Exchequer bills, circulated in England in the later seventeenth century, the establishment of the Bank of England in 1694 inaugurated a new era in the issuing of paper money (Desan 2014: 304–27). These notes were not widespread, however: from 1696, the Bank only issued notes of £50 and above, more than twice the average yearly income in England, and did not start issuing small-denomination notes until the end of the eighteenth century. Bank of England notes, at least for the first fifty years, were handwritten and signed by cashiers, bearing little resemblance to the printed banknotes of the nineteenth century.

Paper money came to America to service the costly military expeditions of European empires in the interior. In 1685 in Canada, French military expeditions began using a new form of paper money to pay soldiers. Made from repurposed playing cards, this *monnaie de carte*, or card money, stood in for payments until the regiments received coin from France. Those responsible for the payroll divided playing cards into quarters, wrote denominations on them by hand, and local intendants signed them and marked them with a seal. Dutch colonists in Surinam resorted to a similar system, though in Surinam, these playing card notes were issued against bills of exchange and later against property values, rather than being redeemable for coin (de Vries 2001: 135).

Soon, British colonies in North America began to issue money for the same purpose. Without a tax revenue sufficient to pay soldiers, the colonial governments of Massachusetts, South Carolina, New Hampshire, Connecticut, New Jersey, Rhode Island, and North Carolina began to issue paper bills of credit as emergency wartime measures during expeditions against the French, the Spanish, or Native Americans in Canada, Florida, and further into the North American interior (the earliest was Massachusetts in 1690).

In 1723, the colony of Pennsylvania began to print paper money that was novel in its scale, longevity, and purpose. The Pennsylvania Assembly established a General Loan Office, which functioned as a land bank, issuing bills of credit in a wide range of denominations as fixed-term mortgage loans. The bills circulated freely, and the Assembly frequently passed acts over the next three decades to replace old bills with new emissions, keeping paper money in continuous circulation (Grubb 2006: 1–4; Grubb 2008; Newman 2008: 9–10). This was a new kind of paper money: Pennsylvania's bills were not designed as a way for the state to make emergency payments or solve the problem of expenditures that exceeded revenues; rather, they were designed to answer the problem of currency shortage among Pennsylvania's population at large. Unlike Bank of England notes, American paper bills were printed in a wide range of denominations: from a penny all the way up to £100 and everything in between, though most of the early bills were between 1 shilling and 20 shillings. Those who promoted the idea of paper money in Pennsylvania explicitly linked the new paper currency to the development of manufacturing industries and internal trade in the province (Rawle 1721; Franklin 1729). Paper money in Pennsylvania was an economic stimulus project, not a stopgap measure to meet the exigencies of wartime expenditures.

Paper money in Pennsylvania was vulnerable to counterfeiting and confronted the problem of trust in an even more immediate sense than did copper money in Britain before Boulton's minting reforms. The cost of replication was low, and the rewards were extremely high. Counterfeit bills were easy to transport, and counterfeits were often printed in Europe (Newman 2008: 26). Furthermore, some inhabitants of Pennsylvania worried about how the bills would retain their value over time, and sought to restrict the quantity of bills that the Loan Office issued out of fear of inflation. While other colonies' paper currencies experienced high volatility and inflation, especially in Massachusetts and Rhode Island, Pennsylvanians' fears never materialized: its paper currency was notably stable. But counterfeiting was a constant and pernicious problem, and Pennsylvania's printers and politicians constantly experimented with strategies to combat it. As a result, paper money in Pennsylvania was the site of intense experimentation and innovation in printing techniques.

The techniques to deter counterfeiting began simply and became increasingly complex. Some of the early strategies were no different from what had come before. Authorized signers would sign each bill manually, often in different colors of ink. Bills were numbered consecutively by hand. If anyone receiving a bill doubted whether it was authentic, they could request that the payer sign the back, and the extant bills have lists of names that enable the tracing of their

FIGURE 1.5: Pennsylvania paper 20s note, 1739, printed by Benjamin Franklin. Jim Halperin at Heritage Auctions.

circulation. Bills were "indented": that is, bound into a book, numbered, and then cut free along a jagged edge, so that the bills could be tested against the stub when they were redeemed. But these methods did not protect Pennsylvania's new currency, and the first two emissions had to be taken out of circulation completely because they were too laden with counterfeits from Britain.

In response, the technologies of making paper money soon became more sophisticated, and with them, the safeguards against counterfeiting grew stronger. Many of these innovations were the work of Benjamin Franklin, one of the early proponents of paper money, who obtained the contract to print Pennsylvania's paper bills in his own print shop after the publication of his wildly popular and eloquent defense of the paper currency in 1729 (Franklin 1729). Franklin and his business partner David Hall imported typefaces from abroad and mixed many different kinds of type in a single bill. They sometimes included Hebrew and Greek letters and zodiac symbols that would be difficult to find. "Secret marks," such as a single letter slightly askew, a small ink blotch, or an incorrect accent mark helped to detect counterfeits. "Pennsylvania" was frequently spelled in different ways on bills of different denominations. Franklin and Hall began to use difficult-to-obtain paper, such as rag paper with colored fibers or flecks of mica, watermarked paper, or imported marbled paper. They began printing with two different colors of ink on the same side, which took longer to complete but was a more difficult technique to master, and hence difficult to imitate. But the most novel of Franklin's strategies was "nature printing," where he used unique natural forms to make the bills distinct. In order to make the bills virtually impossible to copy, Franklin would make a plaster cast from a leaf—often a sage leaf—and from there, he would make a lead casting with the shape of the leaf, which he could mount on a wood block for insertion into the printing chase as he would for any other engraving. The textures and vein patterns on the leaf castings were so delicate and detailed that no engraver could hope to replicate them by hand, and since no two leaves found in nature are exactly alike, no counterfeiter would ever be able to make the same cast. While it did not eliminate counterfeiting altogether (one small-scale method of counterfeiting involved ironing the bill against moistened muslin and then using the cloth to transfer the ink to new paper), the deceptively simple but ingenious technique was among the most effective counterfeiting deterrents of the age (Newman 1964; Newman 2008: 19–28).

CONCLUSION

The technologies of making money changed dramatically over the course of our period. Mints in Europe gradually transformed from hand-hammered coinage to mechanized, "milled" minting; mints in Spanish America soon followed. The introduction of steam power to minting at the end of the eighteenth century further revolutionized the production of money. Paper money became central to colonial economies, especially in North America, and rudimentary receipts were supplanted by sophisticated and difficult-to-copy printing techniques. In each of these cases, technological transformations were an answer to the problem of trust. New inventions that changed the production of metal and paper currencies sought to solve the persistent problems of culling, clipping, and especially counterfeiting.

Money in early modern and Enlightenment-era Europe and its empires was always at risk of a collapse in public confidence, whether it was made of paper, copper, gold, or silver. Some currencies, such as gold and silver coins, had a commodity value by virtue of the precious metals they contained, and as states tried to maintain some equivalence between their "intrinsic" values and their nominal values, any irregularities between coins exposed these currencies to culling, as people hoarded or exported the heavier coins and left the lighter ones in circulation. Coin clipping further reduced the precious metal content of coins, and left a larger chasm between the face values of coins and the market values of the materials they contained. Most damaging, widespread counterfeiting undermined confidence in the authenticity of the money that circulated. For European monarchies and states, the integrity and reputation of the money they issued was intertwined with their own credit and political legitimacy. In times of political and economic crisis, these states took on the risks and costs to implement new technologies of making money that could reduce or eliminate these problems of counterfeiting, culling, and clipping. Mechanical blank-cutting machines produced perfectly round coins of uniform weight, making culling unlikely. Screw presses and edging mills created intricate and difficult-to-copy coins with lettered edges that would not allow clipping to go undetected. Currencies without a significant commodity value, such as copper and paper money, were especially vulnerable to counterfeiting, and depended even more starkly on confidence in the institutions that issued them. Steam-powered minting made copper coins more intricate, uniform, and difficult to counterfeit, providing a reliable supply of small change that made it possible to pay wages during Britain's Industrial Revolution. Nature printing and the use of secret marks and rare papers protected American paper currencies from widespread counterfeits, and enabled the circulation of paper notes in a wide volume of denominations, facilitating colonial development and internal trade.

When states transformed the techniques of making money, however, they often encountered the resistance of those who worked in the mints, such as the Corporation of Moneyers or the Cour des Monnaies. The successful opposition of mint workers and administrators to new coinage technologies, both because of the defects they detected in those technologies and because of those technologies' threat to moneyers' very status and existence, delayed the introduction of mechanical coining technologies in Europe for centuries. At last with the introduction of steam-powered minting, moneyers' expertise and privileged status became obsolete, as craftsmen were replaced with interchangeable laborers who operated the machinery. The absence of a protracted struggle when Spanish American mints converted to milled coinage may be because these mints did not rely on an established body of mint workers who safeguarded traditional coining methods; rather, they relied on enslaved people of African descent to provide skilled labor in refineries and mints, as well as on the labor of indigenous people and recent migrants. The contrast is telling. Further research on minting and other industrial operations in places that relied on unfree labor, especially the Spanish mints at Potosí and Mexico City and the Portuguese mints at Minas Gerais and Rio de Janeiro, would help to illuminate the relationship between labor relations and technological change in the manufacture of money.[18] As industrial minting technologies undermined traditional labor relationships in Europe, these technological changes made it possible to produce currencies that were difficult to counterfeit and easy to trust in, especially the small change that was so crucial to the growth of large-scale industrial enterprises.

CHAPTER TWO

Money and its Ideas

Enlightenment Debates about the Morality of Money

CARL WENNERLIND

If you were alone and happened to come by some accident to the land of an unknown people, and if you see a piece of money, you know that you have reached a civilized nation.

—Montesquieu, *Spirit of the Laws*

When money and riches bears all the sway in the rulers' hearts there is nothing but tyranny in such ways.

—Gerrard Winstanley, *The Law of Freedom*

Many Enlightenment philosophers regarded money as a signature achievement of civilization and a crucial mechanism for the improvement of society. Together with private property, money was considered necessary for economic prosperity, state formation, and the globalization of commercial networks. The new understanding of money that emerged in the seventeenth century was an integral part of the broader Enlightenment vision of progress. Drawing on Anthony Pagden's recent work, it is possible to consider money a quintessential Enlightenment institution. Money was the result of a complex sociability that struck a balance between "human rationality" and "human benevolence"; money was regarded as a product of and an instrument for the "general human capacity for self-improvement"; money was seen as freeing people to "shape their own ends for themselves"; and money was perceived as a powerful conduit for "universalism," "globalism," and "cosmopolitanism" (Pagden 2013: x–xi).

Indeed, it would be next to impossible to contemplate the Enlightenment, Pagden's or anyone else's version, without a well-functioning monetary mechanism.

Far from everyone, however, was impressed by money's capacity to foster human improvement. Some philosophers suggested that the rapaciousness on display in early modern Europe was caused or, at least, accentuated by the prevailing pecuniary culture. Thomas More, in his controversial book *Utopia* (1989 (1516)), had earlier noted that gold and silver, in their role as money, had the potential to severely undermine good morals. To ensure that precious metals would never again be able to corrupt society, the Utopians decided to only use gold and silver for the production of urinals and jewelry exclusively worn by convicted criminals (More 1989 (1516): 104). More than a century later, during the English Civil War, Gerrard Winstanley offered an even more damning critique of money. He insisted that money is a tool of the devil, fostering nothing but hostility and greed. "Money must not any longer," he wrote, "be the great god that hedges in some and hedges out others, for money is but part of the Earth; and after our work of the Earthly Community is advanced, we must make use of gold or silver as we do of other metals but not to buy or sell" (Winstanley 1649a: 2). Similar sentiments were later echoed by Jonathan Swift, Jean-Jacques Rousseau, and others. These thinkers contested the mainstream Enlightenment perspective on money, arguing that far from promoting sociability and conviviality, money facilitates covetousness and strife.

This chapter is organized in two sections. First, I explore how eighteenth-century philosophers understood the foundation of money. In their minds, what was the essential quality of money that enabled it to serve as such? To what extent did they believe it was possible to establish an "unsocial sociability" that allowed people to trust the monetary mechanism? In the second section, I explore the many ways whereby philosophers regarded money as central to progress or, alternatively, as a critical force for moral decay.

PART I: THE SOCIABILITY OF MONEY

As the intensification of commerce destabilized traditional hierarchies and challenged time-honored ways of understanding society, Enlightenment philosophers began to rethink the basic foundation of society. In their efforts to offer a secular account of human sociability, they often focused their attention on the foundational institutions that shape and order human interactions in society. Most agreed that money plays a powerful role in coordinating the behavior of heterogenous human beings. Money frees the individual to make autonomous decisions, efficiently distributes society's wealth throughout society, and facilitates the creation of a powerful fiscal system. Money, in short, was seen as essential to liberalism, capitalism, and the modern fiscal-military state. Of course, money had been appreciated for its indispensable contributions to the formation of society for a very long time. Ever since Aristotle, if not before, money had been seen as a mechanism that facilitates exchanges by enabling commensurability between different commodities and different producers. Money thus enables specialized labor and mediates between classes. The problem, as Aristotle declared, is that money not only facilitates exchanges, but also enables boundless accumulation. By providing a means to store up a limitless amount of value, money promulgates greed and selfishness. Money was thus Janus-faced, literally and figuratively. The challenge was therefore to find ways to harness the benign powers of money while steering clear of its negative uses. The extent to which money was used appropriately would shape the future trajectory of society. The understanding of money was thus deeply rooted in a conversation about the nature and future of society, as well as specific understandings of power and authority.

In addition to the debate about money's moral valences, philosophers also deliberated on money's indeterminant social ontology. If everyone had agreed that money was an object that circulates because of its intrinsic value, money would have engendered much less disagreement. It would simply have been regarded as any other commodity, with the peculiar characteristic of entering into every exchange. But because many Enlightenment philosophers argued that money circulates because of its extrinsic value, grounded either in the authority of the state or a society-wide culture of trust, the ontology of money was more difficult to grasp. Early modern thinkers had to find a plausible explanation for why self-interested people were willing to accept symbols serving as representations of promises of future reciprocation in exchange for valuable goods. While some philosophers, such as Shaftesbury and Francis Hutcheson, insisted that people's natural sociability restrains their self-interest and therefore allows them to create a culture of trust, most Enlightenment philosophers assumed that there was no such internal psychological mechanism that could be relied upon. People, they believed, were fundamentally and inescapably motivated by a regard for their own wellbeing, which made it difficult for them to trust others and for money to circulate widely (Force 2003 and Hont 2015).

The English philosopher Thomas Hobbes, for example, suggested that in the state of nature, before any institutions had been formed, self-interest generated a constant animosity between people, making it difficult to form societies. He noted that "competition, diffidence, and glory" pitted people against each other and incited perpetual violence. "The first maketh men invade for gain; the second, for safety; and the third, for reputation." This created an untenable situation in which "every man is an enemy to every man" (Hobbes 1991 (1651): 88).

FIGURE 2.1: *Thomas Hobbes* by John Michael Wright. National Portrait Gallery, London.

To overcome this "war of all against all," Hobbes suggested that it is essential for humanity to dedicate themselves to a set of rules or agreements that limit the extent to which people indulge their covetousness. The first two types of agreement necessary for the formation of society are that people respect other people's property and commit themselves to the performance of contracts in which the rights to certain properties are conferred to others via exchange. Given that words and promises are not binding in themselves, there has to be an external power, a strong state with the power to punish, in order for property and contracts not to be continually violated. Once the requisite fear of punishment is instilled in people, property and contracts provide a solid foundation for society. Moreover, in order for such a society to truly flourish, a slightly more advanced category of contracts had to be established. Because most trades in commercial societies involve the transference of a right to a good or service in the future, it is therefore necessary for people to forge what Hobbes referred to as covenants. These were contracts whereby one person delivers a good or service today, leaving the others "to perform his part at some determinate time after, and in the meantime be trusted" (94). Covenants thus constituted a form of credit contracts. These credit agreements were absolutely essential to modern societies. If society failed to establish property, contracts, and credit, there would be "no place for industry, because the fruit thereof is uncertain: and consequently no culture of the earth; no navigation, nor use of the commodities that may be imported by sea; no commodious building; no instruments of moving and removing such things as require much force; no knowledge of the face of the earth; no account of time; no arts; no letters; no society." And, "worst of all," he added in a phrase that has become synonymous with Hobbes, in the absence of property and credit, people will live in "continual fear, and danger of violent death; and the life of man, solitary, poor, nasty, brutish, and short" (89).

Credit soon became recognized as the operative principle of money. Although all earlier monetary thinkers had not believed that money had to be comprised of precious metals, most writers had viewed money and credit as separate phenomena. Money was understood as coin, while credit was discussed in the context of private and public borrowing and lending—resulting in non-circulating contracts. For example, the discussion in England during the commercial downturn of the 1620s centered almost exclusively on the lack of circulating silver coin—the so-called scarcity of money problem—and paid little attention to the extensive networks of private credit that social historian Craig Muldrew (1998) has documented. This changed in the early 1650s. In a series of proposals for the substitution of paper notes for silver coin, members of the so-called Hartlib Circle suggested that all forms of money—paper notes and silver coin—are at the core based on credit (Wennerlind 2011). William Potter, for example, argued that originally people had come to an "*Agreement* to put a certain value or estimation upon mettalls, and accordingly to accept thereof" in transactions of goods and services. But, to him, it was not the silver or gold content of the coin that was ultimately responsible for the coin's ability to function as money. Instead, he argued, "there is not at all any true worth (I say) in the best *money* or *mettall* that this Earth can afford, further than as by being *generally accepted* for things of *real value*, it gives to him that so *accepts* thereof, *security* for obtaining some other Commodity of *like* or *greater value*."

Potter therefore argued that money is really nothing but an "*Evidence* or *Testimony* (that is as it were a TOKEN or TICKET) *to signifie how far forth, other men are indebted for, and ingaged to recompence the fruits of their Labors or possessions by Commodities of some other kind, instead of those that for such money they parted with*" (Potter 1650: 38). That is, people are willing to exchange their goods and labor for money if they feel comfortable that the money will be accepted by others at a later date. Money represents the value a person gives up in a transaction and how much the person can realize in a subsequent transaction. Money thus serves simultaneously as a repository and a claim-check. Since the essential quality of money is not its intrinsic value but its capacity to be exchanged for other goods, there was no real reason why money could not be made up of a material other than silver and gold. Potter suggested that paper money would work perfectly well. He made a number of different suggestions for how paper notes could circulate as money, either by making them redeemable for land or by creating a network of merchants who agreed to redeem paper with silver coin on demand, within a few months of presentation.

Hobbes and Potter agreed that modern commercial societies relied on the existence of credit. According to Hobbes, people honored credit contracts primarily out of a fear of punishment, while, for Potter, people agreed to uphold the monetary mechanism because they recognized the potential economic benefits. In either case, money functioned because people were willing to curtail their immediate self-interest and agreed to honor their obligations. As such, money serves as a social glue, facilitating the stability of society. This was a far cry from Winstanley's scathing criticism of money's role in tearing people apart. Addressing himself to the modern merchant, he wrote:

> For Covetousness is thy God, Pride, and an Envious murdering Humor is thy God, Self-love, and slavish Fear is thy god, Hypocrisie, Fleshly Imagination, that keeps no Promise, Covenant, nor Protestation, is thy God: love of Money, Honor, and Ease, is thy God: And all these, and the like Ruling Powers, makes thee Blind, and hard-hearted, that thou does not, nor cannot lay to heart the affliction of others, though they dy for want of bread, in that rich City, undone under your eys.
>
> —Winstanley 1649b: 21

For the remainder of the seventeenth century, a spirited debate ensued about what type of paper money would be most likely to succeed. The major difference between the designs was in the type of asset or revenue stream that would serve as security for the paper notes. Soon, in 1694, the Bank of England introduced Europe's first generally circulating paper notes, backed by profits from the Bank's commercial banking operations, interest payments from the government on loans issued by the Bank, and the initial capital acquired when the Bank's stock was first issued (Carruthers 1999 and Murphy 2012). The new system of public credit worked well from the start, enabling England to marshal substantial resources for its armed forces, which allowed them to successfully challenge Louis XIV's military might in an exhausting series of battles that went on for twenty years, with only a two-year hiatus (Hoppit 2002).

The success of the Bank of England spawned even more writings on money and credit, including John Law's famous tract *Money and Trade Considered* (1705). He argued therein that with the aid of land-backed paper notes, a national bank could multiply the quantity of money in circulation and thus ignite industry and contribute to a massive increase in the nation's wealth. While the infamous credit money scheme he eventually ended up creating in France was different from his earlier proposal, both systems shared an exuberance about the potential of credit money to promote progress (Murphy 1997).

During the Financial Revolution, most writers accepted the idea that credit was at the core of money. Yet many remained confused as to what exactly credit was. The English MP Charles Davenant famously proclaimed "Of all Beings that have Existence only in the Minds of Men, nothing is more Fantastical and Nice than Credit" (Davenant 1698: 38). The prolific author Daniel Defoe similarly stated his befuddlement with the essence of credit. He proclaimed, "I am about to speak of what all People are busie about, but not one in Forty understands: Every Man has a Concern in it, few know what it is, nor is it easy to define or describe it." He cautioned, "If a Man goes about to explain it by Words, he rather struggles to lose himself *in the Wood*, than bring others out of it. It is best describ'd by it self; 'tis like the Wind that blows *where it lists*, we hear the *sound* thereof, but hardly know *where it comes*, or *whither it goes*" (Defoe 1710: 6). Unable to find a satisfactory explanation of credit, Davenant and Defoe gravitated back to the same basic solution: credit is trust in other people's probity and punctual fulfillment of obligations (Pocock 1975). As long as people behaved appropriately, money would be able to circulate and commerce would flourish.

It should be noted that not all philosophers agreed that the essence of money is credit. The English philosopher and member of the Board of Trade, John Locke, for example, reverted back to an earlier conception of money, arguing that the intrinsic value of the coin dictates its value in exchange. He contended that "*a little piece of yellow Metal*," by not wasting or decaying over time, had the capacity to serve as a repository of value (Locke 1960 (1690): 294). That is, if a person produces more wealth than she needs to feed herself and her family, she can exchange the surplus production for coin, and thus store the additional value until she wants to buy some other good or service. It was the intrinsic value of the coin that allowed it to serve as a store of value. Yet, while Locke theorized money as circulating because of its intrinsic value, he could not entirely escape the notion that money was based on a subjective valuation and a collective agreement. He acknowledged, much like Potter had done earlier, that it was "Fancy or Agreement," not the actual use-value, that had led people to ascribe value to gold and silver in the first place (300). Yet, once the value of precious metals had been set and the mint had determined the weight and fineness of the coin, it was absolutely essential, Locke insisted, that money remained incorruptible. Indeed, in the famous recoinage debate of the 1690s, Locke lobbied the British government to remint the badly clipped coins at the traditional full-bodied standard, in order to protect and uphold the integrity of the coin, even though the quantity of coin in circulation would be drastically reduced and commerce would suffer. He refused to remint the currency at a lower weight, as this signaled that the government had been forced to accept the new standard created by clippers and counterfeiters (Caffentzis 1989; Kelly 1991; Cary 2011; Desan 2015). No one, Locke insisted, should have the right to meddle with money, in particular not members of the criminal underworld. Authority and trust had to be re-established by upholding the monetary standard and by severely punishing the money manipulators, who, according to Locke, constituted a more formidable threat to Britain's safety than the armed forces of Louis XIV.

Locke had a complex relationship with paper money. As an investor in the Bank of England he cannot have been absolutely opposed to the issuance of credit money. And it appears as though his adamant insistence on protecting the old mint standard was at least partly motivated by the fact that the Bank of England notes would never be able to circulate if the underlying currency securing the notes was not entirely incorruptible (Wennerlind 2011). That said, Locke was also deeply concerned about the sustainability of paper money. While he recognized that paper money certainly had the capacity to circulate domestically, because of the fact that foreign merchants or governments would not accept them in transactions, there was a real limit to the extent that paper could substitute for coin or bullion. As the nation kept on issuing paper money, eventually all the silver and gold coins would flow out of the country, leaving the nation impoverished and exposed (Carey 2011).

While few writers worried about people's capacity to honor their promises and uphold their obligations during the Financial Revolution, with the cataclysmic bursting of the Mississippi and South Sea Bubbles and the publication of the expanded edition of Bernard Mandeville's *Fable of the Bees* (1723), philosophers embarked on a lively debate about the feasibility of trust in a culture of greed. If Mandeville were correct that all people are fundamentally selfish and greedy, even when they appear to have noble and respectable aims, how was it possible for people to remain sociable enough to uphold money? In the resulting discussion, some philosophers questioned the viability of the social fabric undergirding money, while others focused on how governments and banks jeopardized the stability of money.

FIGURE 2.2: *John Locke* by Michael Dahl, oil on canvas, *c.* 1693. National Portrait Gallery, London.

The Irish philosopher, George Berkeley, also following in the footsteps of Potter, suggested that it does not matter what material money is made of— "Gold, Silver and Paper" serve equally well as "Tickets or Counters for Reckoning, Recording, and Transferring" goods (Berkeley 1735: 7). Indeed, he believed that money's intrinsic value is entirely secondary. Even if a nation's bullion disappears, as long as money retains its function as a measure of value and medium of exchange, people will still be able to carry out their transactions and industry will continue to flourish.

Berkeley even suggested that gold and silver might actually promote idleness, a suspicion he based on Spain's experience in the sixteenth century, during which a massive inflow of gold and silver from the Americas coincided with a prolonged economic slump. Berkeley thus concluded, in his characteristic style, by asking, "Whether other Things being given, as Climate, Soil, etc., the Wealth be not proportioned to the Industry, and this to the Circulation of Credit, be the Credit circulated or transferred by what Marks or Tokens soever?" (6). He believed that any type of paper money might work, but that the "ruinous effects of Mississippi, South Sea, and such schemes" had revealed that it would be safer to have public banks issue credit money, as they were "less subject to frauds and hazards" (41). He concluded by asking, "Whether, therefore, a national bank would not be more beneficial than even a mine of gold?" (10). Berkeley's opinion was thus that people in general were capable of respecting and upholding the rules of the monetary mechanism. The problem was that bankers had gained the power to manipulate money, enabling them to make massive profits and in the process undermine the integrity of the currency and people's trust therein. In some ways similar to Locke, Berkeley was opposed to any private agent enjoying the privilege to manipulate money. Only the government, as a representative of the public interest, should be allowed to manage money, and should do so only in the interest of promoting industry.

The French philosopher Montesquieu, with whom this chapter began, commenced his analysis of money by suggesting that the absence of money is the mark of a savage nation. He exemplified this by offering a conjectural account of how trading relations were organized in Africa—and in the process added further nuance to his notoriously complex perspective on non-European cultures (Spector 2007). He suggested that "the Moorish caravans that go to Timbuktu in the heart of Africa to barter salt for gold need no money." Instead, they rely on simple barter. "The Moor," he wrote, "puts his salt in a pile; the Negro, his gold dust in another" (Montesquieu 1989 (1750): 398). This type of transaction can continue for long periods, but when people begin to transact larger quantities of commodities, the need for money arises. Trading people, he asserts without explanation, will then organically choose some metal that is durable, easily divisible, and not too heavy, to serve as money. The state later finishes the process of money creation by stamping the coin as a guarantee of its weight and fineness. Instead of suggesting that metallic money is able to mediate transactions of all other commodities because it contains intrinsic value, Montesquieu argued that money is "a sign representing the value of all commodities" (399). Similar to Marx's analysis of the money form of value in Chapter 1 of *Capital*, Montesquieu noted, "Just as silver is the sign of a thing and represents it, each thing is a sign of silver and represents it." A nation is developed to the extent that "silver indeed represents all things ... [and] all things indeed represent silver, and they are signs of one another" (399). In serving as the measure of all value and medium of all exchanges, money thus takes on the role of universal equivalent.

Even though Montesquieu argued that money is the product of a broader cultural transformation, determined by the extent of a nation's commodification, he nevertheless insisted that money is not an arbitrary social construct. Indeed, once established, the currency must never be manipulated. "Nothing," he

FIGURE 2.3: *Charles de Secondat, baron de Montesquieu (1689–1755)*. Photo by: Christophel Fine Art/UIG via Getty Images.

argued, "should be as exempt from variation as that which is the common measure of everything" (401). Similar to Locke, he therefore suggested that the metallic content of money should not be subject to manipulation, either by criminals or governments. "Ideal monies" and "real monies" should therefore always be the same. And, he added, when money is well managed and secure, it is entirely possible for paper money to be substituted for silver. "As silver is the sign of the values of commodities," he wrote, "paper is a sign of the value of silver, and when the paper is good, it represents silver so well that there is no difference in its effect" (399).

The French philosopher Jean-François Melon offered an explanation of money that combined various features of his predecessors. He suggested that "Gold and Silver are, by general Consent, the Pledge, the Equivalent, or the Common Measure, of all the Things that serve to the Use of Man" (Melon 1738: 207). Metallic coin thus played an important role in facilitating transactions between people, but it also laid the foundation for credit. The latter role was extremely important in that credit "is a thousand times more valuable" than coin (328). When money is allowed to be manipulated, by private or public actors, credit sinks and commerce is left at "a stand" (328). Melon, as well as Locke, thus argued that the integrity of the coin had to be inviolable, not solely because of the coin's own importance to commerce, but because of its centrality to the broader culture of credit.

While Berkeley, Montesquieu, and Melon did not offer particularly deep and probing analyses of the origins of money, the Scottish philosopher David Hume engaged in a rich analysis of how self-interested people were able to create a monetary mechanism based on trust. He argued that self-interested subjects were able to develop property, markets, and money by shifting their time horizons. Instead of doing what is in their immediate interest every single moment, such as expropriating the fruits of other people's labor or reneging on contracts, they learn by trial and error that they are much better served in the long run by honoring the basic commercial institutions. In a dynamic process, "I learn to do a service to another, without bearing him any real kindness; because I forsee, that he will return my service, in expectation of another of the same kind, and in order to maintain the same correspondence of good offices with me or with others" (Hume 1978 (1739–40): 521). That way, people learn that they can feel secure in their property, transactions, and contracts. If a society fails to develop fidelity in commercial relations, Hume noted, not unlike Hobbes, "the mutual commerce of good offices [is] in a manner lost among mankind, and every one reduc'd to his own skill and industry for his wellbeing and subsistence" (1978 (1739–40): 520).

Similar to his predecessors, Hume viewed money as a subset of credit contracts. He referred to monetary transactions as *"symbolical"* exchanges, in which a sign or symbol representing promises and obligations was accepted in

FIGURE 2.4: *David Hume* by Allan Ramsay. National Galleries Scotland.

return for goods or services. By using "certain *symbols* or *signs*"—or a "*certain form of words*"—people convey to each other that they have recognized that it is in their own long-term interest to respect the rules of the institution, and have accordingly resolved to honor their promises and agreements (1978 (1739–40): 522). This *form of words* thus provides a standardized way to express that whoever uses them is committed to honoring their promises and accepting the negative consequences of failing to do so. "After these signs are instituted," Hume noted, "whoever uses them is immediately bound by his interest to execute his engagements, and must never expect to be trusted any more, if he refuses to perform what he promis'd" (1978 (1739–40): 522).

In arguing that money is fundamentally based on trust, Hume was open to the use of paper money. He argued that as long as it was properly managed, it can definitely circulate within a nation's borders. However, there were certain complications that circumscribed his support of paper money. First, a nation could not issue too much paper money because it would drive out silver and gold, which would leave the government at a disadvantage in their diplomatic and military endeavors. Second, Hume was concerned that paper money was subject to easy manipulation. He, like Locke and Montesquieu, insisted that once a symbol has been agreed upon to represent a certain amount of value, no one should have the right to alter the meaning of that symbol by multiplying its quantity. He was thus opposed to counterfeiting and repeated government debasements, as well as exogenous increases in paper money. Contrary to Berkeley, however, Hume believed that the government was much more likely than private banks to overissue money. The reason was that the government issued paper money backed by an ever-expanding national debt, whereas private issuers of credit always secured paper money by some existing asset or future revenue stream. Because of this securitization, he believed that private credit would be kept in approximate proportion to the nation's wealth. Similar to the specie-flow mechanism, which ensured that each nation ended up with a money stock appropriate to the circulation of its wealth, private credit also had a self-regulating mechanism. Hence, Hume was open to the use of privately issued paper money, but was adamantly opposed to the use of publicly issued paper notes (Wennerlind 2005).

Writing toward the end of the Enlightenment, Adam Smith offered an elaboration on money inspired by many of the writers already considered in this chapter. Similar to Montesquieu, Smith argued that trading people will inevitably gravitate toward the use of some commodity that "few people would be likely to refuse in exchange for the produce of their industry" (Smith 1976 (1776): 27). There is no inherent reason why this commodity had to be a metal. Smith gave a number of examples of places where the medium of exchange was a non-metallic commodity, such as dried cod in Newfoundland and tobacco in Virginia. It was not uncommon, he mentioned, in small villages in his own Scotland, for "a workman to carry nails instead of money to the baker's shop or the alehouse." Yet, he asserted, in all countries "men seem at last to have been determined by irresistible reasons" to choose metals over all other commodities (27). Soon, in order to reduce the risk of fraud, governments step in and, by way of a public stamp, guarantee the weight and fineness of money. Unfortunately, he lamented, most governments have a tendency to do more than that. In "every country of the world," princes and governors have abused their power and manipulated the amount of silver and gold in the coin, thus "abusing the confidence of their subjects" (31).

Smith was careful to point out that money was not wealth in itself, but rather "the great instrument of commerce" (309). Although Smith saw money as first having appeared as a metallic coin, he did not have any philosophical problems with substituting paper notes for metal coins. He suggested that such a shift "replaces a very expensive instrument of commerce with one much less costly, and sometimes equally convenient." The critical word here is *sometimes*, because Smith, like Hume, did not endorse all forms of paper money. He offered a rather lengthy analysis of which types of paper money would work and how much could be prudently issued. At the end, he concluded, with his famous phrase,

> The commerce and industry of the country, however, it must be acknowledged, though they may be somewhat augmented, cannot be altogether so secure, when they are thus, as it were, suspended upon the Dædalian wings of paper money.
>
> —Smith 1976(1776): 341

In sum, for the most part, Enlightenment philosophers who engaged analytically with money were open to the use of paper money. Some argued that all forms of money were in essence credit and therefore relied on the general probity and honesty of all market participants. They recognized that people did not respect their fellow citizens out of generosity or goodwill, but rather out of a fear of punishment or a slightly redirected self-interest. Hence, credit was part of a broader culture of "unsocial sociability." For the philosophers who argued that money is fundamentally a commodity with intrinsic value, most often a metallic coin, paper money had the potential to work as long as it was firmly backed by and redeemable for coin. This had less to do with trust among money users in general, and more to do with confidence in the entity—private or public banks—responsible for issuing the notes. In both of these cases, money was the result of a complex mix of self-interest, rationality, and sociability.

PART II: THE BENEFITS OF MONEY

Money was at the core of the Enlightenment project of promoting economic development, diffusing power through the market, and gradually refining morals. Many thinkers believed that without money it would be impossible to create the kind of economic affluence necessary to free people from drudgery, to form sophisticated governments, to develop the arts and sciences, and to develop refined cultures. We have already seen earlier how Hobbes suggested that credit is absolutely essential for there to be extensive industry, scientific knowledge, architecture, and navigation. His contemporary William Potter added that the only "feasible means, whereby both to revive and multiply the decayed Trade and Riches of this land" was to establish a system of credit money (Potter 1650: 37). For Locke, money was the catalyst that freed people from subsistence production and launched them onto a path of ever-expanding prosperity—the kind of quest for boundless accumulation that Max Weber would later label the "spirit of capitalism." Locke reasoned that it only made sense for "industrious and rational" people to work diligently and apply their ingenuity to the multiplication of wealth after money had been introduced. The fact that surpluses no longer went to waste or spoiled, gave people an incentive to enclose the land and cultivate it as efficiently as possible. Contrary to those, like Winstanley, who vehemently opposed the privatization of land, Locke argued that enclosed land yields ten times as much as common land and thereby promotes the general prosperity of the nation. He asked,

> ... whether in the wild woods and uncultivated wast of America left to Nature, without any improvement, tillage or husbandry, a thousand acres will yield the needy and wretched inhabitants as many conveniences of life as ten acres of equally fertile land doe in Devonshire where they are well cultivated?
>
> —Locke 1960: 294

Locke also suggested elsewhere that money provides a standardized language in which people can interact and transact their wealth. By providing a universal metric, it facilitates the translation of quality into quantity and thus makes all things commensurable. By facilitating the valuation of goods and the negotiation between people, money is part of a distributive mechanism that enables society's wealth to flow freely throughout society. While money is relatively invisible when it works well, its centrality to society was apparent for all to see during moments of monetary instability. During the above-mentioned Great Recoinage crisis of the 1690s, a great deal of dissonance characterized commercial interactions, as people were no longer able to rely on money as a stable measure of value and medium of exchange. Instead, people had to haggle not only over the price of commodities but over the price of money; soldiers rioted over the kind of currency in which they would be paid; and the government was unable to remit funds to their allies abroad (Kelly 1991). But when money functions well, it facilitates the matching of buyers and sellers, thus contributing to the widening of the extent of the market. This, Adam Smith insisted, was vital to the intensification of the division of labor and thus the promotion of general opulence.

But money did not only provide economic benefits. Money also contributed to the decentralization of power in society. Enlightenment philosophers who advocated for greater individual rights and freedoms often saw money as an important practical tool for the reordering of authority in society. As money became a more central institution in society, increasingly mediating economic, social, and political life, it freed people to interact and transact with whomever they wanted. While power had traditionally been situated and structured by birth, titles, and pedigrees, according to both Berkeley and Smith, power was now increasingly conferred on those who had command over property and labor. For Berkeley, the "Aim of Men" was to acquire power—"the power to command the Industry of others" (Berkeley 1735: 9). Similarly, for Smith, "Wealth ... is power"—"the power of purchasing; a certain command over all the labour, or over all the produce of labour which is then in the market" (Smith 1976 (1776): 35). As money represents this form of power, the marketplace became the primary space in which power was negotiated and mediated. Considering that the market, at least ideally, was comprised of many buyers and sellers, no person or body was able to exercise non-pecuniary control over anyone else, which meant that power was negotiated in a more liberal and free environment (Rothschild 2001). Berkeley even added that it ought to be the aim of any well-governed state that each citizen "according to his just Pretensions and Industry, should have Power" (Berkeley 1735: 4). Money thus facilitated the development of a new decentralized power dynamic in society.

Some writers also praised money, together with markets, for promoting the refinement of morals. Most famously, Montesquieu submitted that "it is an almost general rule that everywhere there are gentle mores, there is commerce and that everywhere there is commerce, there are gentle mores" (Montesquieu 1991 (1750): 338). Others, such as Joseph Addison in *The Spectator*, focused on how the universality of money and trade brings people together from all parts of the world to promote peaceful and, even friendly, relations. He noted:

> Factors in the trading world are what ambassadors are in the politick world; they negotiate affairs, conclude treaties, and maintain a good correspondence between those wealthy societies of men that are divided from one another by seas and oceans, or live on the different extremities of a continent.
>
> —Addison 1711: 281

David Hume agreed with this view on the potential conviviality of mercantile relations. He too argued that the universal adoption of money brings the most vibrant classes—the middling sorts—across the world together and promotes the development of the most refined customs and manners. He described how the mercantile elites "flock into cities; love to receive and communicate knowledge; to show their wit or their breeding; their taste in conversation or living, in clothes or furniture" (Hume 1985 (1752): 271). He optimistically believed that people copy the most refined manners and customs they encounter in other cultures, so that when people from different parts of the world come together, they add to each other's refinement.

Hume did not just believe that global markets and monetary flows contributed to the formation of a sophisticated cosmopolitan culture; he also argued that the flow of money between nations had the beneficial effect of promoting balanced economic growth throughout the world. He argued that the specie-flow mechanism ensures that rich countries, as their exports increase and they attract more money from abroad, experience an increase in wages and prices. While this is desirable to wage earners in rich countries, it creates a competitive disadvantage that poor countries can exploit. While the rich countries can still continue to grow by promoting technological improvements in the more advanced, capital-intensive, sectors, because of the lower wages in poor countries, the latter will ultimately be able to take over the more labor-intensive sectors and thus gain a foothold in the global economy. While this does not necessarily generate a convergence between rich and poor countries, it ensures that a small number of countries will not be able to monopolize the world's wealth (Hont 1993, 2008).

Hume thus believed that the international monetary mechanism facilitates cosmopolitanism and global economic growth. However, he acknowledged that there were limits to money's capacity to forge truly global ties. He noted that there were places on the globe where commercial institutions had not taken root and that these places would not be able to partake in the favorable commercial march of progress. Similar to Locke and Montesquieu, Hume referred to these countries as "uncivilized" or "barbarous." Hume argued that barbarous countries were most often found in the tropics. While Montesquieu put forward a controversial theory blaming the climate in the tropics for its people's inability to thrive economically, Hume claimed that there were deeper causes of the alleged inferiority of Africans. He suggested in an infamous footnote in the essay *Of National Character* that "[t]here scarcely ever was a civilized nation of that complexion, nor even any individual eminent either in action or speculation. No ingenious manufactures amongst them, no arts, no sciences" (Hume 1752: 208). Hence, according to Hume, the only way for all nations to join the march of progress was to create modern commercial institutions. Whether Africans or people of African descent would be able to do so was left unclear by Hume (Ince 2018).

It should also be noted that not all Enlightenment philosophers thought of money as a mechanism for a favorable cosmopolitanism and globalization. Indeed, Berkeley favored paper money for the reason that it did not circulate outside the nation's borders. This, he thought, would be advantageous to the deeply depressed economy of Ireland. He and many of his countrymen had grown tired of seeing English landowners using gold and silver to transport the profits from their landholdings to London or Paris, where they spent the money on foreign luxuries. If Ireland were to shift to a paper currency, the landowners would have to spend their profits in Ireland, which would promote the local woolen trade and perhaps spark the development of other industries (Caffentzis 2000).

The above-mentioned list of benefits of money is far from exhaustive—it merely serves as a representative sample. There were also plenty of critical voices. Among the writers who pointed to money's crucial role in the ongoing moral decay of society was the Irish clergyman and satirist Jonathan Swift. In his *Gulliver's Travels* (1726), he described the *Yahoos*—a thinly veiled account of modern commercial people—as filthy and malodorous creatures whose sole preoccupation was to gather pieces of gold and silver. They were hairy and had sharp claws and lacked any "disposition to virtue or wisdom." He continued in *A Modest Proposal* (1729), a satire in which the poor sell their offspring to the rich as food, to describe the effects of money and commodification on the way people treat each other in commercial societies.

Swift was, of course, not only critical of money; he also submitted criticisms of a litany of other facets of modern society. Sharing a similar disdain for most things modern and commercial, Jean-Jacques Rousseau offered a systematic critique of modern governance, property, science, and culture. He found commercial societies detrimental to what he regarded as a good and virtuous life. The pursuit of wealth and luxury not only distracts people from that which really matters for happiness, but it forces them to organize their lives and relationships in a manner that saps their freedom, removes their civic and military courage, and undermines their sense of patriotism. Commerce transforms people's congenital disposition toward self-preservation into a perpetual quest for vanity. He was not opposed to money in principle, but argued that its centrality to society was detrimental to true human flourishing. "At bottom," he noted, "money is not wealth, it is only a sign of it; it is not the sign that should be multiplied, but the thing represented" (Rousseau 1997 (1772): 228). Nations and their people should focus their energies on producing things that are conducive to a good life and that promotes the "public good and freedom." Plenty of money in a nation is therefore not an indication that its people are happy. On the contrary, wrote Rousseau, because prices of foodstuffs tends to be higher in nations with an abundance of species, the more money a nation attracts, "the more poor people it must have, and the more the poor must suffer" (Rousseau 2003: 401).

Given that money is solely a sign or representation of value, it did not matter significantly whether money was comprised of gold, silver, or paper. Echoing both Locke and Hume, Rousseau pointed out that since "money has no real value in itself, it assumes one by tacit convention" and, he added, all "operations made to fix the values of currencies are thus only imaginary" (2003: 398). This also meant that modern systems of credit and finance added nothing of use. "I see nothing good or great come from them," Rousseau declared (1997 (1772): 225). He added that "ancient governments did not even know the word *finance*,

FIGURE 2.5: *Jean-Jacques Rousseau* by Allan Ramsay. National Galleries Scotland.

and yet what they accomplished with men is prodigious" (1997 (1772): 225). Rousseau's advice was thus for people to "cultivate your fields well, without worrying about the rest" (1997: 225). "If you want to stay happy and free," he suggested, "what you need are hearts and arms: they are what make up the force of a State and the prosperity of a people" (1997 (1772): 226). Similar to Swift's account of the greedy Yahoos, Rousseau noted that "as soon as all one wants is to profit, one invariably profits more by being a knave than by being an honest man" (1997 (1772): 226). While money and credit could play a beneficial role in society, the problem was that money had morphed into idols or fetishes. People pursued them at any cost and at the expense of all other interests.

> In all hearts there is naturally a reserve of great passion; when the only one left is the passion for money, it is because all the others, which should have been stimulated and encouraged, have been enervated and stifled.
> —1997 (1772): 226

To Rousseau, money had profoundly negative effects on people's moral psychology. The interest that it creates "is the worst of all, the vilest, the most liable to corruption" (1997 (1772): 226). In claiming that the modern monetary and financial system creates "venal souls," Rousseau prefigured John Maynard Keynes's famous quip, "The Love of money as a possession . . . will be recognised for what it is, a somewhat disgusting morbidity, one of those semi-criminal, semi-pathological propensities which one hands over with a shudder to the specialists in mental disease" (Keynes 1963 (1930): 369).

CONCLUSION

Whether we employ Anthony Pagden's definition of the Enlightenment or the historian John Robertson's recent suggestion that the Enlightenment entailed a new understanding of humanity's place in the world and a new belief in the "radical improvement in the human condition," it is difficult to conceive of the Enlightenment philosophers' vision of the future in the absence of a well-functioning monetary mechanism (Robertson 2015: 1). While modern economists, from Karl Menger onwards, tend to think of money as a natural and inevitable part of social life, Enlightenment philosophers were acutely aware of what a tremendous achievement it was for humanity to have created a functional monetary system. Money, they argued, constitutes one of the most complex societal institutions, requiring an advanced sociability to function.

While some writers argued that money must consist of objects embodying intrinsic value, many others argued that money has the capacity to carry out its main functions—measure of value, means of exchange, and store of value—even when it is virtual or represented by paper notes. The key is that people use it to evaluate wealth and are willing to accept it in exchange for labor and commodities. Once a society had become, in the words of Montesquieu and Hume, "civilized," it is able to take advantage of the many advantages that money provides. By using money, people contribute to the formation of an ever more advanced internal market, in which more and more aspects of human life become exchangeable. By widening the extent of the market, people are able to enjoy greater material prosperity and more individual freedom. For others, such as Rousseau, life in modern commercial societies is anything but free. Because modern pecuniary cultures reify and disenchant the human experience, divorcing it from religion, morals, and honor, it is difficult to think of the individual as free in any meaningful sense. To Rousseau, the human cost of affluence is simply too great.

These contrasting views on money were not invented by the Enlightenment philosophers, nor did they find a way to settle the disagreements. Indeed, Hume and Rousseau's thinking continues to fuel the discordant discourse on money, from the disagreement between Karl Menger and Karl Marx in the nineteenth century to that of Niall Ferguson and David Graeber in the present. When Georg Simmel wrote his monumental work *The Philosophy of Money* (1990 (1900)), he used money as the primary analytical prism not because he was particularly fascinated with money itself, but because of money's inescapable centrality to modern society. While money had taken on an even more important role by the time Simmel authored his masterpiece, many of the Enlightenment philosophers had already recognized the importance of money to every facet of modern life. Fighting wars, forming complex polities, and engaging in scientific pursuits would have been impossible without money; promoting justice, progress, and opulence would have been far more difficult without money; and liberalism, capitalism, and globalization, for better or worse, would never have materialized without money.

CHAPTER THREE

Money, Ritual, and Religion

A Secularization Story

DWIGHT CODR

The Enlightenment takes shape when set against religious worldviews it is understood to have replaced or superseded. The story of the modernization of money, part of the story of the Enlightenment, thus plays a vital role in the way we understand religion. In this chapter, by "the story of the modernization of money" I mean not simply the rise of mobile property and the tokens and instruments that are used to acquire such property, but the modernization of commercial practice at large, the spread of empire across the globe, the development of the science of economics around the end of the eighteenth century, the massive transformations in political economic organization that took place in the later eighteenth and nineteenth centuries, and the birth of such modern financial institutions and tools as stock markets, banks, lotteries, and insurance contracts. Money is nothing without all of these and these are nothing without money.

I will be suggesting that these events, as well as the people and personalities they called into being, are intimately bound up with stories concerning, specifically, the decline of religion in modern, Western societies. But, more importantly, this chapter aims to complicate this aspect of the story of Enlightenment. Rather than regard Enlightenment and religion as opposed to one another, and the modernization of economic life as *reflecting* a more fundamental change in outlook, I will be suggesting that money—in the broad sense described above—serves as a critical cultural location for the articulation of differences between Enlightenment and religion. The story of money—a story of immanence rather than transcendence, power rather than ethics, the human rather than the divine, and so on—thus becomes one of the ways that both Enlightenment and religion define themselves in and into the modern age.

That Enlightenment and religion stand in such sharp opposition would seem to be evident from the very definitions given to Enlightenment, or from the motto that was famously applied to it by Immanuel Kant in his 1784 essay "What is Enlightenment?" That motto, *Sapere aude!* (Dare to know!), was advanced by Kant in the context of an all-out assault on superstition and ecclesiastical biases: "I have placed the main point of enlightenment, of emergence of human beings from their self-incurred immaturity, chiefly in *religious matters* . . . because . . . that immaturity being the most harmful, is also the most degrading of all" (2005: 119, 124–5). What emerges in Kant, though, is an openness toward something uncertain and other. To pose the question of the dare is to speak of and act on the hope of—one might say *a faith in*—a certain unknowable quantum. The pitting of Enlightenment against religion, that is, was a more complex affair than may at first seem the case and only dubiously can the two be clearly distinguished. Such dares count as a kind of religion within what Charles Taylor has called "the immanent frame" of modernity, a space wherein one can find a kind of fullness that does not require a transcendental reference.[1] That the dangers the Enlightened subject may confront in the course of his maturation are immanent rather than transcendent is testimony not to a departure from a religious worldview, however, but evidence of a structural commonality linking together different leaps of faith. In other words, to define the Enlightenment against religion requires a very particular definition of the religious, and the minute we begin to understand religion in more capacious ways—as fullness, as faith, as hope—such a distinction begins to break down. Indeed, the Enlightenment itself begins to look rather religious, marked by forms of faith and ritual. This brief identification of a moment of faith within the quintessentially Enlightenment *Sapere aude!* is designed to adumbrate the approach to religion and the Enlightenment that this chapter will take with specific reference to money and economic life in the eighteenth century. This chapter suggests that the orthodox story of the gradual splitting of economy and religion over the course of the Enlightenment—what social scientists sometimes refer to as the differentiation of spheres—is neither adequate as a means of understanding the long sweep of economic history nor useful as a baseline for the interpretation of local events and specific persons' lives and works.[2]

This chapter is divided into two sections. First, I outline some of the ways in which religion in the eighteenth century remained tied to economics. I discuss harmonies between religious and secular authorities, religious dimensions of the modern commercial experience, and the way in which the divinity that underwrote providentialist theories of property and the distribution of wealth remained operative, albeit transformed, in discourses surrounding the nature of commerce and trade. This section questions the fundamentally secular nature of economics by demonstrating that at least through the end of the century most associated with Enlightenment, economics and religion were less differentiated than we take them to be today. Most importantly, I argue that far from reflecting a transition in worldviews, money and its associated themes and problems become issues in and around which ideas concerning the difference between the secular and the sacred were developed and tested.

In the second section of this chapter, I attempt to answer a question that arises from the first. If the economy remained or was always in some way religious, how did the economy *come to seem* a secular affair? What produced the illusion of differentiation? Why was the history of money constituted as a secular moment of splitting away from the religious past rather than as a continuation of an already-validated set of religious beliefs and practices? These questions have many answers; I will focus on the way that a Eurocentric approach to so-called primitive cultures helped to form the idea of modern property and the modern economic subject through a series of self-gratifying contrasts that had the unintended consequence of appearing to align religiosity with backwardness and immaturity on the one hand, and economics with progress and maturity on the other.

1: ENLIGHTENMENT MONEY AND THE RELIGIOUS–SECULAR DIVIDE

According to many accounts of economic history, the Enlightenment marks the point at which money and religion finally part ways. To synopsize this story and its principal figures: the pre-modern eye has its sights set on the transcendent, the divine, the spiritual, and, as a corollary to these, the ethical. Those possessing such eyes are often presented as flat, ascetic, willfully obtuse, principled and possibly stubborn, anti-intellectual, and perhaps even a bit goofy. By contrast, the story of secularization, which is coordinate to the liberation of the economy from religious restrictions, teaches us that advocates of commerce and trade represent rationality, wisdom, complexity, and a spirit of compromise. The religious worldview is idealistic; the modern worldview realistic. Thanks to an amalgam of empirical science and the unstoppable current of freedom, the modern eye is happily washed clean of the murky, superstitious film that had long clouded its vision; it now sees clearly the value of all things material. Religious persons of the past, because of their belief in and reliance upon a transcendental authority beyond knowing or control, found their behavior constrained by imperatives that more often than not prohibited the unbridled pursuit of "worldly goods." The modern, Enlightenment subject—whose faith in the human replaces faith in God and whose world is therefore manageable and manipulable in ways that the divinely suffused world was not—operates according to the logic of power, efficiency, and speed. Whereas the pre-modern worldview looks on the world and sees magic and spectral presences, the modern's worldview is thoroughly disenchanted.[3] The pre-modern trusts in Providence; the modern in prudence. Over time the moderns gain the ascendancy: the truth reveals itself, ghosts and angels dissolve, and humanity becomes responsible for itself.

These oppositions and the narrative of displacement in which they are placed grows from a variety of influential histories of the West written over the last three centuries. They can at best be hinted at in a note.[4] However large a territory, the persistence of such a history of opposition in the twentieth century owes its longevity, perhaps paradoxically, to a work written in 1905 that aimed to better understand the intimacy of religion and money: *The Protestant Ethic and the Spirit of Capitalism*. In this rather short book, whose title has become a shorthand for explaining capitalism's rise in the West, Max Weber attempted to show how religious identity became capitalist identity. The long-term effect of his thesis—that what began as an attempt to consecrate time to God through orderly and continuous work became the standard for behavior that characterized capitalist societies—has been to suggest a tension between two irreconcilable outlooks.

The reason for this irreconcilability is simple: the mechanism whereby the consecration of time became profit-generating activity freed from spiritual limits and unencumbered by salvational goals was not explicated by Weber in any detail. At most, Weber speaks of a gradual forgetting of the original grounds of belief. But because of his imprecision on this point, readers are left with a gap in the conceptual history that encourages them to believe that no bridge can cross that gap quite adequately enough. To explain how the one transitioned into the other, the most typical move is to pathologize those on the far side of the gap (where religion and enchantment lie; the loonies, as it were) and assume they were simply superseded by a more intelligent, Enlightened worldview. Doing so means, however, failing to recognize the similarities between faith in a transcendental realm and faith in money, progress, human potential, and so on, that Enlightenment encourages and, as Marx had observed, that markets fully require.[5]

The cumulative effect of Weberian and other such histories has been the widespread adoption of the idea that to *be economic* means to *not be religious*. Conversely, figures emblematic of religion—particularly ecclesiastical authorities—are often characterized as the great dam that prevented the tide of commerce from irrigating the vast, fallow plains of primitive civilization. To take one example, Anthony Pagden recently writes that during the Enlightenment, commerce was "looked upon with intense suspicion by all those, most obviously the religious, who had no wish to be relieved of their 'destructive prejudices' and had the most to lose from the possibilities of diversity that commerce seemed to offer" (Pagden 2013: 262). There is obviously much truth in such claims; writers such as Turgot, Marx, Bentham, and Smith were not simply imagining an antagonism with religious spokesmen.

As with all generalizations, however, there are exceptions. In the same passage as that concerning the Church's hostility toward commerce, Pagden describes the Reverend Alexander Carlyle as an "opponent" of Adam Smith and a reviler of modern commerce. It is worth noting, however, that Carlyle's only stated objection to *The Wealth of Nations* was that it was "tedious and full of repetition" (a criticism to be sure, but one hardly indicative of opposition to commerce as such), and that he spent much leisure time with early political economists. "[A]nd a fine time it was," writes Carlyle in his memoirs, "when we [myself, John Home, and William Bannatyne] could collect David Hume, Adam Smith, Lord Elibank, and Drs Blair and Jardine" for dinner (275).[6] Carlyle also praised Josiah Tucker—whose writings on trade, he notes in a way that testifies to a rather robust understanding of the subject, "anticipated some of the established doctrines of political economy"—as one of the many "excellent people" he met while staying with John Blair at Westminster (511). Carlyle, like many Enlightenment divines, saw the value of political economy and had no trouble reconciling its discoveries with his spirituality.

Given our current global crises of religion, the appeal of secularization narratives and the binaries they depend upon is understandable. To speak of Enlightenment as synonymous with secularization and commerce as a cure for dangerous fundamentalisms would seem a sensible narrative to promulgate.[7] However, the biographies of religious people in the Enlightenment do not support the terms of such a story; and the door swings both ways, for political economists were often deeply religious. As Courtney Weiss Smith has recently argued, John Locke's foundational ideas concerning political economy "were underwritten by a conviction in a meaningfully designed natural world, a 'tangible' world that God created such that it could prompt insight into the best kinds of economic order. For . . . Locke . . . material things provide a kind of ethical guide, a source of knowledge about what should or should not be done with financial systems" (113). I have argued elsewhere that it is possible to see in one the great manifestos of the financial revolution—Daniel Defoe's 1697 *Essay upon Projects*—clear traces of Defoe's commitment to the idea of deference to God in the modern, commercial order of things (2016: 112–17). This is to say nothing of the late eighteenth-century's leading political economist: Thomas Malthus, a Church of England curate. The secularization narrative charted at the outset of this chapter cannot easily accommodate such inelegancies in the progress of history, except by regarding such moments as errors in a field of facts, as striking juxtapositions, or as structures of compensation (one is religious to offset the guilt of commerce, or one is commercial in order to ground one's religious ideals, and so on). Rarely do histories contemplate the deeper and more systematic ways in which religion and money evolved in tandem. Throughout the Enlightenment British subjects, at least, continued to pay homage to the deity and pursued their imperial and commercial initiatives under the banner of religion and with good-faith soteriological objectives very much in mind.[8] We are thus unwise to ascribe to such persons motives of which they were purportedly unaware, to assume that their professions of faith were really just mystifications of a more real economic desire that would only reveal itself as such once Christianity had ceased to mystify. Churchmen consorted freely and happily with political economists, while other churchmen actively lobbied for a more just commercial order; few, if any, believed in a world altogether free from commerce and most saw the unpredictability of the market as in effect no different from the hazards and risks associated with life in a post-Edenic world. Further, as a century of pro-slavery writing attests, Christians often and easily reconciled their pieties with commercial interests that even in the eighteenth century were suspect. One such writer, John Newton, known for his hymn "Amazing Grace," continued to participate in the slave trade after his spiritual awakening and religious conversion (Hindmarsh 2018: n.p.); leading a life of such juxtapositions, Newton would later preach at a church across the street from the Bank of England, which itself had long been flanked by two other churches (see Figure 3.1).

But "juxtaposition" may not be the right word here, at least according to the logic of religion and money that Newton would have understood. For Newton, and many others, there was no tension between devotion and economic life; each was a part of the other. In short, the history of the relationship between religion and economy needs to be understood in terms other than those of opposition, hatred, or exclusivity. Indeed, one must approach the history of money with one central fact in mind: for the vast majority of economic history the idea of such an opposition would simply not have occurred to even the most venal of merchants, tradespersons, adventurers, or even moneylenders.

In what remains of this section I will suggest some of the stronger ties between religion and money, focusing on writers who, because of the gap mentioned above, have been pathologized—made into representatives of an obsolete world—or, conversely, whose religiosity has been erased or ignored. Consider the following two passages. The first is from an outwardly religious, pre-modern political economist, Edward Misselden; the second, from Adam Smith, champion of modern commerce and supposed opponent of the unenlightened religious minds of his era:

FIGURE 3.1: *St. Christopher's Church, The Bank of England, & St. Bartholomew's Church*, etching (1770). Illustration to Chamberlain's *New and Compleat History and Survey of the Cities of London and Westminster*. Photo by Guildhall Library & Art Gallery/Heritage Images/Getty Images.

And to the end there should be a Commerce amongst men, it hath pleased God to inuite as it were, one Countrey to traffique with another, by the variety of things which the one hath, and the other hath not: that so that which is wanting to the one, might be supplied by the other, that all might have sufficient.

Which thing the very windes and seas proclaim, in giving passage to all nations: the windes blowing sometimes towards one Country, sometimes toward another; that so by this diuine iustice, euery one might be supplied in things necessary for life . . .

—Misselden 1622: 25

[E]very individual necessarily labours to render the annual revenue of the society as great as he can. He generally, indeed, neither intends to promote the public interest, nor knows how much he is promoting it. By preferring the support of domestic to that of foreign industry, he intends only his own security; and by directing that industry in such a manner as its produce may be of the greatest value, he intends only his own gain, and he is in this, as in many other cases, led by an invisible hand to promote an end which was no part of his intention.

—Smith 1981: 456

Whether we consider the overt religiosity of early modern mercantilists or the cryptic "invisible hand" allusion in the anti-mercantilist Smith, a hidden force that guides and subtends the exchange of goods is plainly in evidence in both works.[9] That God underwrote and steered the course of trade in pre-modern Europe is as much as saying that for writers such as Misselden the goods of this world were placed by Him for humankind and that for a writer like Smith the dynamics of the marketplace were invisible, mysterious, but totally determinant. What Misselden and others of his era all stated openly and without equivocation was the presence of the divine in the ordinary course of commercial traffic; for them, the divine and the commercial were inseparable since God was part of all things.

As for Smith, the matter is more complicated; whether the invisible hand is a secular or sacred figure has been hotly contested. Some argue that Smith's invisible hand is a metaphor that helps to express the elegant operations of a fundamentally disenchanted marketplace; others see it as a metaphor for God in control of the market (testifying, as it were, to God's approval of the modern economic order). As early as 1899 we find Thorstein Veblen remarking that for "Adam Smith the ultimate ground of economic reality is the design of God, the teleological order; and his utilitarian generalizations . . . are but methods of the working out of this natural order" (412). More recently, Adrian Pabst writes that for Smith, "God's benevolent providence for the world takes the shape of a kind of predetermined harmony among all actual and potential things" (2011: 118).[10] For Emma Rothschild, by contrast, Smith's invisible hand, and Condorcet's indissoluble chain, principally entail judgments about the secular order, "judgments about how people might live, in a world without sublime truths" (Rothschild 2001: 246). For Rothschild, Smith was disenchanted and the economic order was a manifestation of the loss of the transcendent or divine.

But while it is possible to argue that Smith's "invisible hand" is a sacred or secular figure, to ask that question at all is to first assume that such a distinction is a material one. What is perhaps most important in all of this is that Smith's figure enables both readings of the economy to be true. What scholars on either side of this debate do not seem to consider, in other words, is precisely the figurality of the figure that is the "invisible hand" and the consequences of such figuration itself. That Smith's invisible hand can bear the weight of both a secular and a religious reading is what gives it force and enables its adoption and application. As a figure, "the invisible hand" rhetorically gathers together myriad, ostensibly separate putatively "economic" phenomena and makes it seem as though they operate as an organ, limb, or otherwise integrated entity. It is this gathering-together that figuration entails that also allows the market to be "embodied" such that it can be critiqued; this, ironically, gives the abstract and heretofore non-existent thing called an "economy" a kind of substance or substantiality even as the figure makes that "economy" available for criticism (now objectified, the "hand" can be slapped). In this regard, figuration newly substantial*izes* the marketplace, and it is a substance that is *both* secular and religious; or, rather, the substance cannot be convincingly said to be purely immanent or purely transcendental. Secularity and religion thus play with and against each other within Smith's figure. Refusing to openly declare itself as a religious figure but offering nevertheless an image richly evocative of the supernatural, Smith's "invisible hand" is partly responsible for producing the secular–sacred opposition that scholars such as Pabst, Rothschild, and others use to explain it. It is unsurprising that the debate appears intractable: the very terms scholars use to assess the figure's meaning were partly engendered by the figure's own inherent doubleness.

Figuration, translation: these terms help us to better understand the relationship between a religious and a secular economy, not as one of transition but as one of translation. Taylor sees the emergence of polite, moral, civil order in the West as, in effect, a translation of what had been religious order. Christian in all but name, this new order, he writes, "was shorn of much of its 'transcendent' content" such that its basic forms and values could be "embraced outside of the original theological providential framework" (2010: 305). But the emphasis here on a transition—from sacred to a secular that hides or mediates its inner, unavowed sacredness—nevertheless keeps alive the notion that some spheres may be truly secular while there remains some fundamentally religious core within variations of the secular. I would prefer instead that we think about the two as one thinks through Smith's figure: as variations on a theme, as metaphors aiming at a certain level of ambiguous clarity, as substantialized abstractions, but as, in any case, a place where the tensions and similarities between the secular and sacred appear with special color and intensity.

For an example closer to home, consider the phrase that has appeared on virtually every piece of US currency since the 1860s—the United States' national motto since 1956—"In God We Trust" (see Figure 3.2). It would be absurd to regard one's use of American currency as an exclusively or even primarily religious moment of daily life, like counting rosary beads or driving past a notable church on the way to work; it is not as if buying a morning latte or paying a toll reaches the same devotional intensity as taking communion. This is not to say that such moments cannot be compared to more recognizably religious rituals, merely that if asked we would allow that some difference between crucifixes and lattes exists, and that that difference can be expressed in terms of the difference between the religious and the secular. At the same time, it would

FIGURE 3.2: 1864 US two-cent piece. The first coin to display "In God We Trust" was the 1862 two-cent piece. Heritage Auctions. Wikimedia Commons.

be equally absurd to deny the religious meaning of the phrase, and, thus, the religious aspect of the transaction: not only does the phrase, and thus the object bearing that phrase, expressly name a deity (much to the chagrin of many vocal proponents of Church–State separation), the phrase was made the national motto specifically in opposition to Soviet anti-religious ideology and policy.

"In God We Trust" is a phrase that manages to be palpably sacred and bluntly secular at one and the same time. But, and this is the crucial point, it is only in the act of *explicating* the text—the text being the phrase "In God We Trust" and the explication being this very paragraph, as well as many other such ruminations on the phrase—that money manages to become a place where the difference between the secular and the sacred is dialectically established and where the identity of money as secular or sacred takes on and takes up meaning. This is the legacy of the Enlightenment as regards money and religion: the constitution of the economy as immanent in and through a language of transcendence, sacral formations, and divinity AND the constitution of the divine in and through an assessment of one's or one's country's economic wellbeing.

One final translation or mediation along these lines is worth considering before moving on. While early modern writers like Misselden avowed the divinity of the economy, Enlightenment writers and their successors neutralized some of those religious inflections—without losing them entirely—through the language of nature and natural law. Enlightenment discourse transformed the figure who had subtended the economy since the expulsion from the Garden of Eden, the Christian "God," complete with all of His explicit theological, ecclesiastical, hierarchical, and ritualistic contexts and associations, into a relatively decontextualized, deracinated, and abstract "Nature." Take, for example, the "God" of one of the first tracts of Enlightenment political economy: Thomas Hobbes's *Leviathan*. According to Hobbes, the "Nutrition of a Common-wealth consisteth" in the distribution, preparation, and conveyance of commodities for "Publique use" (Hobbes 1651: 127). For Hobbes, "God hath freely layd" "this Nutriment" in or "neer to the face of the Earth; so as there needeth no more but the labour, and industry of receiving them. Insomuch as Plenty dependeth (next to Gods favour) meerly on the labour and industry of men" (127). While Hobbes was unequivocal in his transcendental point of reference, by the time these very words appeared on the opening pages of J.R. McCulloch's important 1845 index of political economy, *The Literature of Political Economy*, Hobbes's phrase "God [who] hath freely layd" had been paraphrased by McCulloch as "the free gift of nature" (3).

This was a translation that had been made possible by a century of thought. Regarding the international balance of trade, for instance, whereas Thomas Mun declared in 1621 that it was "by the prouidence of almighty God" that England was "inriched with treasure brought in from forraine parts," Joseph Addison, a century later, observed that the distribution of goods was owing to "Nature," who has "an eye to [a] mutual intercourse and traffic among mankind, that the natives of the several parts of the globe might have a kind of dependence upon one another, and be united together by their common interest" (Mun 1621: 3; Addison 1711: 264–5). At a glance the alteration seems slight, but that is precisely the point. The very slightness of the shift posed a question—when Addison says Nature does he mean God?—that spurred a debate about the nature of economic life: is the economy the space of God or the space of Nature? This debate, in turn, gave shape to the development of the notion that the secular stood in opposition to the religious sphere, since the idea that it might be both was anathema to an Enlightenment logic founded upon these and similar binaries.

McCulloch went on to further summarize Hobbes's view: "Nature is not niggard or parsimonious. Her rude products, powers, and capacities are all offered gratuitously to man. She neither demands nor receives an equivalent for her favours" (4). Again, these are not Hobbes's words, and by swapping "Nature" for "God" in accounting for the history of political economy, McCulloch gives the impression not only that political economy was always already in some way ahead of the game, intellectually speaking, not dependent upon transcendental concepts, but that political economy in his own time had no element of religion within it and did not require a transcendental reference for its structural coherence and practical legitimacy. McCulloch is by no means special in this regard; he was able to make this move because the Enlightenment had made possible the erasure of the divine in the economy even as it preserved something ineffable in terms as arguably vague as those of religion: invisible hands, nature, and so on.

To turn Hobbes's "God" into "Nature" required the rewriting of the history of political economy; this new history would proceed *as if* the economy occupied a position of secular importance as opposed to the pre-modern world of religious veneration and superstition from whence the Enlightenment promised release. The "economy" would thus become not only the path toward imperial prominence, it would be the path into a future unencumbered by the spiritual limits and ethical meditation that had long guided economic decision-making. A new politics of secular time would be driven by a deracinated "Nature" cooperating with the forces of commerce to free the West from its stagnant, superstitious past. Even so, as modern American currency attests, the West does not wish to entirely free itself from its religious origins; this is not because it guiltily "remains" religious in spite of its outward, secular appearance, but because its true addiction is to the unstable binary which guarantees the unanswerability of the question itself: is the economy a secular or sacred affair?

2: THE PRIMITIVE MIND AND THE EMERGENCE OF A SECULAR ECONOMY

If religion and economy were less differentiated than is often thought, how did we come to understand the process of economic development as one of disenchantment and secularization? In what follows, I would like to argue that representations of British others—primitives, in particular, but not only primitives—made it so that whatever came across as opposed to modern economic thought and behavior could be derogated, directly or indirectly, by associating those other forms of thought and belief with lesser and more deviant forms of religion and faith. Superstition, enthusiasm, divination, fetishism, priestcraft, witchcraft, and other aberrant modes of reason and worship became points of emphasis in a larger project of trumpeting British superiority over its imperial adversaries and the indigenous peoples its imperial ambitions saw as obstacles.

Central to this process of secularizing the economy was a reimagining of the way in which Westerners understood and represented what they took to be their unique ability to think about time, especially future time. In the eyes of Enlightenment thinkers, the primitive—a figure located both in the historical past (pre-modernity) and the geographical present (Africa, the Americas, and so on)—was said to be locked into a confined zone of sensation and temporal experience and therefore ascribed supernatural significance to contingent and unforeseeable events; modern subjects, by contrast, were thought capable of forming elaborate plans for the future, which made him or her (usually him) better at participating in the secular, immanent, economic order. Coordinate to primitive religion, then, was primitive economics; both were characterized by credulity and a fascination with whatever was

FIGURE 3.3: Frontispiece ("Dutch Weight") to *A History of New York, From the Beginning of the World to the End of the Dutch Dynasty* by Diedrich Knickerbocker [Washington Irving]. Hathi Trust Digital Library.

nearby (that is, within reach, within earshot, within one's sight, within "the circle of sense"). As a consequence of this, figures presented as primitives often serve as the butt of a certain joke about European commercial cunning (see Figure 3.3). The engraving shows a Dutch merchant tricking two American Indians into receiving less money for the pelts they have brought with them by applying his own weight to the scale and thus tipping it in his favor. Similar tricks are also reported in the travelogue of Louis Armand, Baron de Lahontan (1703: 257).

Before proceeding, I should quickly mention that my thinking on this problem takes its bearings from the French anthropologist Johannes Fabian, whose 1983 book, *Time and the Other*, revealed some of the assumptions that underlie the concept of "primitive culture." Principally addressing anthropologists, Fabian argued that an uncritical application of the term "primitive" to designate cultures living today made that culture seem comparatively inferior; what was needed, Fabian rightly demanded, was a recognition of the coeval temporality of anthropologist and the culture undergoing study such that the anthropologist did not implicitly consider his or her temporality to be of a superior or more advanced kind.

Recently, Kathleen Davis has critiqued Fabian's claim on the grounds that even Fabian presupposes the division between a "sacred–medieval–feudal" past and a "secular–modern–capitalist" present (4–5). How, asks Davis, were these categories naturalized? When did the opposition itself begin to become useful? For Davis, the opposition grew out of late medieval claims to sovereignty. I would suggest that one of the later episodes in the history of the naturalization of an opposition of the kind Davis analyses was the politicization of temporal imagination in a joint discourse concerning religion and economics, a politicization that occurred around the end of the eighteenth century, but one that had earlier roots and later efflorescences. At stake was not a *realization* of the primitive as religiously backward and economically underdeveloped, but the *constitution* of an opposition between the modes of religion and economic life that characterized the West and its others, an opposition both between the historical primacy of these systems as well as between the mentality of the individuals who made up these systems. The Enlightened mind was thus of an Enlightenment order that focused on the future while the primitive mind, trapped in a primitive order, was regarded as incapable of forming abstract and complex ideas about the future.

Adam Ferguson's characterization of the primitive mind captures these many nuances and illustrates how Enlightenment discourse concerning prudence—calculative rationality oriented toward the future—was positioned against religion and superstition:

> Their superstitions are groveling and mean: . . . They are . . . derived from a common source, a perplexed apprehension of invisible agents, that are supposed to guide all precarious events to which human foresight cannot extend.
>
> [In] strange and uncommon situations, [the mind] is the dupe of its own perplexity, and, instead of relying on its prudence or courage, has recourse to divination, and a variety of observances, that, for being irrational, are always the more revered . . . A Roman consulting futurity by the pecking of birds, or a King of Sparta inspecting the intrails of a beast, Mithridates consulting his women on the interpretation of his dreams, are examples sufficient to prove, that a childish imbecility on this subject is consistent with the greatest military and political talents.
>
> —149–50

Ferguson seems here unwilling to consider the complex web of social, psychological, affective, and cultural forces that, woven together, render the divinatory mode appropriate *regardless* of its efficacy when viewed from the standpoint of Enlightenment-era instrumental rationality. It is as if the primitive has the choice either to be Enlightened (prudent) or to be religious (divinatory) and, further, it is as if the worlds in which the primitive and modern exist are somehow distinct from the instrumental rationalities each chooses to employ in their respective worlds. Although he does not say it outright, Ferguson suggests that the primitive might change the rationality he or she employs as if the world that rationality approaches or attempts to modify would not also have to be changed. In short, it is as if the primitive's approach to the unknown is being measured against prudence only in order for it to be found wanting. The effect of Ferguson's portrayal—and many of its kind—is to consider divination (and related practices) a kind of instrumental rationality of which prudential, economic reason is really just a better and more useful type. Indeed, it is significant that Ferguson allows the ancients and primitives certain "military and political talents"; this allows Ferguson to claim, in effect, that the primitives or ancients *might* have used more appropriate rationality had they chosen to do so.

These and the like oppositions, in which calculative rationality of an instrumental and economic kind is pitted against a divinatory or prophetic approach to the unknown, seems designed specifically to legitimate the former at the expense of the latter and practitioners of the former against the prophets and magicians of an exploded pre-modernity. Hume, similarly, had written that

> [There are events] which are not very remote, and which *reason foresees* as clearly almost as she can do any thing that lies in the womb of time. And though the ancients maintained, that in order to reach the gift of prophecy, a certain divine fury or madness was requisite, one may safely affirm, that, in order to deliver such prophecies [as that a national debt will in time lead to economic misfortunes], no more is necessary, than merely to be in one's senses, free from the influence of popular madness and delusion.
>
> —"Of Public Credit," 365

It is not simply that ancient, pagan, or superstitious minds are different from those of the minds of the present. Hume, who aims to demonstrate the perils of national debt, does contrast a calm, prudential, economic sensibility to an inspired prophetic mode. But, in drawing a comparison between the two— however facetiously—he forces his reader to suppose that the prophecy and reason aspire to the same kinds of knowledge (notwithstanding the bathetic effect of, say, the oracle at Delphi foretelling changes in Mediterranean interest rates). For Hume, as for Ferguson, reason is simply a more effective tool of "prophecy," and this functional equivalence enables and requires a ranking of civilizations according to a logic that is the express by-product of one of the civilizations—the prudential—whose rank is at stake.

How primitives imagined time, and specifically future time, with "childish imbecility" or "divine fury," was one of the central ways in which writers of the Scottish Enlightenment in particular went about delineating the differences between the modern and pre-modern self, which played into the discourse of prudence—the virtue of calculating future economic consequences, as it came to be defined in the eighteenth century—and the mentality requisite for full and successful participation in the new economic order of the eighteenth century.[11] Superstitious or prophetic modes of knowing were cast in opposition to the Enlightened mind insofar as the latter was capable of determining causal outcomes within an immanent frame while the prophetic mode was based on magic and naive credulity.

The connection between the religious and the economic in the discourse concerning primitives becomes even more apparent when looking at the work of another Scottish Enlightenment writer, namely, Dugald Stewart. Stewart justified the political economy of reason in terms of its opposition to the "depravity of rude tribes":

> [T]he farther back we carry our researches into those ages [of the past] we are the more struck with the numberless insults offered to the most obvious suggestions of nature and reason. We may remark this, not only in the moral depravity of rude tribes, but in the universal disposition which they discover to disfigure and distort the bodies of their infants;—in one case, new-modelling the form of the eye-lids;—in a second, lengthening the ears;—in a third, checking the growth of the feet;—in a fourth, by mechanical pressures applied to the head, attacking the seat of thought and intelligence. To allow the human form to attain, in perfection, its fair proportions, is one of the latest improvements of civilized society; and the case is perfectly analogous in those sciences which have for their object to assist nature in the cure of diseases . . . and in the regulations of *political economy* (emphasis in the original).
>
> —Stewart 1866: 452

"Perfectly analogous" aptly summarizes the kind of discursive alignment that the Enlightenment proponents of a modern British economic mentality wished to create between, on the one hand, the extravagant rituals of non-British cultures and, on the other hand, a defective or unnatural understanding of political economy. The same impulse that prompted primitive cultures to interfere with the natural development of the human form would no doubt lead to rash interferences in the market. For Stewart, who demands a passive approach to the human form, the invisible hand that molds flesh should be left to mold the economy as well.

Again, this is not to say that money in the Enlightenment had no religious element. What distinguished Enlightenment from primitive economies was the deracinated quality of the divinity associated with the former, a divinity that was as abstract and immaterial and intangible as primitive figures of worship were concrete, particular, and embodied. The God of the Protestants in particular lent itself to a translation into "Nature," whereas the brute and intentionally graphic quality of the primitive ritual or fetish, as it was described and caricatured by Stewart, rendered the religion of "others" more or less untranslatable into anything other than forms of unreason and hypervisible pagan rite (which is to say, only back into itself). Unlike the heathen gods, whose determinate characteristics opened them up to ridicule and insult—concreteness conducing to satire—and unlike heathen ritual, which when compared to the comparatively sterile Protestant ceremonies—at least as they appeared to Protestants—took on a similar degree of concreteness in those rituals' attitude toward both bodies and the natural world, the Protestant God and the Protestant ritual appeared relatively abstract in theory and aloof in practice. It was precisely this ability to abstract God that marked an Enlightened attitude; hence, in an interesting exception that proves the rule, the Enlightened "Savage" of Baron de Lahontan's *New Voyages to North-America* is praiseworthy and distinct precisely for "the most abstracted and spiritual manner" in which he expresses adoration for the deity (1703 [2]: 19).[12]

While Enlightenment writers generally disagreed with Lahontan's portrayal of primitive religion, they would have concurred with his claims made elsewhere that the natives of America were economically undeveloped. For Rousseau, the primitive's

> ... soul, agitated by nothing, is given over to the single feeling of his own present existence, without any idea of the future, however near it may be, and his projects, as limited as his views, hardly extend to the end of the day. Such is, even today, the extent of the Carib's foresight. In the morning he sells his bed of cotton and in the evening he returns in tears to buy it back, for want of having foreseen that he would need it that night.
>
> —126

It is not at all coincidental that Rousseau would describe the mental disposition of the primitive in the context of trade, for facility in commerce and trade would increasingly become the index for human intelligence *in general*.

William Robertson, more a historian and geographer than political economist or moral philosopher, expressed a similar sentiment:

What among polished nations is called reasoning or research, is altogether unknown in the rude state of society. The thoughts and attention of a savage are confined within the small circle of objects, immediately conducive to his preservation or enjoyment. Every thing beyond that, escapes his observation, or is perfectly indifferent to him. Like a mere animal, what is before his eyes interests and affects him; what is out of sight, or at a distance, makes no impression. There are several people in America whose limited understandings seem not to be capable of forming an arrangement for futurity; neither their solicitude nor their foresight extend so far. They . . . are entirely regardless of distant consequences, and even of those removed in the least degree from immediate apprehension . . . [T]hey set no value upon those which are not the object of some immediate want.

—309–310

For Robertson, "American Indians were creatures of appetite without the use of reason, and consequently incapable of forming an idea of futurity" (Bickham 2005: 197).[13] Again, though, neither Robertson nor Rousseau were simply describing the intellect of natives. They were helping to forge new definitions of terms like "understanding" and "reason"; to wit, "understanding" and "reason" meant the cultivation of a principally economic relationship to the world and to the future. For writers such as these, the appetitive disposition that purportedly arrested calculative reasoning amongst primitives squared with what were considered superstitious forms of thought. As Hume famously put it regarding the source of superstition, when the sources of one's misery are "invisible and unknown, the methods taken to appease them are equally unaccountable, and consist in ceremonies, observances, mortifications, sacrifices, presents, or in any practice, however absurd or frivolous, which either folly or knavery recommends to a blind and terrified credulity. Weakness, fear, melancholy, together with ignorance, are, therefore, the true sources of SUPERSTITION" (1987: 74). The widely held assumption regarding primitive religious action was that its goal was an objectively measurable alteration of the external world; personal edification, community building, or ritualistic affirmation of a particular relationship to nature were never considered possible motivations or justifications for religious practices, perspectives, or enthusiasms. The Enlightenment can thus be seen as marked by a peculiar incapacity to grasp or contemplate relationships between self and world in terms other than the instrumental.

As a way of pursuing into the nineteenth century this complex affiliation of the religious and economic defects of the great mass of humanity beyond Britain, it is worth noting the writings of British explorers Richard Burton and John Hanning Speke. This is partly because they show the legacy of the Enlightenment construction of the primitive mind but also because they reveal the toxic forms of racial-scientific understanding to which such notions gave rise. The "East African," according to Burton, "has stopped short at the threshold of progress; he shows no signs of development; no higher and more varied orders of intellect are called into being ... His mind, limited to the objects seen, heard, and felt, will not, and apparently cannot, escape from the circle of sense, nor will it occupy itself with aught but the present" (489). Likewise for Speke, Burton's travelling companion, "experience will not teach the negro, who thinks only for the moment" (25).

On one occasion, Speke reports asking an African man "what advantage he expected from sacrificing a cow yearly at his father's grave" (236), and later telling him that Britons, "instead of trusting" to magic and omens "put our faith only in skill and pluck" and that "England formerly was as unenlightened as Africa, and believ[ed] in the same sort of superstitions ... but now, since they had grown wiser, and saw through such impostures, they were the greatest men in the world" (237). Speke's anecdote gathers together the many strands that this chapter has covered. In the first place, it plays upon the analogy between Enlightenment and religious "faiths" in order to privilege one over the other; second, it effectively conflates pre-modern and foreign belief systems together under an implicit category of the "primitive"; and, finally, it considers Western imperial, economic supremacy the direct causal result of the overcoming of superstitious beliefs and in so doing authorizes empire by way of the familiar Kantian distinction between Enlightenment and superstition.

Such moves by writers from Ferguson and Smith to Burton and Speke to cast the primitive mind as devoid of an understanding of futurity drew upon characterizations of the irrationality of the primitive that grew out of an unmistakable astonishment with the superstitions and rituals of a monolithic non-Protestant world. Those moves also fed back into celebrations of the prudential character of moderns. Crucially, though, depictions of primitives—their religion or their sense of property—had no bearing on the faith dimensions or the transcendental reference points of the modern economy. Indeed, Speke's astonishment at the African man's sacrifice of a cow is only slightly more intense than his astonishment at the godlessness of the Africans in general (236). It was simply that the abstract and dematerialized reference points of Christianity were more difficult to see *as* religious when they were juxtaposed with such things as animal sacrifice, with the gory and garish spectacles of other people's faiths.

CONCLUSION

By the end of the eighteenth century, and certainly by the nineteenth, the primitive was marked by religion in a way that the Protestant was not. Superstition and ritual of this primitive variety came to define what it meant to *be religious*, a religion whose characteristics were associated with a lack of calculative reason, an inability to think of future consequences, and a defiance of "nature" that rendered those who exhibited such characteristics unfit for the prudential world of modern commerce. Even so, it cannot be said that the economy was any less religious than it had been in earlier times; risks and dares, invisible hands, just desserts, the language of good fortune, and, finally, the faith that underwrites local systems of credit as well as fiat money continued to give impetus to modern commercial institutions and practices. However, when set against the extravagance of primitive religion, such facets of economic life took on the appearance of not being religious at all. Indeed, to speak of good fortune in the modern marketplace would come to seem a category mistake or quaint anachronism.

By redefining religion as the preoccupation of the primitive, of man in his nonage, Enlightenment society defined itself in a way that seemed to exclude religion altogether, even when one of its most defining features—a modern economic order—was, in the final analysis, still very much bound up with matters of faith and an invisible order of things. So, if we are to say that the economy became a sphere differentiated from that of the religious sphere, it is not because it was secular, but because its religious origins had been rendered *comparatively* secular in appearance. We would perhaps do well to ask whether, in accepting a straightforward narrative of economic and religious differentiation, then, we are also accepting the problematic differentiation upon which it is based: the eighteenth-century differentiation of the primitive and civilized.

CHAPTER FOUR

Money and the Everyday

New Practices in the Enlightenment

CRAIG MULDREW

On April 29, 1740 the self-taught local scrivener John Cannon recorded the sale of a piece of land near Glastonbury in Somerset. This land had been mortgaged by John Semer for a loan of £20, two and a half years earlier, to Cannon's aunt, the widow Elizabeth Pope, and was now being sold to a third party, George Fear, to pay back this loan. Fear and Semer met with Cannon, who had written the mortgage, Mrs. Pope, and one other witness. At the meeting the £20 together with £2 10s. interest was paid in cash. After the transaction was completed, Cannon and Mrs. Pope went to the alehouse when Fear arrived unexpectedly and . . .

> feigning a frivolous excuse, request[ed] Mrs. Pope to let him see the money paid her imagining a mistake, to which she readily condescended and forthwith drew out of her bosom a yellow silk knit purse in which were the very principal money and interest which she had just before received at Merriott's house viz. 20 guineas, a moidore and three silver shillings which made up £22 10s and no more. It was observed that the said Fear, Semer and his wife did fumble in counting the consideration money especially in that part of the same which was above Mrs. Pope's part or share. However, let the mistake be designedly or otherwise, it was not found to be in Mrs. Pope's money.[1]

This passage is a rare example where we can witness how people used money in the form of coins in the Enlightenment. Twenty-two pounds was an exceptional amount to carry around, and the purchase of land was one of the few instances when someone would walk around with such an amount, and twenty guineas would have been a lot to keep in one's bosom. Much less was needed, or available as we shall see, for day-to-day transactions. However, the company at the alehouse would have provided some safety from potential theft and thus the counting could take place openly. Mrs. Pope's yellow silk purse is indicative of her wealth and standing in the community, just as the purchaser's nervousness in getting the value right indicates an anxiety about matching the value of gold and silver coins to the units of money of account. At this time a moidore was valued at 27 shillings, indicating that the guineas were worth 21s. each, which with 3 shillings makes £22 10s.

Three years before this, on November 3, 1737, Cannon recorded another rare mention of a new form of currency in Glastonbury. Over the course of four days, besides other work, he drew up over 200 bills for the Widow Swanton, although he did declare it was the "most intricate business I ever took in hand." Swanton had taken over her husband's plumbing and glazing business and all of these bills would have been for work done. But Cannon provides evidence that once written they could circulate as a form of local paper currency until they were destroyed. They could be passed on to a third or fourth party with the endorsement of a signature as a continual obligation, thus making credit more fluid, as long as the value stated on the bill was willingly met by someone else, as in the following example: "19th November Received a bill of goods of David Bell, value £3 1s ½d for which I gave a note payable the 1st December next and took up and cancelled a former note" (Money 2011: 588).[2] Crucially their value depended on people knowing that scriveners or minor attorneys like Cannon had written them up.

These two examples, together with many others which could be cited from Cannon's *Memoirs*, nicely illustrate both the changes and continuities in the everyday use of money in England in the age of the Enlightenment. While metallic coins continued to be used, increasingly this was an age in Europe which saw more use of transferable paper instruments to augment coins. The history of such paper credit is most well known in the form of the shares and banknotes issued as a part of the financial revolution by civic or state institutions such as the Bank of England or the Bank of Naples. These were used to facilitate the growth of public debt, or by large trading monopolies such as the Dutch and English East India Companies (de Vries and van der Woude 1997; Dickson 1967; Murphy 2009). But at the same time merchants and tradesmen were issuing bills of exchange which were being traded all over Europe and some around the world. At the lowest level, informal notes were being arranged by local attorneys and small-scale scriveners such as John Cannon in England. The creation of such informal bills and notes would eventually combine with the business of clearing bills of exchange in the form of numerous local county banks in England in the 1760s and similar urban banks elsewhere (Pressnell 1956).

Of course this happened in different ways and to different degrees in the great number of political units which existed with differing intuitions and economies. Here, I will begin by providing a basic outline of the reasons for this change, but the main aim will be to provide concrete examples of the "every day." In this chapter I will try to show how people in everyday life facilitated this change by first examining the inheritance of the use of coins together with personal credit from preceding centuries. I will then examine the ways in which different forms of paper currency came to be used. Finally I will use the wonderfully detailed, published summaries of trials from the London Criminal Court, the Old Bailey, to provide examples of how both cash and paper money came to be used in Britain's capital.[3]

COINS AND INTERPERSONAL CREDIT

To get a lived sense of how individuals like Mrs. Pope interacted with things that were thought of and called money, I will define money as a type of circulating material object with a value supported by institutions representing some form of social agreement. In addition, one could also, of course, discuss the central role of money of account as a form of *measurement* in everyday use as well. In memory, account books, daily transactions, and reckonings, people all thought about the value of things and services in a numerical measurement based on forms of monetary value such as English pounds, shillings and pence, or French livres and sous, or Venetian ducats and scudi. Such use of money as a tool of measurement also had an "everyday" history which could be told based on the social practice of numeracy. Ways of measuring goods and services, such as the changing size of a penny loaf of bread so it was always worth a penny, or measuring work by the hour, or measuring drink by standardized sizes, were methods to deal with numerical illiteracy. The ability to keep basic accounts, moving up to double-entry bookkeeping, gave households and businesses an advantage in determining their worth and earnings and expenditures. As we shall see, the development of such techniques was essential for the increased use of paper currency as a circulating object, but it will be the use of monetary objects that this chapter focuses on, because while accounting ability undoubtedly increased during the eighteenth century, this occurred primarily amongst the middling sort, especially those involved in retailing, and estate farmers. Coins were used by all, and paper forms of currency also circulated much more widely throughout society in the form of naval tickets and small banknotes used to pay workers, as well as what seems to have been the most common form of paper money (at least in England): notes of hand for work done or things sold, which circulated only for a short time within local villages and districts.

Throughout the whole of the early modern period, including the eighteenth century, it was common throughout Europe to use credit rather than cash for many payments, which was the primary means of using money of account. At one very simple level, this was because there was simply not enough gold and silver coins to meet the needs of the developing market economy in most places. Because all European polities relied primarily on a system of bimetallic gold and silver precious metals as a form of money, they also relied on their scarcity to maintain the value of the small amounts in the alloy of these precious metals included in denominations of various coins issued under the authority of political rulers. Even if people had preferred coins in every transaction, there would not have been enough.

There were areas of Europe that possessed more cash than others. Spain during the sixteenth century suffered much higher inflation than other parts of Europe because of all of the New World treasure being looted and then mined in South America and then transferred to the Old World (Braudel and Spooner 1967). However, this new money did not distribute itself equally around Europe. England and Scotland, for instance, suffered an especially acute shortage during the century. Little of this new gold and silver found its way into monetary circulation there for any great length of time because there was a net outflow of bullion because of foreign trade deficits and England's need to pay for wars in Ireland and in the Low Countries. As a result of these factors, the value of the circulating medium at the end of the sixteenth century in England might have been as low as only £1.5 million (Wordie 1997). If this was the case, it means that by the end of the century there would have been only about £1 16s. per household.[4] But, between 1540 and 1600 food prices also more than trebled, while industrial prices doubled, and the amount of goods being consumed on the market also, roughly, doubled during this period (Brenner 1962: 270; Phelps Brown and Hopkins 1962: 179–95; Muldrew 1998: 99–103). As a result, by the end of the sixteenth century the demand for money had probably increased by something like 500%, while the supply of coins hardly expanded at all, resulting in a vast expansion of the use of sales credit in transactions. Thus, the reality in England was that the economy grew faster than the supply of gold and silver, which was never anywhere near large enough to meet the needs of the economy.

As England's involvement in overseas military action declined and the trade deficit was eliminated by the 1630s, the volume of the coinage gradually increased. But by the Restoration, clipping of the edges of unmilled silver coins reduced the value of most, and good money either left the country for foreign exchange, or was kept out of circulation by merchants to use in payment with each other. Samuel Pepys estimated that there was probably only £7 million worth of money in circulation in 1665 because so much was hoarded (Latham and Mathews 1970–83: IV, 147–8, VI, 23). This situation reached a crisis point in the 1690s because there was not enough money to meet the huge demand of taxation to pay for the Nine Years War against Louis XIV. This resulted in the Great Recoinage of 1696 which produced almost £9 million in silver coins and some £4 million in gold. However, the undervaluing of the Mint price of silver in England by Sir Isaac Newton meant that most of this new good quality silver left the country by 1720. Subsequently, in most years before 1750 less than £5,000 was minted and much less after the turn of the century (Challis 1992: 434, 691–3). At the time of the gold recoinage in 1774 it has been estimated that only about £800,000 in silver was in circulation (Feavearyear 1931: 153–4; Mayhew 2000: 106–7).[5] In contrast, gold from new mines in Brazil was accumulating in England from her Atlantic trade and successful woolen exports, resulting in the new gold coins being worth £18.2 million.

As Jan Lucassen has shown, the Low Countries attracted both gold and silver currency in the fifteenth and sixteenth centuries for various reasons, one of which was the Spanish money which flowed to pay for warfare there. Lucassen has termed this situation one of "deep monetization," defined as a society which has a monetary stock of over five times the hourly wage, which enabled the latter to be paid more regularly, facilitating economic growth (Lucassen 2014: 73–121). But, by the second half of the seventeenth century, huge amounts of silver coins were being shipped to Asia by the Dutch East India Company to pay for imported spices and other goods, leading to a reduction in the stock of coins to only two times the hourly wage. However, this situation was remedied by the successful introduction of new copper coins with milled edges. England, as we saw, never attracted much silver coinage, and also sent much to Asia by the eighteenth century.

But the amounts of gold and silver bullion available do not tell the whole story of the availability of coins. As has been noted by many authors, there was an especial shortage of small coins because they were expensive to produce using silver, which tradesmen and merchants preferred to see minted into coins that could be used for larger transactions and overseas trade (Sargent and Velde 2003: 4–14, 45–68). Because the value of gold was about fifteen times that of silver, gold coins had always been minted in larger denominations. The smallest English gold coin in Elizabeth I's reign was 10s., and from 1663 the guinea rapidly became the main form of gold currency, which circulated slowly because of its value (Kelly 1991: 44; Lowndes 1695: 52–6). As a result, by the time of the Restoration the circulating currency was almost entirely composed of silver coins.[6] Almost all small change was coined from silver, but because inflation had reduced the value of the metal since the Middle Ages, this meant that coins of a penny or less contained less silver and had thus become very small and uneconomical to manufacture. In 1601, for instance, it was stipulated that only four percent of silver coined by the Mint was to be in small money of less than a shilling, but during the seventeenth century this fell to only one and one half percent. By the 1670s this had fallen further to only one half of one percent, and the lowest denomination minted during the recoinage of 1696 was the sixpence.

This was an acute problem for the poor. They had to rely on cash more than their wealthier neighbors. Because of seasonality and the high elasticity of demand, work, especially industrial work, was often irregular, which made debts hard to pay back on time. This damaged the credit of the poor and lowered their ability to buy on credit. As a result, most depended on weekly wages, and any local lack of small change would mean they might not be paid for long stretches of time (Muldrew 2007: 394ff.).

Occasionally governments were strong enough to force mints to produce small silver coins, as was the case in the northern Netherlands in the sixteenth century, but more often they added to their money supply by issuing non-precious copper coins only in small amounts, which formed a fiat coinage used in small-scale transactions, and especially for wage payments. Such use of copper was a common feature of most Asian currency systems in the early modern period as well as in various European states (Lucassen 2014: 79–81). However, the problem with copper was that its market value as a metal was not high enough for a small coin to be minted in which the value of copper was as great as the value of the amount of money of account stamped on the face of the coin. This made counterfeiting a great temptation, and the value of the coinage then had to be protected by the criminal law. In England, counterfeiting base metals such as copper was only designated a misdemeanor, in contrast to the coining of precious metal coins and counterfeiting which carried the highest punishment possible, that for treason (Styles 1980). As a result, copper coinage was only intermittently used by the English Mint as it always led to a glut of false coins developing (Muldrew 2001: 102–3). But even when copper was used the poor still needed to rely on credit.

Other countries, especially the Netherlands and France, were more successful in producing copper coins that remained in circulation, although what methods were used to prevent counterfeiting are not immediately clear (Lucassen 2014: 90–8; Sargent and Velde 2003: 97–8). In Sweden for a time in the seventeenth century the shortage of gold and silver was so acute that copper (which was mined in Sweden) began to be used for larger-scale currency in which the market value of the copper was matched by the face value of the currency. This led to the famous copper plate money where plates worth 10 riksdaler weighed almost 20 kilos (Wiséhn 1995: 14). One other potential solution was for private tradesmen to issue their own local currencies called tokens, again made of a base metal such as copper or lead, or brass which could be quickly withdrawn if counterfeiting began (Mathias 1979).

Coins suffered from other problems apart from counterfeiting. Before milling presses were invented, the most common of these was clipping away the edges thus reducing the intrinsic *vs.* the face value, making the weighing of coins a common practice. Although, during the great coin shortage in England during the Nine Years War, before the Great Recoinage, quite often silver shillings which had been badly reduced in size by clipping continued to circulate at face value, effectively making them a fiat currency (Jones 1988: 30–9, 95–126, 228–48).

The use of coins was generally reserved for certain types of transactions. Wage payment was undoubtedly the most important, but other uses included overseas payment where there was a trade imbalance precluding the continuing use of bills of exchange, or in payment for land as in the example cited above, or as part of a marriage portion or dowry. Another common use was for payments of small amounts in alehouses and markets where the purchaser was unknown and could not accumulate regular credit. Generally the use of credit was much easier and more flexible, and the use of money always worked in tandem with credit. Furthermore, if one was literate and could keep accounts, debit and credit could accommodate the exchange of much larger sums. As Adam Smith facetiously put it, a great merchant might take up to a week to count out £10,000–20,000 if he had to make a large payment in guineas and shillings.[7] The use of credit in economic transactions could take many different forms. The most common was in sales credit. In England this type of credit vastly predominated.

The scale of the relationship between small-scale credit and the use of money in the seventeenth century can be seen by using the example of English probate accounts (the final document in the probate series required by the ecclesiastical courts). These documents are invaluable for the study of credit because they list all the payments by the executrix, or executor, out of the surviving estate of the deceased, including funeral expenses, money for the raising of minor children, bequests, and the final payment of the deceased's debts still existent upon their death (Erickson 1990: 273–86). The following table shows that most credit was extended for goods and services, and not on the basis of money loans before 1715 (Muldrew 1998: 103–11).

TABLE 1: Types of debts occurring in probate accounts from Hampshire 1623–1715

Sales credit, services, work done:	1006	(74%)
Bills and bonds:	193	(14%)
Rents:	90	(7%)
Servants' wages:	27	(2%)
Wages:	24	(2%)
Tithes:	5	
Mortgages:	4	
Herriots:	3	
TOTAL:	1352	

All of these numerous debts, of course, had to be paid eventually, and the means by which this was done with the limited amount of cash available was to "reckon" or compare accounts, cross out equivalent debts, and then settle only the difference in cash or with a bond. Because credit was so common, most people eventually accumulated numerous reciprocal debts over time, and these were either remembered, or recorded in account books, and then mutually cancelled, at convenient intervals. Henry Best recorded one set of complex reckonings over the course of three months with a farm laborer:

> sett off Leonard Goodale's reckoning for 11 days work for himself and 6 days his wife 5s. 1d. 15 July: a cheese sold him 1s. 5d. and rye 2 pecks 2s. 6d. 20 July 1623: reckoned with Leonard Goodale and paid him for his mowing and his wife's *lowking* and hay making 12s. He oweth me yet 1s. 4½d. More a cheese 1s. 5d. (these entries continued until 7 Sept. when Best recorded paying Goodale and his wife 7s. 8d. for their labour).
>
> —Bird 1971: 255[8]

Such reckonings were a common social practice, and occurred between all members of communities, as well as between wholesalers trading over long distances. Nicholas Blundell's diary is full of entries recording when he reckoned or compared accounts with people from all across the social scale. He regularly did accounts with his steward, with his lawyers, with his servants for their wages, and many others as well. On one occasion he mentioned stating accounts with his milkmaid Mary Howard for goods he had bought from her worth 18s. including a pound of old pewter, a brass pan, and a brass spoon, "and for Wages, as also for something she ought me, upon the Stating the Accounts I gave her the whole Ballance." On other occasions he reckoned with laborers for work done, canceling their wages against money lent, and things sold to them (Tyrer and Bagley 1968–72: I, 120, 144, 191, 198, 278, 289, 300. For other examples of reckonings, see I, 17, 18, 24, 26, 29, 41, 49, 65, 75, 82, 86, 90, 107, 119, 122, 135, 140, 168, 178, 93, 203, 204, 208, 221, 222, 224, 234, 242, 252, 292, 300).

TYPES OF PAPER CURRENCY

Usually when we think of paper currency, we think of it being issued by a bank which is trusted to redeem the note at the value written on it, thus allowing others to also accept its value. The earliest banks to actively introduce paper currency in Europe to address the problem of a diminishing number of metallic coins were the public banks of Naples as early as the 1580s. Of course the Song dynasty had introduced a form of paper currency in twelfth-century China, but by 1400 this had ceased functioning as viable currency and by the eighteenth century China relied on silver and copper coins (von Glahn 2016: 262–87, 365–70). The acute currency shortage in Naples was caused by increasingly high taxation by the Spanish Crown to pay for Philip II's wars. However, to make the currency work at this early date it was legally required that every transfer had to be officially endorsed at the bank itself, thus reducing the liquidity of the paper issue and, of course, its use elsewhere. The notes were also returned to the bank when no longer used and as a result there still exist 300 rooms of archival stores with many millions of notes (De Rosa 2001: 497–532). There were many forms of government debt issued by both monarchs, and, most sophisticatedly, Italian city-states in the form of annuities or simply small and long-term interest-bearing bonds written out on paper which could change hands, although quite often this had to be recorded (Mueller 1997: chs. 9–12; Tracy 1984).

The creation of the Bank of Scotland in 1696 provides perhaps the best example of a direct government policy to use a national bank to create a banking system with the aim of overcoming the limitations of oral credit, especially in paying wages to kick-start economic growth, or "improvement," as it was known at the time. Although the Bank of Scotland was created around the same time as the Bank of England, reform of the Scottish economy became politically urgent after the terrible famine of 1696–7 that killed perhaps 15% of Scotland's population. Schemes were put forward to improve Scotland's agricultural production as well as trade and industry (Cullen 2010; Hont 2005). The bank was organized around a central office in Edinburgh with branches in other major towns, and the security of the notes was based on efficient bookkeeping and a fractional reserve of one-fifth of the amount of notes in gold. Initially, notes of £5 and £10 denominations were issued with cut counterfoils to prevent fraud. Certain notes could be accepted at branches if so designated (so that the counterfoil could be sent there), and from 1704 £1 notes began to be issued (Saville 1996: 22–32, 48). Although there were initial problems in finding enough coins to meet the needs of full convertibility, with government support the Bank survived, and as the eighteenth century progressed, more branches were added and competing note-issuing banks such as the Royal Bank of Scotland and a linen company bank were also set up (Saville 1996: 37–8, 49–52, 97–108, 125–6). This system was remarkably successful until the 1760s when the so-called Ayr Bank failed in 1772, causing 114 bankruptcies and leaving debts of over £650,000 (A. Smith 1976 (1776): 313; Saville 1996: 156–66; Phillipson 2010: 206–8). But before this the Bank of Scotland, and other banks created in its wake, including the Linen Bank which was used to pay workers in this industry, successfully created a circulating currency.

Other non-banking institutions could also facilitate credit which might have been able to circulate to some degree, although this is hard to establish definitively. In countries like France and Italy, most towns and villages had registered notaries through whom loans had to be registered for a fee, which was intended to provide security (Hoffman, Postel-Vinay, and Rosenthal 2001: ch. 2; Menant 2004). However, as historians have pointed out, most loans that were registered with notaries were usually of quite a high value, owing to the high administrative cost, and that for poorer individuals smaller sales credit predominated. Julie Hardwick, Michael Sonenscher, and Steven Kaplan have all noted the extent to which small-scale credit was necessary in France below the level of notarial debt (Hardwick 2009: ch. 4; Sonenscher 1984: 307–9; Shaw and Welch 2011: chs. 4–5; Kaplan 1996: ch. 5). Another interesting difference with England is that many Catholic countries had institutions which provided charitable credit for the poor. In Italy and France, the Monte di Pieta, Church-sanctioned pawn shops, offered cheaper credit to the poor (usually 5 percent interest) on receipt of pledges. Work by Maria Giuseppina Muzzarelli and Mauro Carboni and others has also shown how crucial the possession of goods of lesser value was in the economy of the poor. They needed certain sorts of goods that were not too expensive to be placed at pawn in order to obtain cash to purchase food, healthcare, and other daily needs in relation to consumption. These institutions provided money to the poor, who, as we have seen, were more likely to be denied sales credit and who had less access to the more valuable forms of money. Such institutions, if they did not have access to enough small change, could also issue tickets, which became a form of local paper currency (Muzzarelli 2012: 23–38).

The degree to which notaries might act as bankers in issuing paper documents regarding loans that might be endorsable and enter into circulation has not attracted much study (Hoffman, Postel-Vinay, and Rosenthal 2001). However, some work has been done on the degree to which even local tradesmen were using bills of exchange drawn from around Europe in the mid-eighteenth century (S.D. Smith 2001: lxvi–lxxii, 787–8; Denzel 2002). However, it should be stressed that the circulation of a bill of exchange was limited to individuals trading over long distances between towns. Early Venetian banks and other Italian banks facilitated credit by transferring money by book, but they did not actively issue transferable paper (Mueller 1997: ch. 1, *passim*; Marshall 1999: chs. 4–7). The same was true of the Bank of Amsterdam in the seventeenth century. In the eighteenth century, however, increasing numbers of banks began to be created on the fractional reserve principle of turning invested savings or mortgaged land into paper instruments of credit. To do this they obviously lent money with interest, but they also issued paper currency using discount fees to earn small profits. Such banknotes were valuable to them and their customers because they oiled credit markets by increasing liquidity, thus making their interest-bearing credit able to do more work as an investment.

In England the institutional use of notaries was much less common than in most other Western European polities, and it is likely that sales credit predominated to a greater extent in England because of this. Also, the Bank of England was primarily established to attract interest-paying investment to loan to the government on the security of taxes. Although it initially issued some £5 banknotes, thereafter it rarely issued anything less than £20 notes (Clapham 1970: I, 146). But note issue was not its major function; rather, its priority was to issue shares that were initially purchased mostly by a wealthy metropolitan clientele before spreading to provincial towns. Few beyond the middling sort held shares (Dickson 1967: ch. 11), and it was not until the 1760s that local county banks began to evolve out of businesses with large wage bills, or many customers (Fiske 1990: 15–112). The main social and institutional change needed to make paper instruments work was that people who accepted them could rely on the fact that what was written on a note was accurate. If it was issued by an institution, it was important that the institution kept accurate accounts and was solvent. Notes also had to be backed up by laws which recognized their value (Desan 2014: 23–69). Crucially, the value stated on the instrument issued had to be trusted by anyone accepting it, which was achieved in different ways. The degree to which this process happened in different parts of Europe is impossible to say, but we can use England as an example because sources exist to examine everyday use in great detail.

As noted above, in the eighteenth century, England experienced a chronic shortage of small silver coins, during a period of increasing production and consumption. Although many proposals for different sorts of banks that would issue paper currency to speed up circulation were suggested in the late seventeenth century, in the end only the Bank of England was created, which did not issue small notes (Wennerlind 2011: 54–79). However, credit networks were also changing at the informal level, where people began to use personal notes and bills, a development rarely recorded in histories about the financial revolution (McCurdy 2007: chs. 3, 6). In this way, the system of sales credit continued, but with informal written notes which were much easier to transfer locally to third, fourth, or even more parties through endorsement. Although almost none survive, by 1684 it is clear that bills were negotiable by endorsement because John Scarlett in his legal manual on Bills of Exchange noted that endorsements could be made as many times as there was room in the bill (McCurdy 2007: 70, 76, 83, 128, 161). (Transferablity by endorsement did not, however, endow a paper instrument itself with an underlying legal value separate from any individual transaction.) If, for instance, a farmer wrote a bill to pay a laborer for £2 for making a hedge, and the laborer assigned it to his baker for one pound of bread, and then the baker endorsed the remainder as a £1 note to pay for a watch, only the individual transactions could be taken to court as individual cases of debt, if the initial issuer of the bill was found not to have had sufficient liquidity to issue the bill in the first place. The paper itself had no legal value. Credit circulated on such a basis required, therefore, that those holding it trust that the transactions it was used for could be enforced in court.

The *Chronicles of John Cannon*, from which the example at the start of this chapter was taken, give us a detailed sense of how common informal bills and notes had become by 1730 in the small town of Glastonbury. Cannon was a poor Somerset husbandman's son who became an Excise man and then a local schoolteacher and scrivener for the less wealthy of Glastonbury. In his *Chronicles*, Cannon listed over 800 transactions involving bills, notes, bonds, and mortgages, sometimes of great complexity, although only a tiny minority were carried out for significant amounts of money. He mentioned either using, or writing out and witnessing, over 120 notes of hand and over 250 bills. These are also clearly minimal numbers as they are those he wrote down when he thought a record needed to be kept. It is obvious from reading Cannon's *Chronicles* that the circulation of thousands of such bills was becoming an accepted form of evidence of a transaction which in most cases precluded going to court to establish the nature of an obligation. They could also serve as a type of local currency, being passed on to a third or fourth party with the endorsement of a signature as a continual obligation, thus making credit more fluid as long as the value stated on the bill was willingly met by someone else. Such bills could circulate by being endorsed by each party in the progress of the bill, but this left parties open to the risk of a forged signature. Cannon worked assiduously to build up a local reputation for accurate scrivening and accounting and thus became a key trusted individual in the new system of paper credit (Muldrew 2018: 133–59).

Over the whole course of Cannon's memoirs, however, he mentioned only about fifteen transactions involving guineas and eleven with shillings. Copper coins or tokens were not mentioned at all, and neither were bills of exchange, even though there were mercers, grocers, and maltsters in the vicinity mentioned in the diary. But perhaps they wrote out their own bills of exchange, which would only have circulated between other towns such as Wells and Bristol.[9] However, on one occasion, when describing a recent robbery of the Western Mail post boy by an armed highwayman between Sherborne and Crewkerne in April 1739, Cannon noted that,

> ... he broke open the Western Bags and took out what bank bills, accepted bills and notes of hand he could find which he took with him and made back to Salcomb near Kingsbridge, where he agreed with a master of a sloop to carry him to St. Malo in France for eight guineas. He lodged a bank note of £20 in the master's hand for payment of the same and set sail on Wednesday last but were forced back to Dartmouth by contrary winds, when endeavouring

to change the said bank notes which was endorsed by one Follet of Topsham and sent in the same mail for London gave some suspicion (which he suspected) . . . The notes and bills he took amounted to near £7,000 which he left with the justice except the £20 bank note.

—Money 2011: 479

These bags were intended for over twenty towns, including Axminster, Taunton, Bridport, Exeter, Totnes, Barnstaple, and Bodmin, which certainly implies that there was a very large circulation of merchants' and tradesmen' paper credit between these towns and London by this time.

EXAMPLES OF THE USE OF MONEY IN CRIMINAL TRIAL RECORDS[10]

The exceptional detail of John Cannon's financial transactions in his *Chronicles* give a strong sense of how paper was being integrated into his rural community and how trust was generated and how disputes took place. Other less detailed journals from around Europe can also provide information on some transactions. However, a wonderful source exists with literally thousands of descriptions of how individuals in London dealt with many different sorts of money in their day-to-day lives, including new forms of paper, and it is very accessible. These are the online *Proceedings* containing accounts of trials that took place at the London Central Criminal Court, the Old Bailey, which covered the City of London and the County of Middlesex. The first published collection of trials at the Old Bailey dates from 1674, and from 1678 accounts of the trials at each session (meeting of the court) were published regularly at an inexpensive price, and targeted initially at a popular audience.[11] Although there are some gaps in the early years, since the publication was validated by the Mayor of London it is assumed by criminal historians that the publications contain accurate reports of the great majority of trials, of which there were about 78,000 before 1820. The descriptions of the trials are not, and were not intended to be, an official transcript. But in many cases the level of detail contained in witnesses' descriptions of the events relevant to the crime in question provide accounts of quotidian life simply unavailable in such quantity from other sources. Elsewhere in England, witnesses' depositions exist for criminal trials held at local assizes, but since much evidence only needed to be reported orally, this documentation is not as rich, and only exists in written manuscript. The latter is true of other criminal jurisdictions around Europe, where undoubtedly similar sorts of cases were tried.

It is also the case that when dealing with examples of the use of money, criminal trials, of which over 80 percent concerned property theft, are in no way a neutral source from which any kind of accurate statistical pattern of monetary use can be determined. Thieves undoubtedly targeted people and premises that were likely to possess or contain valuable items worth stealing, of which money was the easiest to dispose of. Furthermore, the great majority of cases originated in the heavily built-up urban environment of metropolitan London, which had a population of over 600,000 by 1750. Not only was London much wealthier than the rest of the country, it was also its economic and financial entrepôt. Although northern towns like Liverpool, Manchester, and Birmingham were growing rapidly, it was not until the turn of the nineteenth century that even their combined populations came near that of London's. However, in cases of theft, useful *comparisons* can be made between the amounts of different sorts of money stolen from people's purses or households including copper, pennies, shillings, guineas, and foreign money in addition to paper notes of hand and banknotes. In addition, a great deal of information is available as to where and how people of different status and occupation kept money in their dwelling places. We simply need to remember that probably most poorer people had much less money on their person, although there are cases of poor individuals being robbed which can be used as examples.

There is also a significant amount of qualitative evidence to suggest that much of the kingdom's money flowed into London for payments of tax as well as wholesale goods and rent for country gentlemen's London townhouses. In Peter Earle's sample of especially detailed inventories of the London merchant and trading elite taken from the London Court of Orphans for the period 1665–1720, the average value was £5,283, and the amount of cash possessed was £254 (Earle 1989: 121). London Goldsmiths obviously had a considerable amount, and larger merchants and tradesmen needed a great deal of money for overseas trade. A cross section of all the inventoried London population would most likely give a much lower average, but even so, the amount of cash held by this tiny percentage of the population was enormous. Using the same records, Richard Grassby estimated there were 8,350 London businessmen with assets worth £500 or more, with an average net worth of £2,829, after 1660. This means that they might theoretically have been in possession of over £2 million, or 25–35 percent of the cash in the Restoration period, and around 15 percent thereafter (Grassby 1995: 247–50; Earle 1989: 32, 121; Muldrew and King 2003: 158–60). Thus in all of the cases given as examples below, we must keep in mind that London was a much more cash-rich society than rural England and undoubtedly most of rural Europe, even where copper coins were circulating. Since cities were centers of trade and industry, even small coins tended to gravitate toward the center of networks and transactions.

Almost all of the cases in which money is mentioned fall under categories outlined in Figure 4.1 below. Grand larceny was the most common offence, and it involved the theft of goods of the value of one shilling or more, but without any aggravating circumstances such as assault or breaking and entering. Many

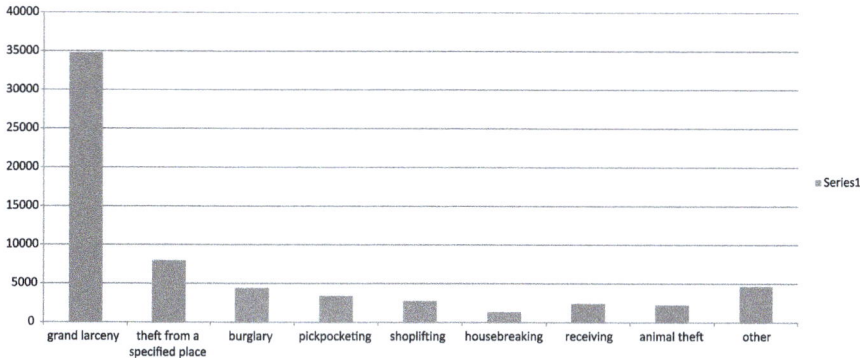

FIGURE 4.1: Total number of theft offences of all kinds in the Old Bailey proceedings (1678–1820). https://www.oldbaileyonline.org/static/Crimes.jsp#theft (accessed March 17, 2018). Author's own.

of these cases were what we would understand as pickpocketing, but at the time the statutory definition of pickpocketing involved "privately" stealing goods worth more than a shilling from the person of another, which meant without their knowledge. The difficulty of proving that the victim had no knowledge of the crime meant cases were difficult to prosecute. Many involved prostitutes stealing from their clients' clothing while they were in bed. Burglary was defined as breaking into a dwelling house at night with intent to commit a felony (normally theft), or actually doing so. Offences of this sort committed during the daytime were defined as housebreaking. Theft from a specified place included thefts from warehouses, ships, manufactories, churches, lodging houses, and domestic houses (where no breaking and entering took place). Shoplifting was defined as "privately stealing" 5 shillings or more worth of goods from a shop, and was made a capital offence in 1699, reflecting concern over its apparent increase as shops became more numerous.[12] Violent theft was the most serious and usually involved highway robbery.

To begin with petty larceny and pickpocketing, a few examples can suffice to show that people took the precaution of securing the cash they carried around with them in different pockets, purses, or fobs. A fob was small, snug and sewn in like a modern pocket on men's trousers, while a pocket was a small bag which could be tied to a belt or placed inside a jacket. In a case of grand larceny from 1716, John Mason was convicted for stealing a "Pocket-Piece," "a Tuscan Crown, value 4 s. 6 d. as well as 1 Dollar, value 4 s. 6 d. 10 Iron Keys, value 1 s. and 2 Shillings in Money from the Person of Mary Wenham."[13] In another case of violent theft from 1770, Benjamin Hall, a cheesemonger, deposed:

> I had been round among my customers as usual, to see what they wanted. I received the money, and was returning with my pans for butter under my arm . . . Bowers, one of the prisoners, came up to me, and asked me what it

was o'clock … and then bid me stop, and put a pistol to my head … Milbank unbuttoned my breeches to see for my watch. I had none. Then he took three guineas and a half out of my fob, a quarter guinea and sixteen shillings out of my breeches pocket; they felt in my other pockets, and found nothing else … They cut off my waistcoat pocket, with seven shillings worth of halfpence in it.[14]

In another case—one of highway robbery from 1736—"an iron Key, value 1 d. a Nutmeg, value 1 d. a Copper Ticket for the King's private Road, value 1 d. three Copper Medals, value 2 d. two Pieces of Silver Coin, value 2 s. 10 d. five Guineas and a half, and 13 Shillings and 1 d. in Money" were all taken.[15] These examples and many more show that it was common to carry a wide assortment of different types of coins on one's person, even when wealthy, undoubtedly to make small daily purchases. The case of Anne Keys, who was tried for theft on December 3, 1729, but acquitted for lack of conclusive evidence, presents us with a detailed account of how money was used in a small market purchase, and again how it was common to carry money on the body in more than one purse or pocket:

Elizabeth Miller depos'd, that the Prisoner came to her Stall on the 15th of November, cheapned some Meat, and after some time, agreed with her for a Piece of Beef that weighed 4 Pounds and a half, at two Pence a Pound, which came to 9 d. the Prisoner offered her a Shilling, but she seeing some half Pence in her Hand, this Deponent desired the Prisoner to give her 15 d. and she would return her 6 d. but, upon looking for Change, she [the seller] had lost all her Money which she had just before; upon which the Prisoner was seized … upon searching her, they found upon her One Guinea, Ten single Shillings, and a half Crown … there was three Shillings in one Pocket, One Guinea and half a Crown in another, and 7 Shillings in a third.[16]

Other cases also show how and where people kept their money in households. The following case of a theft from an upwardly mobile gardener, also involved the stealing by his spinster maidservant, Maria Doon, of a number of valuable silver buttons, buckles, and teaspoons:

… a canvas bag, value 2 d. and 47 guineas, 6 half-guineas, a quarter-guinea, 4 half-crowns, 2 silver threepences, 21 pieces of foreign copper coin called doits, value 6 d. a piece of foreign copper coin called a liard, value an halfpenny, and 46 s. and 6 d. in monies numbered, the property of the said Timothy. And a linen handkerchief, value 18 d. the property of Samuel Smith. And a bank note of the value of 20 l. one other bank note of the value of 10 l. one other bank note of the value of 10 l. the money secured by the said notes being due and unsatisfied to the said Timothy Marshall.

Marshall was the gardener victim, and related that he had discovered the theft when he,

> ... went up stairs to see what money I could spare, as I had my rent and other things to pay. I looked over my money. I put my bank notes in a private drawer in my bureau which stood in my bed-chamber. I put forty-seven guineas and six half-guineas in a canvas bag, which I put in the drawer upon the bank-notes. I then told over two guineas worth of silver in shillings and sixpences; there was a half-guinea, and four half-crowns. I put all that into a common drawer which slides in by the side of the private drawer; they were likewise in a bag.

Later in the evening upon going to bed he "saw a hole through the ceiling in the closet which led up into the cock-loft. I went directly to my bureau; I found it broke open, and I missed all my money, the snuff-box, the spoons, the seal, and the other things." Doon was Marshall's servant, and in the witnesses' statements which followed it was discovered that she had changed the £20 banknote by purchasing mercery wares to obtain change which she put in a nutmeg grater for safekeeping. When the note was produced at the trial, Marshall was asked if he possessed a memorandum of it and if he knew its number. Although he deposed that he did not, this question shows how paper credit could be protected with diligent bookkeeping. Another witness told the court that Doon had given her children some of the doits (a small Dutch coin worth half of an English farthing), claiming she had had them from another child. When produced in court, Marshall claimed to identify them by specific marks:

> Here is a Flemish halfpenny amongst them, which has a mark upon the edge by which I know it. There are two of the doits have holes through them; I have had them years, and know them well; they were in a snuff-box with the gold-ring.

Doon attempted to defend herself by claiming that she had had the doits sixteen years, and what she bought at the mercer's "I paid ready money for; I had no Bank-note; the money I had I partly worked for, and part was left me. I had twenty-five guineas left me by my mother." Such bequests were part of the lives of many of the poor, so could be possible, but in Doon's case the court did not believe her and she was found guilty.[17] Here we see how money from Bank of England notes to worthless foreign copper coins was kept together. The copper coins interestingly seem to have been more of a souvenir than active currency. The case also demonstrates how someone with a large amount of money would hide it by locking it in a secret drawer of a desk in a locked room, but all such security was vulnerable to the ever-present access of servants in the houses of the better off (Meldrum 2000: ch. 4). However, another case from 1736 shows that money locked in a desk was also vulnerable to lodgers in the house, which was also a very common situation in London:

> Anne Newman of St. Botolph Aldgate, was indicted for feloniously stealing out of the House of Jacob Busaglo. 21 Guineas, one half Guinea, a Barbery Ducat value 8 s. 6 d. a Barbary silver Ducat, value 2 d., and a green silk Purse, value 6 d.

Busaglo deposed that:

> When my Money was gone I suspected the Prisoners, because they fell out last Saturday Night with another of my Lodgers, and in the Quarrel they taxed one another with pawning my Goods which they used in the Rooms ... to pay me for their Lodging. This gave me some Suspicion, and I got a Warrant to search the House of Mrs. Cooper in Castle street, by the Meuse where I knew the Prisoners frequented; there I found a Trunk with my Leather Bag, and 16 Guineas, a 36 Shilling Piece, three Half Guineas, and two Half Crowns in it.[18]

Shopkeepers, however, seem to have kept their daily float in unlocked tills which were vulnerable to theft when the shopkeeper was purposefully distracted, as in 1678, when a shopkeeper "was upon some urgent occasion call'd out of his Shop, designing immediately to return; the Lesser of [the accused] ran to his Till or Cashbox (which likewise happened to be unlockt) and took out of it Fifteen Pounds in ready Money."[19] Cases of shoplifting and theft show how different sorts of money were kept and hidden. One female apprentice at a public house pilfered "two five-and-three-penny pieces out of the till, and one shilling out of the sarthing-dish," "a paper of half-pence out of the bar, and half a crown in silver." On the Saturday following she took another paper. On the following Monday she took four shillings out of a bag of silver, and after that she took two thirty-six-shilling pieces (probably a Portuguese four escudo gold coin), and some half-pence from a silver tankard under the brandy cask, with money in it. To hide her theft she gave a servant three or four shillings at a time to keep for her.[20]

Although the majority of theft was committed against wealthy victims, the following is a poignant case of the theft from a poor weaver who obviously had little money. It is also one of the few cases to mention copper coins, which he had scraped together for his wife's funeral:

> William Dawson Pilkington was indicted for stealing 192 copper half-pence, value 8 s. one weaver's shuttle, value 6 d. one pair of shears, value 4 d. and one hat, value 3 d. the property of John Whalan.

> John Whalan—My wife lay dead, and I had 192 halfpence, the quantity of 8 shillings, and I suppose more, which I locked up; the neighbours contributed and raised it for me, in order to pay the expences of burying my wife; I locked them up in a cupboard, and went to sleep; there were none knew of it but the prisoner at the bar . . . when I awoke my cupboard was broke open, my lock lying on the ground, my shuttle, shears, and hat, were taken away.[21]

On Saturday night, March 14, 1752, the bricklayer John West had just been paid and was walking along with a hock of bacon under his arm. He was approached by a prostitute who asked him to buy her a pint of beer and then to go to her lodgings, where he had his pocket picked of five shillings he had just been paid.[22]

A similar case from 1726 shows how a laborer could possess capital in the form of a note of hand, and how he kept it. He deposed that "it's well known that I work hard for my Money," and that while on his way home to his wife he also met a prostitute between one and two o'clock on a very cold morning who invited him to a dram shop to warm up by a fire. He continued,

> [T]he Reckoning came to 8 d. and I had got a Brass Box in my Pocket, with 2 Guineas in it, and a Note upon Command for 6 Pounds 6 Shillings, and some other odd Matters. Whereof I takes out this Box, in order to pay the Shot . . . I gave my Landlady a Shilling to change, and put up my Box again, and some other People came in to drink; and by and by my Landlady brings me a Groat, and so I went out with the Groat in my Hand . . . and I goes to put my Money up, and missed my Box, and so I call'd the Watch.[23]

Other cases also show how small material objects could be used as a pawn or pledge in lieu of cash or credit, as in this one from 1754:

> Burk came . . . into our tap-room; he called for a pint of hot; I believe they staid about two hours and a half . . . Burk called, and asked what was to pay? I said, betwixt two and three shillings: Said he, I have no money; but I'll leave my buckles . . . I went and called my father-in-law, and told him Burk had no money; but wanted to pawn his shoe-buckles. My father came in, and said, Mr. Burk, how is this? He said, his ship was at Black-wall, and would be paid in two or three days; and said, if you will lead me some more money on them, I'll pay you in that time: upon which he lent him ten shillings.[24]

Pawnbrokers appear quite often in cases of theft as places where thieves attempted to convert stolen goods into cash. This shows that private pawnbroking certainly played a role in the economy of the London poor, but again, given the nature of the source, it is impossible to tell how common such institutions or individual services were, except to say they were often associated with crime.

Unfortunately, what we can't see in these cases is how often cash was used in payment in comparison to credit since non-payment of credit was dealt with in completely different courts, for which the records have been lost. But there are literally thousands of other examples such as this which give a vivid depiction of what money looked and felt like, as in the case of Edward Lloyd, who was "stop'd by the Prisoner, who would have had him gone with her to drink; but he refus'd it, and immediately heard the clinking of Money, and searching his Pockets, found he had lost 5 s. upon which he call'd for the Watch, who coming up, search'd her, and he saw a Pocket-piece, which was a crooked Shilling remarkably bent."[25] Or there is the case of a soldier and a woman selling a puppy to one Samuel Jennings:

> Jennings thus deposed: . . . The Soldier asked whether I'd have the Puppy or no, and so I took out Money to pay him, which I laid upon the Table, there was a half Guinea, a Shilling, a Six-Pence, and three Fathings. [the] Prisoner presently clapt her Hand upon it, and took it up. What do ye mean by that, says I. D— ye for a Son of a Bitch, says me, I have got none of your Money, and if I had, what then? But by the bye, she gave me the Shilling and Six-pence gain, and swore that that was all that she took up.[26]

Perhaps most importantly for the argument of this chapter, the Old Bailey trials also offer a great deal of evidence of the increasing use of notes of hand and then banknotes, but also of how they were used. A case from 1735 involving the forgery of an endorsement demonstrates how the system worked and how vulnerable it was. Thomas Devenish, a backmaker (iron goods maker), was indicted for forging an endorsement on the back of a promissory note (dated May 25, 1735), which he had signed and written thereon that he promised to pay to one William Morris, on order, £100. The forged endorsement purported to be the writing of Morris to pay one Thomas Green on order, dated May 29, 1735. Witness statements give a good sense of how people used local knowledge to assess the validity of endorsements if there was some reason for doubt. James Graham, a pawnbroker deposed that,

> This Note was brought to me first by James Northall a Scrivener. He desired me to get Money for it. I told him I would try. It was then indors'd [by] William Morris. I enquir'd who Morris was, and Northall answer'd, that Morris was a Smith at the lower End of Broad-Street. Northall came several Times about it, and at last he said he was employ'd by Devenish to whom the Note belonged, and to whom I must pay the Money. After this, [Devenish] came himself, and said it was his Note, and that the Name at Bottom was his own Hand.

Graham then stated that he asked Devenish whom Morris was and how he came to owe him such a considerable sum. Devenish answered that the money was owing for nails and other things in the backmaking trade, and that the sum was not considerable for the trade. Graham accepted this and applied to Mr. Conran, a discounter, and then he in turn to Mr. Green, a jeweler, who offered to give rose diamonds at the market price for the note. Graham also claimed that he had agreed to do this as, "It's Part of my Business, as a Broker, to get Notes discounted. The Brokers don't usually enquire after the Indorsers; though it's what we ought to do, but we leave that to the Person who discounts the Notes." He also noted that Devenish came five or six times to see if it had been done. The jeweler Green further deposed that before accepting the bill for diamonds, he asked his glazier, who lived near Morris,

> ... if he knew Morris, and if he was a Man of Worth. He said he did not think he was worth Twenty Pounds; upon which I returned the Note. Mr. Conran came the next Day to know the Reason of it; I told him it was but a coined Note at best. We went to Morris and shew'd him the Note. He said the Name was none of his Writing, and he wrote his Name before us, and it was not at all like the Indorsement.[27]

This case indicates that in London by this date, pawnbrokers were commonly discounting paper notes, which must have been done on a large scale if it was not common to check the endorsement before taking the note. It also shows how many middlemen were involved in passing on the note and how this was done to maximize the knowledge of the maker of the note and his worth and honesty. Other cases show that notes of hand were often used even in the payment of servants and workers, such as mantua makers.[28]

Banknotes were often carried around together with other money and stolen, as in the following example from 1715:

> Hunt depos'd, That he lost his Pocket-book in his Way from Lawrence Lane to Smithfield, and with it two Bank-Notes, one of 35 l. the other of 15 l. upon which he stop'd Payment; and the Note of 35 l. coming in, it was trac'd by the Evidence, from the Person that brought it, back to the Prisoner; who said in her Defence, she dealt in old Clothes, and received it of a Chapman for 10 l. (10 l. having been already paid off and endors'd at the Bank) to whom she gave a Token, upon the Return of which she was to pay the remaining 15 l. to the Bearer. That she had accordingly received her Token, and paid the Money; but knew not her Chapman's Name, nor where he liv'd. Upon the whole she was acquitted.[29]

Bearing in mind our earlier reservations about the representativeness of the Old Bailey reports, we can still note the number of trials in which different forms of currency are mentioned in order to get a sense of the relative use of various types of coins and notes by the victims. Such a study has been carried out for the period from 1680 until the beginning of 1820, and the results are presented in Table 2 and Figure 4.2 below. The search has been confined to cases of theft and actual accounts of the trials, which consist of the statements of the parties concerned and witnesses. In respect of guineas and notes, this is a straightforward matter of using the word search function since they were not units of money of account. However, for both the plural forms of pence and shillings, only an approximation can be made of the actual use of coins, since many cases state the value of goods by using the written word, as in, for instance, listing a stolen item as "worth six shillings" or "ten pence." Some cases only contain such use of the word for such valuations, but many contain a mention of actual coins, so they cannot simply be eliminated through a Boolean search, and can only be identified on a case-by-case basis.

A similar problem exists for the use of the word "farthing" since in most cases it was used descriptively, such as "worth a farthing," "last farthing," or "not a farthing more." Only in approximately 27 percent of cases do such mentions refer to an actual coin. But the plural "farthings" always referred to the use of coins. Since there are too many cases to examine on an individual basis, I have made an estimate based on a sample of 100 cases from different decades which indicates that in approximately 38 percent of cases where the words "shillings" and "pence" were mentioned, they were used in the context of valuing objects rather than as references to actual coins. No reduction has been made for the counting of the singular shilling or penny or the plural farthings, as there were very few things worth only a penny or one shilling, and most compound values of pounds, shillings and pence were printed as, for example, 1L. 12s. 5d.[30]

TABLE 2: Total mentions of different types of currency in trial reports from the Old Bailey Criminal Court 1680–1820

CURRENCY	Raw amount	Adjusted totals
Farthing	730	197
Farthings	296	
Farthing(s) Total	**493**	
Penny	1,649	
Pence (pennies)	4,143	2,569
Pence Total	**5,792**	
Shilling	4,067	
Shillings	10,124	6,277
Shilling(s) Total	**10,354**	
Guinea(s)	9,362	
Banknote(s)	5,939	
Notes of hand	151	
Promissory note(s)	146	
Total notes	**6,236**	

MONEY AND THE EVERYDAY   117

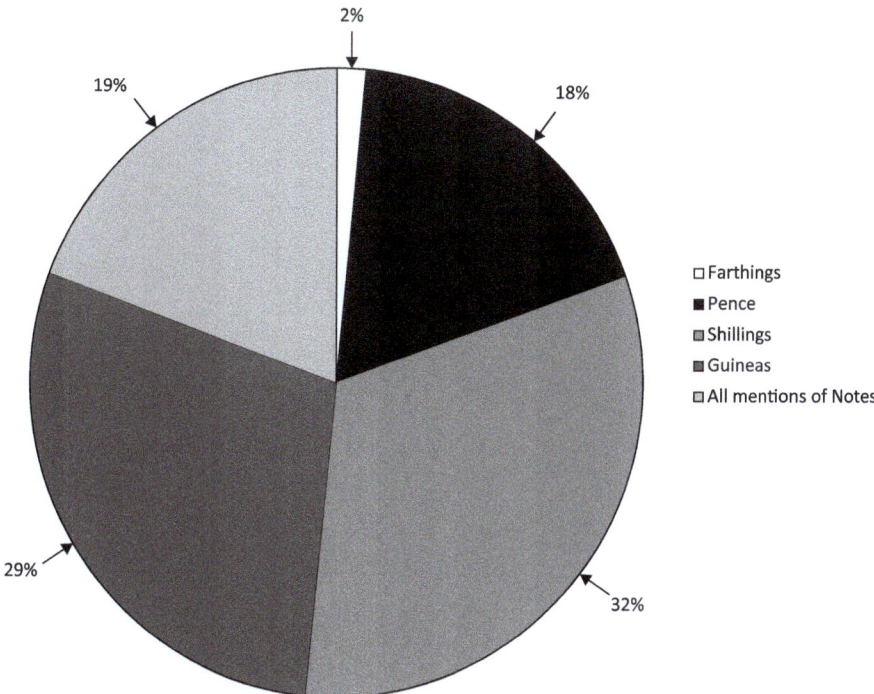

FIGURE 4.2: Total mentions of different types of currency in trial reports from the Old Bailey Criminal Court (1680–1820). Author's own.

Although only approximate, what can be seen from this data is how much the guinea features in the stock of money in cases of theft. Shillings predominate, but only slightly, and as Figure 4.3 demonstrates, this is because they were mentioned much more often at the beginning of the nineteenth century, probably as a result of the introduction of stamped Spanish silver dollars worth five shillings in 1804.[31] We also need to remember that a shilling was worth less than one-twentieth of the value of a guinea. The small number of farthings and the almost total lack of tokens is also notable, but as mentioned above, there were probably a greater number in circulation but held by poor people who would have been robbed less frequently. But it is significant that banknotes form 19 percent of the total. We can further see in Figure 4.3 how the number of mentions of banknotes rose over the course of the century, with a very large increase occurring in the early nineteenth century together with a concurrent drop in the number of mentions of guineas. Since the number of cases obviously varied from year to year, and generally increased over time as the population of the capital continued to rise, it is probably more accurate to examine such mentions as a percentage of the total cases of theft, as presented in Figure 4.4. This figure measures change over time in terms of the percentage of all theft

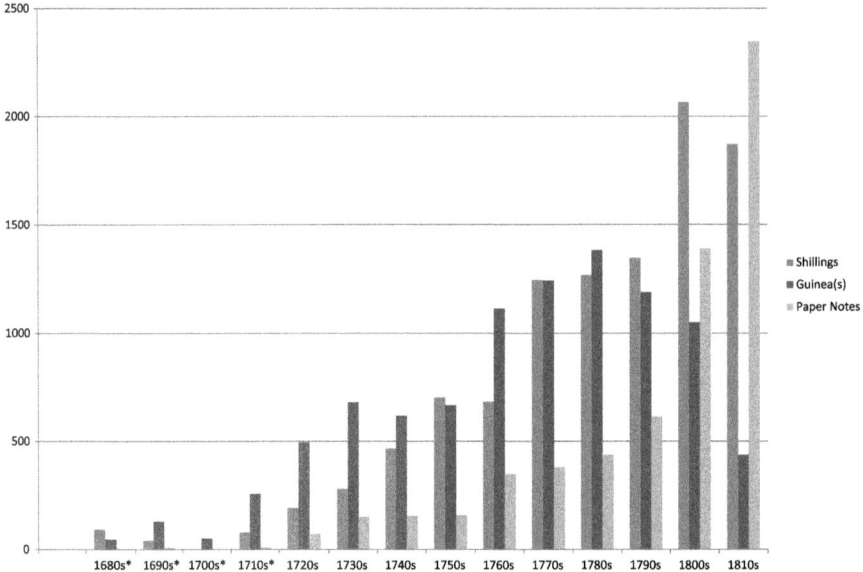

FIGURE 4.3: Number of mentions of shillings (est.), guineas, and paper notes (1680–1820). Author's own.

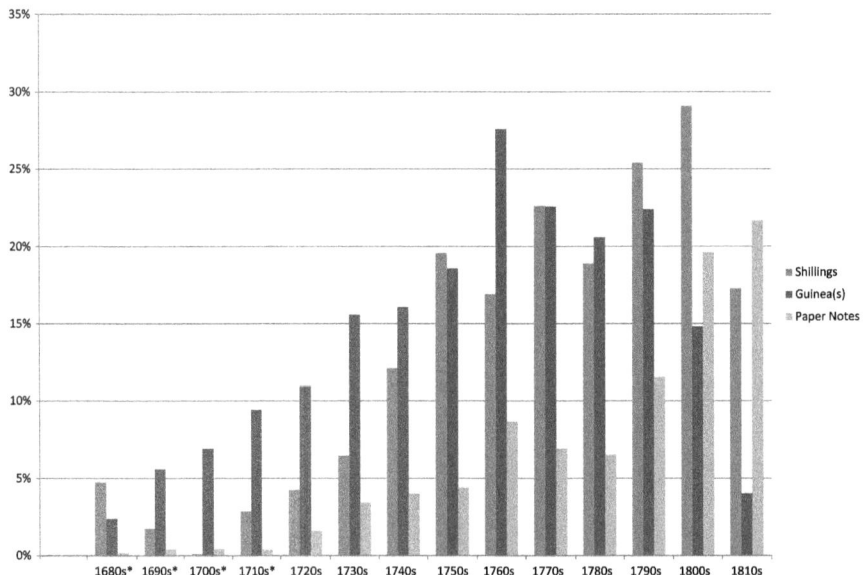

FIGURE 4.4: Percentage of cases mentioning shillings (est.), guineas, and paper notes (1680–1820). Author's own.

cases mentioning each different currency. Here we can see that the trends are roughly the same except for the 1810s, which saw a rise in the number of cases not involving any of these items of currency, but especially shillings.

The sharp decline in the use of gold after 1800 was almost certainly a result of the Bank Restriction Act of 1797 which suspended the convertibility by the Bank of England of its and other local banknotes to gold because of fears that there would be a run on the Bank after the declaration of war against revolutionary France. This restriction lasted until 1821 when convertibility to gold was reinstated after much debate, paving the way for the development of the gold standard. Banknotes were relatively common from the 1760s on, but again, not surprisingly, increased in use after the introduction of the Bank Restriction Act. Looking specifically at Figure 4.4, we can see that the use of gold guineas predominated in almost every year until the 1780s. Estimates of the value of gold coins in circulation indicate a rise from probably around £1 million in 1700 to £17 million after 1750. They then declined in use during the suspension period, when more would have been held in reserve. The infrequent use of shillings before the 1740s is evidence of just how rapidly the newly recoined silver money had left the country due to the undervaluing of the Mint price after the Great Recoinage. However, the rapid increase in the mention of shillings from the 1740s on is quite striking since almost none was being minted in these years. This is evidence that the London middling sort were in possession of a large amount of the country's silver coinage by this time, but why this concentration should have accelerated so much around the mid-eighteenth century is not obvious and worth further investigation (Craig 1953: 179, 219–21, 246–51, 253, 261–6; Feavearyear 1931: 158–60, 169–70).

Finally, Figure 4.5 resets the same data as Figure 4.4 in linear form, where we can see that while coins predominated, there was a continual rise in the use of paper currency throughout the eighteenth century. It should be reiterated that outside of London the percentage of cases mentioning gold and silver coins was likely much less, although without a proper study it is impossible to say how often paper instruments would come up in cases of theft. What we can say is that in Cannon's memoirs, paper notes certainly predominated over mentions of cash.

Hopefully this chapter has achieved its two stated aims of putting flesh on what Marx termed the cold hard impersonality of the cash nexus of exchange, and of showing how people came to use paper money. Metal money, of course, is hard and cold, but the examples given here show that in exchange its use was far from impersonal. Where it was kept on the body and in the home, how it was counted, and what it was used to pay for were all sources of emotional anxiety. It was also precisely through these rituals and emotions of exchange that trust in new paper currency was created. Endorsement and knowledge of

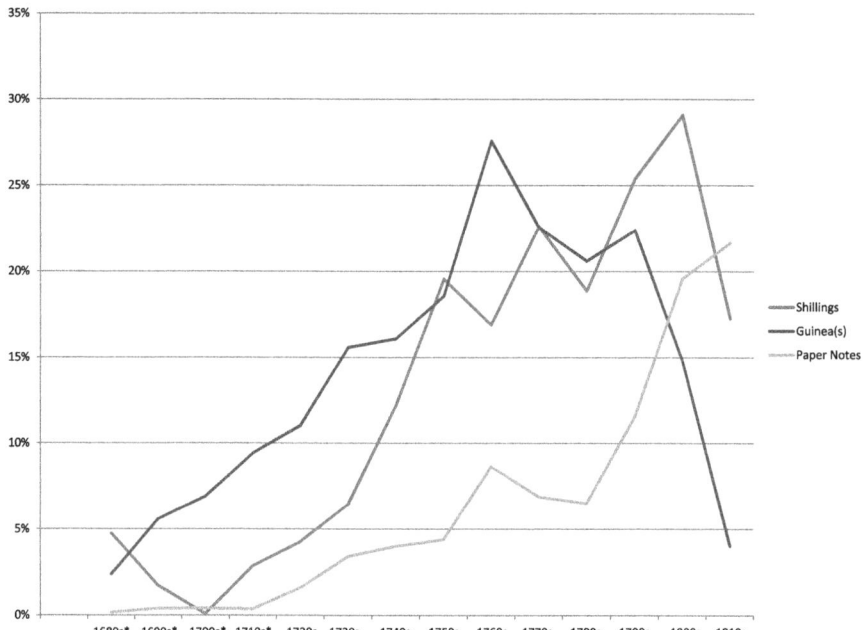

FIGURE 4.5: Percentage of cases mentioning shillings (est.), guineas, and paper notes (1680–1820). Author's own.

endorsements allowed the value to be traced back beyond the note to a certain degree. With banknotes, of course, people also had to trust the institution and the person running the bank, but the *personality* of endorsement remained a key factor in the circulation of their notes.

The beginnings of the use of paper currency were no more impersonal than the use of cash had previously been (Muldrew 2001: 78–120). It was a central argument of Adam Smith in his *The Wealth of Nations* of 1776 that one of the key features of a progressive economy was the existence of institutions that could turn the value of labor into circulating capital like banknotes (Muldrew 2018: 133–59). Smith went to great lengths to show how this value was superior to that possessed by gold and silver coins, and to do so he used the examples of local banks. Here we have seen how the value of local notes evolved gradually to replace oral credit and became a very local paper currency. Banknotes could circulate more widely depending on the extent to which the institution was trusted. In a city like Naples, this was based on the meticulous record-keeping of the bank. In the case of English country banks, it was based on the trust in prominent shopkeepers or businessmen whose success combined with structured accounting allowed them to create named institutions issuing currency (Pressnell 1956: 12–74). But it is only by examining the "everyday" that we can understand how the value of banknotes is always a communal product.

CHAPTER FIVE

Money, Art, and Representation

The Look and Sound of Money

REBECCA L. SPANG

In the opening paragraphs of Charles Gildon's *The Golden Spy* (1709), the first-person narrator recounts how "as [he] lay awake one Night" he was startled to hear a low humming noise "like one struggling to speak, or not awake enough to give his Words their true Articulation." Looking around his bed chamber, then calling his servant to help him do so a second time, the narrator can find nothing amiss and so returns to bed. The humming and throat clearing continues, however, until eventually the speaker is revealed to be an ordinary looking French coin (a *louis d'ore*—sic., italics in the original). In the pages that follow, the coin recounts the scandals and intrigues to which it has been party around the world (emphasizing that coins, though they have faces, lose the ability to speak if they are locked up in coffers and not allowed to circulate). Gildon's talking *louis* launched a fad: over a dozen copycat texts followed. From Joseph Addison's "Adventures of a Shilling" (1710), to Thomas Bridge's *The Adventures of a Banknote* (1770) and beyond, money talked. We could even say it tattled (Lynch 1998; Kibbie 2006; Martinez 2013).

By imagining coins as individuals, eighteenth-century novelists challenged the legal fiction that all money was identical and hence interchangeable (that, in words inherited from the ancient world, "money does not stink"). At the same time, the stories told by these unlikely narrators suggested that people were perhaps more similar than they liked to pretend: all could be bought or sold (and many were willing to buy or sell others). Neither claim—nor, indeed, any cultural product—should be read as a simple "reflection" of social reality or a statement of historical fact. Rather, these texts (like the other images and artifacts analysed below) were all interventions in ongoing debates and developments.

This chapter proposes that if money in the eighteenth century did not literally speak, it nonetheless said different things, in different ways, to different people. By making as much of money's sound as they did of its appearance, Enlightenment-era authors took folk wisdom and made it into a literary subgenre. As was said in a completely different context, "It is easier to tell that a coin is silver by its sound than by its look ... Even a peasant woman can rely on the triple evidence provided by her eyes, ears, and hand (which weighs the coin)" (*Archives parlementaires* 10: 272, 27 Nov. 1789). What we today would call the "visual culture" of money—that is, the learned and sometimes consciously cultivated behavior of *seeing* certain objects, words, or even human actions *as* money—had in fact long been the product of multiple senses.[1] Looking at coins, bills, and other media of exchange was an integral part, but it was *only* a part, of the whole constellation of social practices through which monetary value was created, maintained, and stored. This chapter therefore moves from an introductory discussion of money in eighteenth-century European art to sustained consideration of the look, sound, and even smell of the many money objects that circulated in this period. While the first demonstrates how Enlightenment-era culture envisioned and depicted money's significance, the latter reveals more about money's functioning and circulation. In neither domain was money's value automatic or something on which issuer and user (producer and consumer) necessarily agreed. Interpretation was always required.

* * *

European and North Atlantic art of the Enlightenment era is full of references to—and meditations on—wealth and riches, even as it is comparatively thin on literal depictions of money. Portraits of monarchs, aristocrats, and other social elites almost inevitably showed them *surrounded by* the lavish trappings of their station. When a ruler was depicted without obvious signs of wealth and grandeur, as in Elisabeth Vigée-Lebrun's *Marie Antoinette en chemise* (1783), scandal resulted. Vigée-Lebrun's portrait, showing the Queen of France in a fashionable white cotton dress and wearing a simple straw hat, met with sustained hostility and had to be removed from public showing less than a month after it was first exhibited (Sheriff 2003).

Majesty was expected to manifest itself with clear signs of opulence and material comfort. When those appeared on their own, however, or when they were openly available for purchase, they sent a more mixed message. Some works, such as Watteau's *Gersaint's Shop Sign* (1721), celebrated commercial culture (see Figure 5.1). Originally painted to hang above the entrance to an art

FIGURE 5.1: Jean-Antoine Watteau, *L'Enseigne de Gersaint* (1721), oil on canvas. Watteau's *L'Enseigne de Gersaint* shows an enticing assortment of luxury goods but depicts no money: aristocratic consumers almost always bought on credit. Photo by Charlottenburg Palace/Wikimedia Commons. The Yorck Project (2002), Wikimeda Commons.

dealer's gallery, the large canvas (more than 5 × 10 feet) was initially a shop sign itself and is hence best understood in terms of the fantasies it was meant to conjure and advertise.

On the right (an idealized rendering of Gersaint's actual shop), customers in shimmering silk scrutinize paintings, examine mirrors, and perhaps admire their own portraits and reflections. The art dealer (who supports a large, oval canvas from behind) and his wife (who similarly displays a handsome table mirror) are indistinguishable in appearance from their aristocratic patrons, implying that the market for luxury goods somehow levels social difference. On the left, manual laborers (clearly not the beneficiaries of any trickle-down wealth or transitive glamor) pack up and remove a large rectangular painting in an ornate frame. The workers are in fact crating a portrait of the recently deceased Louis XIV (reigned, 1638–1715), as if to say that the era of absolutist pomp and majesty—focused on Versailles, where even the King's simplest actions were occasions for protocol and status dispute—has been superseded by Paris and the market.

Such open promotion of commercial culture and the pleasures of shopping was an especially common theme in the ornate trade cards of the era (Berg and Clifford 2007). So-called "high art," however, usually took a less sympathetic position. Consider, for instance, William Hogarth's great commercial and critical success, *The Rake's Progress*. Painted in 1732–3, engraved in 1734, and often reprinted, it is a series of eight tableaux charting the brief rise and dramatic fall of "Tom Rakewell," son of a miserly financier. To make the point that his protagonist does not work for his wealth but comes into it by inheritance, Hogarth's first painting (see Figure 5.2) depicts Tom in a dark, dingy, cave-like room almost literally bursting with (or giving birth to) money.

FIGURE 5.2: William Hogarth, "The Rake Taking Possession of his Estate," scene one of *The Rake's Progress* (1734), engraving. As his inherited wealth is chiseled from the wall behind him, Hogarth's "Rake" tries to buy off his one-time affianced with a handful of coins. Photo by Smith Collection/Gado/Getty Images.

Coins tumble from the wall and the fireplace; a starving cat searches fruitlessly for something to eat in a chest of silver tableware. While a tailor takes the measure of our hero (and no doubt finds him wanting), the series' true heroine—the servant girl on the left—reminds Tom of his past commitments by holding out a plain, gold ring. He responds with a handful of gold coins, meant to buy her silence. As the series unfolds, Tom squanders his inheritance on expensive pretension (in the second scene, he is surrounded by fencing and dancing masters, as well as a musician at a harpsichord and a jockey who kneels with riding crop and enormous silver race cup) and late night debauch. He then acquires a second fortune by marrying an aged and wealthy widow, but loses it just as quickly (the sixth scene in a gambling den shows two winners gloating over their fortune while, to the far right, a well-dressed aristocrat borrows from a moneylender, and Tom—in the center—raves at his loss). In the final scenes, we see his descent into a debtors' prison (where his fellow inmates try to make gold from lead and pen schemes for paying off the nation's debt) and, finally, into madness and the asylum. The series' moral is unambiguous: unearned wealth (represented repeatedly by coins) and the fashionable pastimes of high society are roundly condemned. Loyalty (represented by the many dogs in the series, but also by the servant girl who returns and tries to save Tom at several junctures) may be celebrated, but loyalty to such a figure can only go unrewarded.

Artists explored related themes in still life and genre painting as well. The London version of Chardin's *The House of Cards* (1736–7—one of at least four paintings with this title that he completed) shows a boy of eleven or twelve building the eponymous structure on a gambling table (recognizable by its green felt covering). Intent on his task, he has pushed aside a gambling chip (clearly labeled "100") as well as a silver token, but Chardin's point—if indeed he was making one—is harder to read than Hogarth's. Are we to conclude that the best use of cards is not play but construction, or that whatever is built at this table must inevitably collapse (regardless of the builder's own innocence)? In the pastel on paper *Still Life with Lotto Box* (1771–73, Musée d'Art et d'Histoire, Geneva), the Genevan portraitist Jean-Etienne Liotard observed the materiality of "lotto" (a precursor to bingo) with great precision. A small bag of numbered game pieces and a larger bag of silver coins sit beside a well-crafted wooden box on a green-topped table. While the text on the label affixed to the box lid is difficult to decipher—does it identify the game's maker, its owner, or summarize the rules of play?—the numbers on the game card are sharp and clear: 1–23–44–61–80. Random they may be, but they catch the viewer's eye nonetheless and invite us to take those numbers as our own, hoping they will be called and placing side bets on the chance. In the 1780s, Hubert Robert's many paintings of Paris in ruins commented with both excitement and alarm on speculative bubbles and busts in real estate (Dubin 2010).

Eighteenth-century art's concern with the relation of enduring value to speculative wealth was both a response to specific transformations in artists' lives and livelihoods and a commentary on more general cultural trends. Across much of Europe, the art market was shifting from private patronage to public commerce; at the same time, new technologies (such as mezzotint) made art all the easier to reproduce (Solkin 1996). Asserting authorship and ownership therefore became economically more important even as it was logistically more difficult. The Engravers' Act (8 Geo. 11 c 13, also known as "Hogarth's Act") gave artists in Britain copyright protection over their "original" works, much as slightly earlier legislation had done for authors. Artists' creative endeavors were increasingly defined as a matter of property rights—a development that some resisted, and on which many commented. Gambling in many forms—from high-stakes card games and betting on sporting events (horse races, boxing matches, billiards) to dice games, lotteries, and casual wagers—simultaneously pervaded British and French life at all levels of society.[2] Playing cards, subject in Britain to the Stamp Act and in France to a state-controlled monopoly, were both a source of government revenue and themselves used as currency (especially in France's North American colonies). With an individual's name added to the back, stray playing cards were the first calling cards; others survive in archives having been used as "washers" to reinforce sheafs of bundled paper. Edmond Hoyle's *A Short Treatise on the Game of Whist* (1742) was the first book in any language to give the rules of a card game. An instant bestseller, the book's success resulted in a flurry of unauthorized editions. Hoyle's publisher responded to the piracy by having him autograph the title pages of the genuine copies—a solution very like the use of signatures on bills of exchange and paper money (see below) (Levy 2010).

The prominent presence of coins in a work of eighteenth-century art almost always signaled an artist's critical stance toward commercial culture and personal greed. When the Paris actress Anne Françoise Lange took objection to her portrait as painted by Anne-Louis Girodet de Roussy-Trioson and refused to pay him, he retaliated with a new one in which he cast her not as Venus but as Danaë (1799; see Figure 5.3). The story of Danaë, impregnated by Jupiter in the form of a shower of gold, had been treated in medieval iconography as prefiguring Christ's conception, but Girodet presented the actress not as virginal, but venal. Gloating greedily as coins fall in her lap, Mademoiselle Lange seems oblivious to the artist's criticism: she notices neither the cracked

FIGURE 5.3: Anne-Louis Girodet de Roussy-Trioson, *Portrait of Mlle. Lange as Danae* (1799), oil on canvas. Portraying an actress as the mythological Danaë, Girodet implied she could be easily seduced with money. Minneapolis Institute of Arts, Wikimedia Commons.

mirror, the dead dove, the enormous turkey, nor the script of Plautus's *Asinaria* (*The Play about the Asses*)—all of which surround her.

What mattered in all of these works was not the specific qualities of the individual coins depicted but their overall quantity. So too with works that foregrounded paper money, such as the compilations of prints, poems, plays, and commentary bound together to make the eighty-two distinct volumes each known as *Het groote tafereel der dwaasheid* (*The Great Mirror of Folly*) (Goetzmann 2013). Ridiculing the puffed-up speculation (or "wind trade") that drove investment in the South Seas Company (Great Britain), John Law's Bank (France), and dozens of different insurance schemes (Netherlands) in 1719–20, the sixty (or so) copperplate engravings assembled in each volume depict a dizzying variety of scatalogical, aeronautical, gambling, and theater scenes, as well as oversized bellows, mad crowds, winged demons, and dancing monkeys. Captions and titles assert the relevance of each image to the collection's thematics, but because the images mock the idea of making real money on the stock market, they show very few coins or papers from credible issuers. Some do show share certificates and other related papers (such as financial news sheets or projectors' pamphlets and broadsides), but they do so to spoof the idea of their having any lasting value. The great irony here, of course, is that images *on paper* were being used to deride the value *of* paper—and those images have, in fact, survived for nearly 300 years.

At the close of the eighteenth century, a similar thematic pervaded a host of objects—chiefly prints (many hand-colored) but also fans and, eventually, ceramics and tinwear—featuring elaborate *trompe l'oeil* ("eye fooling") scenes of *assignats* (a circulating paper issued during the French Revolution) (see Figure 5.4). Like all representational art, *trompe l'oeil* mimics the real world. Because it does so in order to trick viewers into mistaking art for reality, it thereby calls both the realness of the real world and the faithfulness of art into question. Even "the viewer's perception of illusion as a deception" is challenged (Siegfried 1992).

As with *The Great Mirror of Folly*, the *trompe l'oeils* from the late 1790s depicted paper money in quantity to caution viewers against mistaking it for something of value. In contrast, Jacques Louis David's *Death of Marat* (1793)—showing the radical journalist assassinated in his bath—includes an *assignat* that is far from being the painting's focus (though it is located almost exactly at the center of the canvas (see Figure 5.5). As the art historian T.J. Clark remarks of it, the bill does not carry the "visual weight" of the painting's other components and "One might almost say it is meant to be overlooked" (Clark 1994: 53). David, a committed revolutionary who organized many of the era's most elaborate festivals (including Marat's funeral procession), served in the National Convention, and was later jailed as a Terror-ist, actively believed in the paper currency's value. For that very reason, he did not invite viewers to scrutinize

FIGURE 5.4: "Valeur des assignats" (c. 1796–7), engraving. French Revolution era paper moneys lost value with the collapse of political legitimacy; *trompe l'oeil* prints like this one suggested the bills had never had substance. Photo by Leemage/Corbis via Getty Images.

the bill, but instead presented it as something to take for granted. Hidden in full view (like, as Clark notes, the purloined letter in the Poe story of that title), Marat's *assignat* is naturalized, normalized—an unremarkable detail in a remarkable scene.

* * *

The *assignat* in David's *Marat* reminds us that when a means of exchange or store of value functions normally, it is recognized almost automatically. Identifying one flat, round, shiny piece of metal as a coin and another as a button is something most adults do with little conscious effort, but it is a learned behavior nonetheless. Individuals are socialized and acculturated to recognize money as something of value, but rarely do they remember the learning process.

Most Westerners today have been educated to see (literally and metaphorically) comparatively little as "money." Because of national monopolies on currency issue, centralized design, and highly uniform mass manufacture, a relatively limited number of distinct money objects circulate at any one time.[3] In the eighteenth century, in contrast, a greater range of objects had currency as money (that is, they were "currently" accepted *as* money). Coins made excellent novelistic narrators because they were imagined to go everywhere, crossing

FIGURE 5.5: Jacques-Louis David, *La Mort de Marat* (1793), oil on canvas. The *assignat* on Marat's bath-side table signifies both his faith in the Revolution and his generosity. Photo by Imagno/Getty Images.

class and territorial borders with ease, but in fact money often stayed in its own social and regional channels. Silver in France, for instance, was minted chiefly in the kingdom's interior, while gold (used mainly for international trade) was coined at mints along the border. Only under political pressure did any of those mints produce the so-called "money of the poor," the base-metal small change necessary for daily cash transactions (Dermigny 1955; Sargent and Velde 2001; Spang 2015). For merchants in thriving port cities such as Bristol, Liverpool, Bordeaux, Nantes, Amsterdam, or Cádiz, money consisted of minted metals in extraordinary variety, but also of cowrie shells; at the same time, wholesale traders there and elsewhere made many business transactions with bills of exchange and other forms of credit carefully recorded in ledgers and account books. Europeans in North American colonies could be comfortable—depending on the place and decade—using beaver skins, playing cards, or barrels of tobacco to settle accounts; they also relied on book debt, locally issued papers, and various coins to fill many monetary functions. And for a tax receiver in provincial France, money looked like a canvas bag filled with metal objects: silver coins of various denominations but also worn base-metal coinage and metal blanks, as well as tokens, buttons, and even the heads of nails.

The *variety* of money's look and sound in this period has rarely been historians' chief concern. Instead, scholars have more often focused on episodes such as the South Sea Bubble, the French Revolution's *assignats*, and the Bank of England's wartime suspension of payments in order to describe the eighteenth century as a time in which paper money's eclipsing of commodity money first became thinkable.[4] Writing about money as a proxy for totalizing concepts such as capitalism, consumer culture, and modernity, these scholars have generally followed economists and legal scholars in treating money as "fungible": interchangeable, identical, and measured in quantity alone (because devoid of qualities). The word "fungible" was, however, first used in the mid-1700s and remained something of a term of art for more than the next two centuries[5] (*OED*, "fungible"). This chapter therefore suggests that while artists' representations of wealth and greed often featured masses of indistinguishable coinage, we should not jump from these depictions to conclusions about money's social life and economic functioning. Ordinary people's monetary practices were (and remain) far more varied and complex than economic theory or artistic representation would have us believe.

Men and women in eighteenth-century Europe recognized their "own" money (a definition which had as much to do with region and status as it did with nation or state) and scrutinized others' money with all their senses. They also began the work (completed by nineteenth-century political economy at the zenith of European imperial expansion) of establishing a hierarchy of moneys and money users, one that ranked metals over other materials and things of "real" value over mere fetishes (Pietz 1988). Being able to recognize different moneys was believed to be a sign not just of the objects' legibility but of the viewers' intellectual sophistication. Some moneys (and their users) were deemed more "advanced"; others, more "primitive." Jean-Jacques Rousseau depended for decades on Thérèse Levasseur to manage his basic household arrangements, but he nonetheless mocked her as "dull" and complained that "she can never learn the different value of the pieces of money in any country."[6] European ships in the eighteenth century carried an estimated 10 billion cowrie shells (the mortal remains of small, sea-dwelling, snail-like animals) from the Indian Ocean to Europe and back to the west coast of Africa, but the captains of those ships saw the shells chiefly as ballast and derided those who prized them as money (Hogendorn and Johnson 1986). Even when writing about coin collectors, Joseph Addison (author of the 1710 "Adventures of a Shilling") insisted on distinguishing between those with morally uplifting motives and those who were but vulgar enthusiasts (Alvarez 2005).

* * *

The many transactional media used in our period made value visible in distinct ways. Looking closely at them—as we will do for the remainder of this chapter—confirms that the value of money was never a matter of quantities alone. Some money objects indicated quantity and some monetary quantities could be easily counted and tallied, but numbers were hardly the only (or even the first) thing that eighteenth-century men and women saw when they looked at money. Whether stamped with portraits, inscribed with mottos, or left apparently blank, the various money things of this period also give substantial visual hints about the moral, social, emotional, and aesthetic values of those who held, exchanged, and treasured them.

Coins were probably the most readily recognized money objects in the eighteenth century, but individuals' interactions with them were far more varied than representations of coins in high art might suggest. Men and women could, for instance, credibly claim to recognize individual coins by sight. In one trial proceeding, a woman told a London court that she and her husband had been assaulted on the King's Highway in winter 1767, and been robbed of a "green silk purse . . . [containing] a Spanish dollar, a King William and Queen Mary's half crown, a 4 s. 6 d. piece, a 5 s. 3 d. and some silver." The accused protested that the dollar found on him was his own and brought from New York eight years ago, but this defense backfired when the prosecutor asked him to read the date on the coin (1764). Shown another piece of money at the trial, the plantiff stated, "I believe this to be the same that was in my purse that I lost . . . I know it by this little hole almost punched through it." As for the half crown from seventy years earlier, her husband testified that he had given it to her "about seven years earlier for a pocket piece." This single trial reveals the richness and complexity of money's visual culture in everyday life: people differentiated foreign issues from national ones (but carried them together), they distinguished individual coins by their imperfections and signs of wear, and they treasured others as mementos and easily carried love tokens (*Old Bailey Proceedings Online*, trial of Joseph Guy).

For the polities that issued them, in contrast, coins—especially larger denomination gold and silver ones—were most importantly about asserting legitimacy. As markers of a particular type of sovereign authority, European coins were in many respects visually consistent from one kingdom to the next. A British shilling from 1710 and a French écu from 1765, for example, both depicted a monarch's bust on the obverse side and a shield (or shields) on the reverse. Both were marked with abbreviated, Latin inscriptions and made claims so nearly identical as to compete with each other: Queen Anne's shilling proclaimed her reign "by grace of God" as "Queen of England, France, and

Ireland," while Louis XV's coin asserted his rule "by the grace of God" over "France and Navarre" (see Figure 5.6a/b). On the reverse, the écu carried a further inscription: the abbreviated Latin for "blessed be the name of God." Implied by iconography and inscription alike was the idea that money's worth came from its status as a representation of the ruler's divinely given authority. Value came from the imprint (as life from God) and while the material stuff that received the stamp ought ideally to be as shining and lustrous as the monarch, it did not necessarily have to be so. In many respects, this was a logocentric political and economic theology (that is, one centered on words and names: "blessed be the *name* of God"), not a materialist one.

FIGURE 5.6a: Louis XV écu (1765), obverse. Louis XV, "By the grace of God, King of France and Navarre." Courtesy of South of the Border Coins, Bethesda, MD.

FIGURE 5.6b: Louis XV écu (1765), reverse. "Blessed be the Name of God." Courtesy of South of the Border Coins, Bethesda, MD.

Rich with the vocabulary and iconography of divine-right monarchy, Enlightenment-era coinage also bore small, but important, traces of its human makers. Metal objects produced at a certain time and place, coins indicated the date of their minting and also carried a small mint mark. To the savvy reader, the mint marks tell different stories: the French coin's mark, directly under the bust on the obverse side, literally indicates in which of France's thirty mints the écu was made, whereas the British signifies the source of the metal (since silver and gold minting had been centralized at the Tower of London for over a century). Not marked on the coins nor visible to even the most discerning eye, however, was any indication of monetary value. How many shillings were there to the pound in 1710? How many *livres* (literally, "pounds") was this écu worth in 1765? The coins are mute on these questions, for legally it was the prerogative of the monarch (God's appointed representative on Earth) to set the coin's value. As a matter of domestic law in medieval and early-modern monarchies, it was royal decrees (not physical mass or any other property—visible or otherwise—of the object itself) that determined a coin's legal exchange value. Coinage issued by the quasi-republican Swiss cantons offers in this context an interesting variation: the obverse of the Basel ducat, for instance, depicts the city's heraldic animal (a basilisk) rather than any individual ruler, while the reverse clearly states "New Ducat, Republic of Basel."

Coins of the realm could be found well beyond the territory over which a monarch ruled. Records of London's chief criminal court, for instance, show that housebreakers and highwaymen in eighteenth-century England stole shillings and guineas, but also Tuscan crowns (valued 4 shillings 6 pence in September 1716), Spanish dollars, and coins issued by English monarchs dead for more than a century (in 1753, John Stubbs was held up and lost a Queen Elizabeth shilling valued at six pence). Swedish dollars (made of copper and notoriously heavy) also appear in the lists of stolen goods. Some of these foreign coins clearly arrived in the United Kingdom as souvenirs: Widow Isabella Morgan testified in court that she had "a dollar that my husband brought home from Spain, and gave to me five years ago." We do not know if the coin was looked at carefully when it was first brought to England, but when Morgan tried to buy beer with it, the dollar was thoroughly scrutinized by the pub-keeper, an assistant, and even a caged bird (!)—all of whom concluded it should not be accepted as payment (*Old Bailey Proceedings Online*, trial of Mary Gathney). What this tells us is that eighteenth-century men and women saw even the most obvious money objects (minted coins) as far from fully fungible. Moreover, the verb matters: they *saw* differences in coins—a difference that most visual artists, whether they were representing stashed silver or showers of gold, failed to capture.

While most European states strictly prohibited the export of specie (a policy today sometimes mistakenly referred to as "mercantilism"; Stern and Wennerlind 2013), wealth was nonetheless produced and circulated across territorial boundaries, thanks to the growth of overseas colonies, the expansion of international trade, and the near constant warfare that accompanied both. Merchants relied heavily on credit and bills of exchange (see below), but two European coins in particular became part of monetary sensory cultures far beyond Europe. The Maria Theresa thaler (or "dollar"), for instance, was initially issued for domestic use in the Habsburg Empire and shared many of the visual attributes of Queen Anne's shilling or Louis XV's écu (see Figure 5.7). On the obverse, her bust portrait is surrounded by an abbreviated Latin legend ("Maria Theresa, by the grace of God, Roman Empress of Hungary and Bohemia, Queen"); on the reverse, the imperial two-headed eagle is circled by another Latin inscription ("Archduchess of Austria, Duchess of Burgundy, Countess of Tyrol"). The year of its minting appears, but no numbers or words indicate its monetary value. A large silver coin (approximately 1.5 inches in diameter and weighing nearly an ounce), it was accepted as money in the Middle East, Levant, and Africa, and continued to be used and treasured there well after Maria Theresa's death (though Austrian coinage at that point was redesigned to depict her successor). In the nineteenth and even twentieth centuries, it was produced as a "trade coin"—any merchant could take silver to a mint (including, eventually, those in Rome, London, Paris, and Bombay) and ask for it to be made into Maria Theresa thalers (all marked "1780," the year of her death)—and came to be as much a part of Arab culture as of Austrian. Some of its many names in Arabic—*abu nuqta* ("the one with dots"), *abu tayr* ("the one with birds"), and *abu reesh* ("the one with feathers")—indicate how central its imagery and visual impact were to its value. Its size and its clear engraving of a matronly woman made it popular as jewelry and a fertility charm in Oman, Yemen, Ethiopia, and beyond. Made into a pendant or sewn into clothing, the thalers became part of fashion; used as standard weights in

FIGURE 5.7: Maria Theresa thaler (1780). Minted for more than 150 years after her death, the Maria Theresa thaler may have been the first global currency. Courtesy of the British Museum. Photo by DeAgostini/Getty Images.

markets, they measured mass as well as value (Semple 2005). That they had initially been issued in the name of the Holy Roman Empire did not prevent British colonial authorities in the twentieth century from classifying them, along with cowrie shells and manilas (horseshoe-shaped bars of metal), as "primitive money" (Tschoegl 2001: 448).

Overshadowed by the Maria Theresa thaler in the nineteenth and twentieth centuries, the Spanish Empire's dollars or thalers, also known as "pieces of eight" (so called because they were worth eight *reales* (royals)), rivalled it for international prominence in our period (see Figure 5.8). Nearly as large and heavy as a Maria Theresa thaler, the Spanish colonial coins were minted at or near sites where silver was mined in great quantities—Potosí (in what is today Bolivia), Lima (Peru), Mexico City—and served both as currency and as mass propaganda devices. As with other European gold or silver coinage, the obverse carried an abbreviated Latin inscription announcing the current Spanish monarch to be "By the Grace of God, King of Spain and the Indies." Their reverse iconography made a more audacious claim, however: coins issued before 1772 depicted the Spanish Crown surmounting maps of the Western and Eastern hemispheres and carried a Latin legend asserting "both [hemispheres] are one." The Pillars of Hercules (promontories marking the entrance to the Strait of Gibraltar and an emblem of the Spanish monarchy since the sixteenth century) framed the maps and were themselves embellished with additional crowns and a banner reading *Plus Ultra* ("further beyond"). Circulating well beyond the territories claimed by the monarchy, the imperial Spanish dollar (like the Maria Theresa thaler) was valued far from its place of origin for reasons that were both visual *and* non-monetary: among the Bedouin and Fellahin peoples of Arabia and the Southern Levant, the coins known as "the ones with the pillars" were used as medical amulets (Saidel and Barakat 2007).

FIGURE 5.8: Spanish imperial dollar, or "piece of eight" (1739). The pillars wrapped in banners are said to be the origin of the dollar sign ($). Courtesy of Bill Muldoon.

In their wide circulation, the Maria Theresa thaler and Spanish dollar both seem to confirm one important premise of eighteenth-century "it-narratives": money traveled. Yet, to the best of my knowledge, no novelist ever took either coin as a protagonist. Interchangeable neither with each other nor with other silver coinage, Austrian and Spanish dollars were apparently not perceived as individuals by the French and British authors who made their own coins into such lively narrators. What was distinctive to one set of eyes made little impact on another.

* * *

Coins were a common visual shorthand for money, but they were hardly the only mode of payment, means of exchange, or store of value in Enlightenment-era Europe. Constrained by the shortage of raw materials (most of Western Europe had no significant gold or silver deposits of its own), mint production was inadequate for the monetary needs of growing economies. Early globalization, the first decades of the Industrial Revolution, and the costs of war were therefore supported not by cash flows but by state credit, personal credit, privately issued tokens, and (in England and Scotland) bank-issued paper. In Europe's overseas colonies, an even greater variety of transactional media were in use.

It is impossible to inventory all the different forms of "paper money" used in our period.[7] Even in England and Wales, the state-chartered Bank of England (founded 1694) held only a quasi-monopoly on its issue, and "country banks" (small firms that slipped through a loophole created by the Bank's charter) grew in number throughout the eighteenth century. By the 1810s, there were over 700 such banks, nearly all of which issued their own notes. Each of Britain's North American colonies had its own paper and some colonies authorized "land banks" as well (which issued paper to individuals against mortgaged properties). In France, perpetual annuities (*rentes*) were both transferrable and considered such solid stores of value that they were treated for legal purposes as real estate (Spang 2015: ch. 1). The Austrian monarchy's *Banko-Zettel*, issued by the crown and accepted for all taxes and administrative fees, circulated in Galicia and the Habsburg Empire's Hungarian lands as well. All across Europe and well beyond, merchants used bills of exchange to transfer funds across time and space, but the bills themselves were often used as a means of payment as well. Even personal IOUs might be (and were) transferred to third parties. The following analysis does not try to exhaust this variety, but instead considers how these objects signified value and for whom, in consequence, they were valuable.

As with minted metals, paper transactional media conformed to genre norms that contributed greatly to their visual intelligibility and hence to the ease with which they circulated. If "life" experiences (wear, alteration, circulation) made coins distinguishable by users in a way that issuers never intended, individuality was instead a planned attribute of circulating papers, both private and public (state-issued) alike. When goldsmiths in mid-seventeenth-century London started issuing notes in exchange for coins and bullion they held for safekeeping, they of course specified the value confided to them, the name of its owner, and their own names. When a merchant wrote a bill of exchange, he too dealt in particulars. (No merchant expected *all* his colleagues in some distant city to honor his request!) These bills and notes depended for their value on the reputation of the specific individuals they named, and the status of those individuals derived not from divine appointment but from their own personal histories. In this one context, at least, their names—not God's—were what mattered.

So, too, when the state-chartered Bank of England began issuing notes in the early eighteenth century, they were intentionally and obviously individualized (see Figure 5.9). Printed with text such as "We promise to pay to Mr. _____ or bearer the sum of 20£ twenty pounds at demand, London, the ___ day of _____ 172__" and with space left for a cashier's signature, they look in many ways more like a cheque than like a twentieth- or twenty-first-century banknote. Though their acceptance for tax payments gave the Bank's notes a legal status and public function very different from that of the goldsmith-bankers' bills, the former nonetheless gained in intelligibility by mimicking the latter's appearance. Moreover, while the printed phrase "or bearer" meant notes belonged legally to whomever held them, the Bank continued the conceit of writing them to named individuals because of the legal precedent (established in the case of private bills of exchange) that, in instances of default, any one named on the bill could be sued for payment.[8] The mere appearance of a chain of reliable, named men helped make the notes credible, even as that same degree of individualization would have rendered a coin highly suspect. Even as

FIGURE 5.9: Bank of England banknote (1725). Though partially printed, early banknotes belonged visually to the manuscript culture of bills of exchange. Courtesy of the Governor and Company of the Bank of England.

FIGURE 5.10: John Smith, *The Prince of Wales* (George II) (1716), mezzotint. When the Royal Bank of Scotland reproduced this portrait of George II on its notes, it implied that they derived their value from his sovereign authority. National Portrait Gallery, London.

paper's circulation increased across the century, its visual cues signaled its continued legal status as a freely-entered-into relationship between two individuals. Only for a few months in 1793–4 did the French Republic mandate that *assignats* and coins circulate on a par with each other; only in 1833 were the notes of the Bank of England declared legal tender for all debts.

Belonging to the visual culture of bills of exchange rather than that of coinage, very few eighteenth-century banknotes carried images. The Royal Bank of Scotland's 1727 twenty-shilling note marked a radical innovation by adding an engraved portrait bust of a young George II (see Figure 5.10)— clearly copied from John Smith's 1717 mezzotint (National Portrait Gallery), itself based on Sir Godfrey Kneller's full-length portrait (done in 1716 when George was still Prince of Wales; now in Hampton Court Palace) (Royal Bank of Scotland 2017). Only two decades after the Act of Union and at a time when London's control over Scotland was, at best, tenuous, the first Director of the RBS (Archibald Campbell, Earl of Ilay; also Minister without Portfolio for Scotland) added the portrait to emphasize the new bank's loyalty to Britain's Hanoverian rulers. (In contrast, the rival Bank of Scotland, widely suspected of sympathizing with the Stuart rebels, stuck to the convention of text only.) The note hence sent double, and implicitly contradictory, visual messages about the source and form of its value: did it derive from the reputation of the various individuals named (which differed from note to note) or from sovereign authority (identical on all notes)?

* * *

Legal prohibitions on the export of coin from Europe and the logistical difficulty of shipping it in large quantities meant that overseas European colonies had especially varied and complex monetary systems. British colonists in North America calculated accounts and kept their records in pounds, shillings, and pence, but coins or even paper changed hands far more rarely. (One affluent New Englander recorded cash payments in 23% of his business interactions, a surprisingly *high* figure (Vickers 2010).) Shop and tavern keepers routinely extended credit to established business partners and regular customers who purchased low-value goods, with the understanding that bills would be paid at the end of the month, quarter, or year. Account books and ledgers were hence an important part of the visual culture of money.[9] John Singleton Copley's 1765 portrait of John Hancock (now in the Museum of Fine Arts, Boston), for instance, shows him in an almost completely bare setting, seated at a small table, with quill pen in one hand and enormous ledger propped on a book cradle before him (see Figure 5.11).[10] Hancock's biography at this point was

FIGURE 5.11: John Singleton Copley, *John Hancock* (1765), oil on canvas. Copley's painting depicts a man with nothing to distract him from his ledgers. Photo by DeAgostini/Getty Images.

not unlike that of Hogarth's "Tom Rakewell": he inherited his wealth (his uncle and benefactor had directed the largest transatlantic shipping firm in Boston) and largely ignored the business thereafter. Unlike Tom, however, Hancock was in a position to manage his own image. He therefore chose to have himself depicted not just keeping accounts, but about to make an entry on the right-hand page (where credits were tallied). Meanwhile, his left arm covers the ledger page recording his debts.

Britain and France's North American colonies were so consistently cash poor that *pesos* or "pieces of eight" (the Spanish imperial dollars described above) circulated widely and few (if any) thought of them as foreign. Tobacco, where it could be grown in large quantities, was both a major export crop and a common mode of payment and means of exchange. In mid-eighteenth-century Maryland, for instance, debts, fees, taxes, and salaries were all reckoned in terms of tobacco (Schweizer 1980: 556). Recognizing tobacco as money and knowing its value was not done by eye alone. As the names given to different tobacco strains (sweet-*scented*, *bright* leaf, *dull* oronoco (my emphasis)) indicate, distinguishing one variety from another required sight, touch, smell, and taste. With the introduction of tobacco inspection laws (Virginia, 1730; Maryland, 1747) these commodity currencies were subject to quality control (much as minted coins were assayed) and the notes given by inspectors for warehoused tobacco became a circulating medium of exchange in their own right. Inspection laws both standardized tobacco money and created specialist sensory regimes: the inspector and his crew had to use *all* their senses as they appraised the goods, but tobacco notes could be recognized by vision alone.

In New England and the Middle Atlantic colonies, where tobacco was not widely grown, other goods were used in a similar fashion. One petition from 1700 mentioned that the colonists of "Pennsylvania, East and West Jersey, and New York" had only "Skins and ffurs, Whaleboan and whale-oyl" (sic) with which to pay for British imports and intimated that if England did not approve the creation of a colonial mint, the colonists would simply stop buying British goods ("Memorial from Proprietors and Inhabitants of the English Colonies in North America" 1700, cited in Chalmers 1893: 12). In the twentieth century, European writers (economists and early anthropologists alike) would define animal skins and shells as "primitive" money, but in the eighteenth century it was *European* colonial and commercial expansion that drove their ever-widening use.

Merchant and military activities also prompted the ever-greater use of paper. Massachusetts issued the first North American paper (1690) in order to pay troops returning from an attempted invasion of Quebec.[11] At the time, Massachusetts' charter as an independent colony had been revoked (in part because it had violated coinage laws) and its agents had no legal grounds on which to claim that these paper payments were "backed" by anything. Instead, the Massachusetts bills derived their value from two printed claims about the future: "This indented Bill of Five Shillings due from the Massachusetts Colony to the possessor *shall be* in value equal to money and *shall be accordingly accepted* . . . for all Public payments" (emphasis added). Like other circulating papers of our period, the Massachusetts bills were not money but they were the promise of money (a credit instrument, in other words), and visual signs of individuality were crucial to establishing their credibility. For this reason, the bills were both signed and "indented"—made to look as if they had been torn from a single, matching stub that remained in the issuer's possession (Goldberg 2009). An indented bill (like a servant's "indenture") represented a legally binding contract between two individuals. When, in later decades, the pressures of time and mass production made it impractical to indent the edges of each distinct bill, the word nonetheless appeared on them as a promise of individuality and legitimacy (see Figure 5.12).

The visual culture of money in Britain's North American colonies borrowed as much from print culture as it did from traditions associated with medals, minting, or numismatics. Fractional denominations, values spelled out in words, and Roman numerals (more difficult to counterfeit than Arabic ones) all made for bills that were densely packed with text (Cohen 1993). When images appeared on these bills, they were meant as anti-counterfeiting devices. First pioneered by Benjamin Franklin (who probably earned more printing paper money for Pennsylvania, New Jersey, and Delaware than he did printing their laws or the deliberations of the colonial assemblies), one common technique

FIGURE 5.12: Delaware note for 2s. 6d. (January 1776), obverse, ink on paper. "This indented bill . . ." Department of Special Collections, University of Notre Dame Libraries.

FIGURE 5.13: Pennsylvania note for 15s. (April 1759), reverse, ink on paper. Benjamin Franklin's ingenious anti-counterfeiting technique involved imprinting paper money with actual leaves. Courtesy of Special Collections, Robert H. Gore, Jr. Numismatic Endowment, University of Notre Dame Libraries.

was to incorporate an actual leaf into the bill's design (see Figure 5.13). Probably done by pressing the leaf into plaster and then using the plaster cast in making metal printing plates, the method relied on the uniqueness of nature to give added legitimacy to human, cultural artifacts (Library Company 2006, 2014; Trettien 2016). Only because each leaf was different, could all bills be treated in the same way.

* * *

What did money look like in the Enlightenment era? By turning to two obvious sets of materials to answer this question, this chapter has found two strikingly different answers. In works today classed as high or fine art—chiefly paintings, but also prints—we see that money was largely represented as homogeneous, fungible, and consisting of minted metals. Wise men shepherded it and fools squandered it, but the money itself was all the same. This way of thinking about money was more than a convenient artistic shorthand: attractive to governments and theorists alike, it played an absolutely crucial role in the emerging field of economics and in nineteenth-century liberalism more generally. When we consider specific transaction ecologies and micro-technologies of exchange, however, we find something else. Looking at the objects themselves and understanding something about how they functioned, we confront money's variability and its social specificity. If economics tells us that all money is the same, history tells a very different story.

CHAPTER SIX

Money and its Interpretation

Paper Currency in Early America

JENNIFER J. BAKER

In 1690, the colonial legislature of Massachusetts became the first government in the Western world to issue paper money. There was no gold or silver ore on the eastern seaboard of North America, and British mercantilist policy, which sought to settle trade debts through the shipment of metal specie from colony to metropolis, drastically limited the supply of coins. To cope with the chronic shortage, colonists had relied on barter, IOUs, coins of other European countries, and various experimental media—wampum in New England, tobacco in the South—before turning to government-issued paper instruments.

Printed to finance a military expedition to Quebec, the Massachusetts bills differed from existing European paper instruments, such as banknotes and bills of exchange, in that they were backed by nothing but legislative order: although denominated in Spanish dollars and English pounds, they were only ever redeemable for tax credit and in 1712 the legislature declared them legal tender (Newman 1990: 1). European monetary theorists had long distinguished between a symbolic commercial paper and the "real" metal money it promised, but the Massachusetts bills blurred this distinction by effectively constituting the value they were supposed merely to represent. It was just a matter of time before every British American colony had issued its own public paper money, and in 1775 the Continental Congress turned to the printing press to finance the colonies' move for independence, backing its dollars not with metal reserves but with anticipated tax revenue.

Promoters praised paper money as an imaginative resource suitable for enterprise and as a tool that communities and individuals could use to exceed the limitations of their material capital. There was no need to depend on metal coins, they argued, if abstract reasoning, language, and trust could transform paper into a medium of exchange. In this sense, paper money was the product of Enlightened thinking and resourcefulness: by expanding the money supply in this way, communities could facilitate trade, spur economic growth, and provide debtor relief.

Viewing the matter from a decidedly colonial perspective, these advocates often represented their monetary experiments as New World innovation: just as Robinson Crusoe concludes that a knife is worth more than a pile of metal coins to a man stranded on a desert island, many colonists felt their geographic displacement might foster, and even require, new ways of conceptualizing value and money's operations. The colonies were sorely lacking in raw metals and circulating coins, but they had energy, initiative, and burgeoning print technologies. Critics maintained that paper instruments must maintain full convertibility at all times—John Adams would later declare that every dollar issued beyond the exact quantity of gold and silver in the vaults was a "cheat upon somebody"—but to those who believed in the economic potential of the colonies and new nation, the instrument's convertibility might well just be a matter of time (Adams 1809: 610).

Like Adams, most opponents condemned paper money as a folly that staked false claims to value. Also worrisome was the fact that a paper money not backed by collateral constituted a *debt*, and in this sense threatened to weaken and corrupt communities and individuals alike. At stake in the extensive literature surrounding American monetary debates of the long eighteenth century—political tracts but also poetry, novels, and belletristic writing of a range of genres—was the contested notion of autonomy itself. While this literature celebrated the prospect of colonial self-sufficiency and, later, national independence, opinions differed on the extent to which debt should be the tool to achieve it; and among those who accepted a large public debt as a wartime measure, there was heated debate about whether it should be a permanent fixture in the nation's economy. Moreover, the use of paper money to foster personal independence by providing extensions of credit to individuals sparked debates about opportunity and social mobility in early American communities. Proponents touted paper money as a means by which enterprising people might advance themselves, but opponents condemned it as a source of social unrest, linking the use of paper money to fraud and linguistic manipulation.

These disputes often reflected different views of what defined a healthy state. In elite political circles, the civic virtue necessary for a properly self-governing republic was thought to reside in a governing class of landowners whose fortunes were not tied to the market. According to this classical republicanism, anyone beholden to creditors or investments would necessarily be compromised ethically and susceptible to influence, and so public paper credit created tangled webs of obligation that jeopardized statesmanship and citizenship.[1] But the counter-argument maintained that concentrations of wealth in the hands of a few would upset a republic's balance of power, and by this logic, credit could crucially facilitate the small-scale farmer's or mechanic's ability to achieve independence, creating a healthier distribution of wealth and power. This second understanding of republicanism viewed credit as a temporary form of dependence that made progress possible in the long run. To those who adhered to this second view, the advent of privatized national banking, which tended to benefit wealthy elites and curtail extensions of credit for those of the lower social orders, marked a serious setback for this progress after the revolution.

Complicating this discourse, moreover, was the argument that *permanent* indebtedness might be economically, politically, and socially beneficial. Throughout the century, various writers had lauded paper money for its power to foster communal cohesion by creating webs of interdependence. A tenuous money not backed by metal coins would tie together the fortunes of buyers and sellers, they argued, and make faith in the community necessary to sustain its value. In the post-revolution era, ongoing borrowing—if coupled with responsible debt redemption—was also understood to be a means by which the nation could prove its creditworthiness to its citizens and other nations.

At the turn of the nineteenth century, a permanent public debt was formalized in Alexander Hamilton's Bank of the United States, which used the backing of wealthy subscribers to bolster the nation's credibility. Although Hamilton held himself to high standards of civic virtue, he was perfectly willing to foster "corruption," in the elite republican sense of the term, in order to strengthen the national economy through financial interdependence. As Hamilton sought to harness private interests for pragmatic purposes, however, the era's literature often questioned the very assumption that such interests compromised a person's integrity. Some literature challenged the notion that anyone could ever transcend private interests, and other works considered whether it was even desirable for disinterest and emotional detachment to govern public life. Refiguring "interest" in positive emotional terms as the basis for sympathy, writers worked to imagine how the interdependence wrought by financial entanglements might be the basis for new forms of civic personality, social relationships, and political representation in the new nation.

FUNDING INDEPENDENCE

The 1690 Massachusetts emission was controversial from the start. A paper money issued without backing and not immediately convertible cast doubt on the integrity of the government, and the fact that the government frequently adjusted the value of currency as it depreciated was proof to opponents that it could not keep its promises. Tellingly, the legislature used the linguistic term "tenor" to revalue its currency and, hence, change the purport of its original promise: in 1737 "old tenor" was replaced by "new tenor," which in turn became "middle tenor" when another revaluation became necessary only five years later.[2] Essentially a measure to buy time until the colony could procure funding, the Massachusetts issue also aggravated the Puritan community's fears that it was backsliding with each generation. Lamenting the colony's debts, one anonymous pamphleteer proclaimed sarcastically, "we had found an easy way of paying for them, and shuffling the Saddle off our own backs, on to our Children" (*Second Part* 1721: 311).

Monetary thinkers in the colonies and early United States took very seriously the notion that barter was a cumbersome mode of exchange and the marker of a primitive society. Because the scarcity of coins made barter necessary, paper money offered an appealing form of monetized exchange based on literacy, reckoning, and abstract units of accounting. Metal money was simply a symbol of exchange necessitated by an "ignorance of Writing and Arithmetick," the Puritan minister Cotton Mather argued, and therefore the spread of writing and reckoning skills would discharge metal money of any "Conceited necessity." An educated society, Mather added, could just as easily settle debts through units of accounting, and paper money had the added advantage of being worthless as a commodity, discouraging a love of mammon and hoarding by transmitting "vast summs without the intervention of *Silver*" (Mather 1690: 190–1). Virginia pamphleteer Peyton Randolph argued similarly that whereas metal money appealed to base impulses, paper money appealed to reason and trust. Unlike the "rational Trader," the miser derives "inexpressible Pleasure in the counting and poring over his Golden Guineas" and cannot grasp the symbolic function of monetary media (Randolph 1759: 15).

Defending American paper money to British officials in 1767, Benjamin Franklin argued that the colonies did not have the specie to issue convertible banknotes ("payable in Cash upon Sight," as he put it), but that paper money would be an "excellent Machine for Settling a new Country" (Franklin 1767: 34; 1765: 53). When the British Parliament ordered the Massachusetts colony to retire its bills of credit in 1750, the printer Joseph Green issued a ballad broadside singing similar praises. Green's *The Dying Speech of Old Tenor*, sung by an anthropomorphized paper bill, reminds colonists that he helped settle their land ("I've built you Houses, for to keep you warm, / And bought you Cattle for to plough your land"), funded their wars ("I bought you Guns and

Drums, and Swords indeed"), and provided debtor relief ("I've help'd the *Poor Man* in Distress, / And eas'd the *Widow* and the *Fatherless*) (Green 1750).

As did other paper-money advocates, Franklin emphasized its power to fund improvements and enterprise in cash-poor communities. He understood such currency-financed ventures to be "projects" in the sense that Daniel Defoe had used the term in his 1697 *Essay upon Projects*, a text Franklin cited in his *Autobiography* as a key influence on his own philanthropy. Like Defoe, Franklin saw projection as a form of speculation that was not dishonest but, rather, inventive and communally serviceable. Although he discouraged reckless borrowing in *Poor Richard's Almanac*, he maintained that managed risk was the key to entrepreneurial advancement. A 1771 New York bill of credit, which depicted a trio of figures—American Indian, Commerce, and Britannia—surrounded by ships, shipping barrels, and beavers, similarly emphasized paper money's power to stimulate commerce (see Figure 6.1).

In a number of mid-Atlantic colonies, where colonists had been forced to use tobacco as its medium of exchange, advocates hoped paper bills of credit might eliminate this commodity-based exchange and reduce the unnecessary cultivation of sot-weed. "Money crops," grown solely for the purpose of supplying a medium, glutted the market, ravaged the land, and discouraged agricultural and economic diversification. In this context, paper money was praised as a measure that might reduce the colonies' unhealthy monoculture and provide a medium that would not be hoarded or taken by merchants back to England.[3] William Borden, a North Carolina pamphleteer, declared that the colony's natural resources, which long "served the Inhabitants in the Infancy of the Province, as well for a *Medium* as for Food and Raiment," had "had their Time" and were "almost eaten out and gone." A medium of "no intrinsick Value," he argued, would obtain value by remaining in circulation and spurring industry and husbandry (Borden 1746: 6). Implicit in these arguments about tobacco was a more general theory about money and purchasing power: as the Maryland poet Ebenezer Cooke wrote in his 1730 poem, *Sotweed Redivivus*, it matters not what "sort of Mine" money issues from (be it the ground, tan-pit

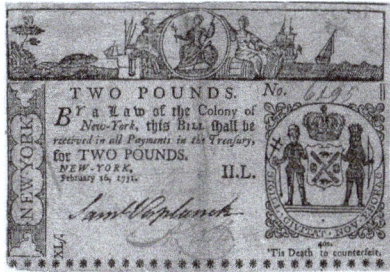

FIGURE 6.1: A two-pound bill, issued by New York on February 16, 1771, bears images of transatlantic trade. Notre Dame, Department of Special Collections, Room 102 Hesburgh Library, Notre Dame, IN 46556.

or paper mill) "since ev'ry Thing / Is worth no more than it will bring" (Cooke 1730: 3–4).

In praising the resourcefulness of colonial monetary experiments, advocates of paper money took care to distinguish paper money from merely fanciful air castles or get-rich-quick schemes. When James Madison declared in 1787 that "nothing but evil" would spring from "imaginary money," he expressed a distrust of dematerialized instruments that had become commonplace in anti-paper rhetoric throughout the century (Madison 1787: 106). By contrast, one Massachusetts pamphleteer, John Wise, applauded the people's "power of thought" and the inventiveness that was born of public necessity and deployed for collective good (Wise 1721: 210). In outlining his remedy for Maryland's economic woes, the speaker of Cooke's *Sotweed Redivivus* also aligned paper money with a publicly serviceable form of imaginative thinking: "And with Submission to the State, / I have a Project in my Pate, / May prove the Making of this Land, / If executed out of Hand; / Which is to give my Fancy vent, / Within my *Pericranium* Pent" (Cooke 1730: 4).

Like Borden, Wise, and Cooke, Franklin emphasized the symbolic power in his widely reprinted 1729 essay, *A Modest Inquiry into the Nature and Necessity of a Paper-Currency*, observing that the monetary medium symbolically "*is* whatsoever it will procure"—it is "Cloth to him that wants Cloth, and Corn to those that want Corn" (Franklin 1729: 345). In the history of money's development, so often recounted in pamphlets like Franklin's, monetized exchange represents an advance over barter by introducing a common equivalent that gauges the relative value of what each party seeks to acquire. In the words of contemporary theorist Jean-Joseph Goux, the medium only represents the absent objects of buyers' and sellers' desires, hence negotiating the conflicts between exchange parties that cannot offer what the other really wants (Goux 1984). The introduction of this "third quantity," philosopher Georg Simmel wrote in 1907, had marked a watershed moment in the "development of the purely symbolic character of money" (Simmel 1907: 146). Applying the lessons of monetary history to an ailing colonial economy, colonial advocates of paper money reasoned that a common equivalent might be fashioned out of any media—gold, silver, leather, tobacco, beads, shells, and, of course, paper.

The notion of a scripted value not based on ready convertibility to metal was the culmination of earlier English experiences with coinage. Throughout the seventeenth century, the continued acceptance of clipped coins at face value had undermined the notion that money derived its worth from either commodity value or legal designation, demonstrating, instead, the power of buyers and sellers to negotiate value in the act of exchange. The passing of debased coins, as well as the introduction of banknotes and paper money, marked an important milestone in what Marc Shell describes as the overarching trend in Western monetary history: the increasing disjunction between "face value (intellectual currency) and substantial value (material currency)" (Shell 1982: 1).

The widespread circulation of clipped coins in England had demonstrated how monetary symbols might retain value despite this disjunction, but economic thinkers like John Law, James Steuart, and Adam Smith went one step further in arguing that this detachment could actually fuel economic expansion. In his famous critique of mercantilist banking in *The Wealth of Nations*, Smith argued that a bank, rather than maintain a one-to-one ratio between metal reserves and circulating banknotes, could maintain a one-to-four or one-to-five ratio, keeping on hand only enough reserves to meet redemption needs and then reinvesting for additional profit. Complete convertibility, he emphasized, was actually the mark of a stagnant economy, and, if banks could free up metal piling up as "dead stock" in the vaults, that money could do double duty in circulation (Smith's advocacy of fractional-reserve banking, which Steuart had advocated a decade earlier, was essentially that of modern-day banking, in which the entirety of deposits are not kept in house but reloaned with interest). Substituting paper for a portion of metal coin, Smith argued, could "convert a great part of this dead stock into active and productive stock" (Smith 1776: 341). Emphasizing its benefits, Franklin had promoted this model of banking almost fifty years earlier: "Money which otherwise would have lain dead in [bankers'] Hands, is made to circulate again thereby among the People: And thus the Running Cash of the Nation is as it were doubled" (Franklin 1729: 348). Rather than see paper money as the mark of deficient specie, he saw it as a source of proliferation and productivity. Fittingly, a 1775 bill issued by the colony of New York featured a bundle of wheat and the words *E Parvis Grandis Acervus* (A Massive Stack from Small Things): like the tiny seed that develops into a plant, paper money spawns production for just the cost of paper and printing (see Figure 6.2).

The fiscal experiments of the colonies laid the groundwork for the Continental Congress's creation of a national paper money in 1776. The

FIGURE 6.2: A one-dollar bill, issued in 1775 by New York, bears the image of a bundle of wheat and the words *E PARVIS GRANDIS ACERVUS* (A Massive Stack from Small Things). The Hesburgh Libraries of Notre Dame.

decision to use paper money to fund the Revolutionary War was based on a conviction that the public debt that had earlier facilitated colonial settlement could now be pressed into service for insurrection. A national currency, issued to pay for soldiers' salaries and military supplies, provided much of the underwriting for the risky, but potentially profitable, venture of war. Recasting dire necessity as ingenuity, Thomas Paine boasted in 1778 that the new nation had brilliantly created money to fund its independence: "We are rich by a contrivance of our own" (Paine 1778: 51).

Reversing the traditional association of debt with dependence, the images and mottos on wartime colonial and Continental bills aligned paper money with liberty. The 1775 "Sword in Hand" bill (see Figure 6.3), engraved by Paul Revere and issued by Massachusetts at the start of military conflict with Britain, featured a soldier holding the Magna Carta and the words, "Issued in defence of American Liberty" (the soldier's Magna Carta was replaced with the Declaration of Independence after its ratification). Two 1777 South Carolina bills also celebrated freedom (see Figures 6.4 and 6.5). One announced *Servitus Omnis Misera*, or, "All Forms of Slavery Are Wretched" (with obvious irony, given the prevalence of chattel slavery in the region), and the other featured a bird fleeing a cage and the motto *Ubi Libertas Ibi Patria*, or, "Where There Is Liberty, There is Homeland." In his 1790 *Report on the Public Credit*, Alexander Hamilton would later call this debt the "price of liberty," an investment undertaken to reap political and economic independence (Hamilton 1790b: 533).

By war's end, liberty's pricetag totaled almost $450 million in state and federal currencies on top of $12 million in foreign loans, and although many

FIGURE 6.3: A Massachusetts four-shilling "Sword in Hand" bill, issued on December 7, 1775, bears the image of a soldier and the words "Issued in defence of American Liberty." The Hesburgh Libraries of Notre Dame.

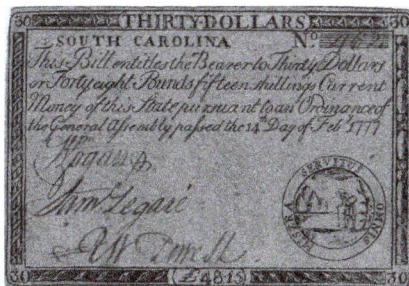

FIGURE 6.4: A South Carolina thirty-dollar bill, issued on February 14, 1777, bears the words *SERVITUS OMNIS MISERA* (All Forms of Slavery Are Wretched). The Hesburgh Libraries of Notre Dame.

FIGURE 6.5: A South Carolina twenty-dollar bill, issued on February 14, 1777, bears the image of a bird escaping from a cage and the words *UBI LIBERTAS IBI PATRIA* (Where There is Liberty, There is Homeland). The Hesburgh Libraries of Notre Dame.

colonists were willing to accept paper money (and deficit spending generally) as an emergency wartime measure, the over-emission of Continental dollars had caused alarming depreciation and by 1781 its complete demise. That year, another of Green's ballad broadsides, titled *A Mournful Lamentation On the untimely Death of Paper Money*, praised an allegorized Continental dollar whose time had been cut short by severe depreciation: "He rais'd and paid our Armies brave. / To guard our threaten'd State; / Whose val'rous Deeds their Country save, / And num'rous Foes defeat." This "doleful tale" celebrates the role of Paper Money in supporting independence and criticizes those "assassins" who refused to credit him (*Mournful Lamentation* 1781).

The author of this broadside lamented the death of Paper Money because he imagined an ongoing role for currency finance in the war effort, but other writers considered the death of Paper Money essential to American success. *M'Fingal*, John Trumbull's 1782 epic poem of the Revolution, for example, proclaimed that the Continental dollar, the offspring of "dame Necessity" who "proves the tale of Midas true," must finally die. Marching to his grave in the vision of the fourth canto, Paper Money appears limping on crutches, draped in tattered robes, and bearing a breastplate that reads, "The faith of all th' United States."[4] Although an admirable patriot supported for a time by popular opinion, he must "perish in his country's cause" and give way to more sustainable fiscal measures (Trumbull 1775–82: 208, 207, 209). Trumbull anticipated the day when the Continental bill would lie buried in eternal peace.

Trumbull's poem indicates the eagerness of many political leaders, including Federalists, to retire paper money as soon as possible. Parting ways with many members of the revolutionary generation and his political allies, Hamilton saw ongoing borrowing as the most efficient way for a nation to build its credibility, maintaining that a nation proves itself by borrowing and paying off its loans in a timely and regular fashion. The "wreath of *punctuality*," the essayist Judith Sargent Murray observed, supports the "character of an honest man," and extending such logic to nations, Hamilton argued that a government's "punctual performance of contracts" would inspire citizens and other nations to invest further in the United States. Because "[s]tates, like individuals, who observe their engagements" and pay off their debts "are respected and trusted," a public debt would be the first step to build trust at home and abroad (Murray 1798: 29; Hamilton 1790b: 532).

Hamilton's program of economic nationalism, strongly influenced by the "trickle down" economics of financier Robert Morris, envisioned elite wealth as the foundation for a strong US economy. As a result, his monetary policies sought to concentrate wealth in the hands of merchants, lawyers, brokers, and politicians—as many historians have reminded us in the wake of Lin-Manuel Miranda's smash Broadway musical *Hamilton* and the recent surge of interest in Hamilton as a historical figure (Frank and Kramnick 2016). Recent scholarship on early American monetary history has also discerned in these policies a major shift from the concept of money as a widely available medium and source of credit to money as an investment opportunity for the already wealthy.[5] As Christine Desan details, colonial money and Continental dollars were communal enterprises, created jointly by legislatures and citizens for mutual benefit, but, by contrast, the banknotes that replaced them were printed at government expense but largely benefited the private investors who both supplied collateral and helped regulate the institution. This transformation, Desan argues, marked "a turn from an early modern to the liberal political economy" (Desan 2008: 27).

This shift in money's design and purpose, Terry Bouton argues, was an essential part of the anti-democratic counter-revolution that followed the Revolutionary War. Focusing on pre- and post-war Pennsylvania, he details how the withdrawal of paper money limited access to financial independence for a democratic majority. To pay the interest on the new banknotes, governments levied taxes and collected whatever paper money and coin were still in circulation, and to make matters worse, lawmakers were reluctant to issue more paper money for fear of depreciating the certificates in the hands of the wealthy. Farmers and mechanics complained that such policies were incompatible with republican ideals aimed at distributing property and fostering independence. They did not imagine that independence might be available to non-white men, Bouton writes, but their protest was nevertheless animated by the then-radical idea that the "Revolution (and the Pennsylvania Constitution of 1776 in particular) gave ordinary people extensive rights to resist policies that threatened economic equality and political liberty" (Bouton 2007: 866).

CREDIT AND SOCIAL MOBILITY

Disagreements over national banking registered disagreements about the true measure of a nation's wealth—and specifically the question of whether large businesses and investors primarily determine a nation's economic wellbeing and so should receive special protections and incentives. Efforts to curtail paper money also reflected deep-seated anxieties about social fluidity. In early American writings, available credit was celebrated as a catalyst for enterprise but alternatively condemned as a tool of linguistic misrepresentation and duplicitous self-fashioning. For states and individuals alike, becoming respectable required the careful management of reputation, but this attention to appearances could also be grounds for suspicion.[6] Unbacked government paper money was particularly implicated in a debt culture that fostered overreaching and social climbing.

In one 1775 magazine sketch, "Considerations on the use and abuse of mottos," for example, government-issued paper money was personified as a charlatan who claims a wealth he does not actually have in his possession. Mocking as duplicitous the mottos on Continental dollars, the sketch featured a character named Paper Money, who speaks words the reader can never entirely trust, casting doubt on the word of the government as well as on the ambitious upstart. In another sketch, titled "The Representation and Remonstrance of Hard Money," the persona of Hard Money provides a foil to his paper counterpart. Hard Money insists that the accurate assessment of personal character and monetary value alike is the prerogative of an elite class of "reading men" who are "able to conceive that first appearances are oftentimes deceitful, and that *all is not gold that glitters.*" He is a man of substance, honorable birth, and fluency in all languages (metal's widespread acceptability making it universally conversant). Paper Money, by contrast, is charged with "affecting an importance, as if he had been equal to the *solid coin*" ("Representation and Remonstrance" 1779: 28).

In "Considerations on the use and abuse of mottos," Paper Money is the offspring of a printer and bears a striking resemblance to Franklin, the tradesman-turned-statesman who designed the Latin mottos and images for colonial and Continental currencies and was an easy target for hard-money advocates. The sketch denigrated Franklin as an imposter who fashions himself as learned, speaking only a smattering of Latin and clichés and twisting words to serve his ulterior motives. Paper Money, who bears those Latin mottos, similarly proclaims a value that cannot be backed up by collateral. In the most obvious sense, Paper Money is the brainchild of Franklin and the product of the Philadelphia printing house Hall and Sellers, but Paper Money's parentage also aligns credit use with the tradesman. In the class-conscious satire of these anti-paper-money sketches, "substance" refers both to the tangible material of metal coins and to the status and capital of landowners.

The lineage of Paper Money in this sketch also linked paper credit to dubious print technologies. By making possible mass-produced and standardized texts, printing lent an aura of legitimacy to paper money, promissory notes, newspapers, tracts, broadsides, and other media. But a man might also hide behind print and assume a false identity in a newspaper or broadside that he could not so easily assume in a face-to-face encounter. And a printed bill might seem official and yet still make promises it could not keep. Worse yet, it might be a fake entirely, for the more standardized and generally reproducible a bill was, the more easily it might be counterfeited.

The alignment of anti-populist sentiments with opposition to government-issued paper money was nowhere more clearly expressed than in *The Anarchiad* (1786–7), a mock-epic poem by Trumbull and three other Connecticut poets. Composed in the wake of Shays's Rebellion, an uprising of Massachusetts war veterans protesting about dire economic conditions and calling for debtor relief, this celebrated political satire attacked rural supporters of paper money and called for a new federal constitution to regulate the nation's finances. Modeled, in part, after Alexander Pope's mock-epic *The Dunciad*, the poem offered a fiscal warning of mythic proportions which forecasted a reign of allegorical tyrants, such as Chaos, Night, and Anarch, if the rage for paper money was not curtailed.

The Anarchiad depicted paper-money advocates as duplicitous upstarts, but equally villainous were the local courts that had mandated the acceptance of devalued currency at face value. In an apostrophe to paper instruments, Anarch revels wickedly in the transformative power of legal language: "Fair from the Gen'ral Court's unpardon'd sin, / Ap'st thou the gold Peruvian mines within; / Wak'd to new life, by my creative power, / The press they mint, and dunghill rags thy ore." Anarch's constitutive "creative power" entails a licentious use of law and letters alike. While the press transforms toilet rags into money, legal tender laws render "fair" the "unpardon'd sin" of roguery and turn debtor crews into "licens'd villains" (Humphreys et al. 1786–7: 15–16). That such instruments "ape" gold—the verb connoting a clumsy imitation of a social better—suggests again that paper money is a charade and also the instrument of provincials on the make. "Self-taught" and "unletter'd," advocates of paper money are said to pervert meaning for the sake of their own social climbing.

The double-layered allusion to Pope and Milton's *Paradise Lost* also reinforced the satire's larger concern that paper money violates a putative linguistic integrity and takes liberties with language itself. In a passage borrowed directly from the fourth and final book of *The Dunciad*, Chaos speaks an "uncreating" word that reverses the genesis of the "new-born state": "Thy constitution, Chaos, is restor'd; / Law sinks before they uncreating word; / Thy hand unbars th'unfathom'd gulf of fate, / And deep in darkness 'whelms the new-born state" (Humphreys et al. 1786–7: 36, 6–7). In Pope's satire the speaker laments the death of Logos: while God's creating Word called forth the world and wrought coherence out of chaos in Genesis, words in Pope's England have only "uncreating" powers. Pope's satiric lament, based on a similarly uncreating act by Milton's Chaos, was aimed at London's deteriorating educational and literary institutions. The satire of *The Anarchiad* predicts that paper credit schemes in the United States will bring a similar kind of linguistic apocalypse. Because the very genesis of the newborn state of the United States, like God's creation of the world, was enacted through words, such corruption will be particularly devastating to a nation so conceived in language. Chaos has been lamentably restored, the stanza suggests, and only the reversal of his uncreation, by way of a legitimate restoration of law and letters through a national Constitution, will bring an end to darkness.

Even privatized national banking, which limited access to credit, aroused fears of social climbing and upended hierarchies. A speculative bubble following the first issue of notes by Hamilton's national bank in 1791 is a case in point. When Hamilton loosened the credit requirements for purchasing bank shares in order to create investment opportunities for those with less capital, what followed was a potentially disastrous flurry of leveraged purchases. Wealthy elites worried that speculation would fuel fantasies of upward mobility and wreak havoc on the structure of American society. Speaking of the "incurable" spirit of gaming, Thomas Jefferson worried that the "taylor who has made thousands in one day, tho[ugh] he has lost them the next, can never again be content with the slow and moderate earnings of his needle" (Jefferson 1791: 74). New York Senator Rufus King expressed similar concerns about the lower orders of society abandoning their positions once tempted by quick riches. The speculation had been "going on in a most alarming manner," he recalled in a letter to Hamilton, "mechanicks deserting their shops, [s]hopkeepers sending their goods to auction, and not a few of our merchants neglecting the regular & profitable commerce of the City" (King 1791: 60).

To understand the counter-argument to these anti-democratic claims, we might turn again to wartime periodical literature and the persona of Paper Money. In two anonymous responses to "Representation and Remonstrance of

Hard Money," the character Paper Money is still a man lacking in "substance," but his insubstantiality takes on a decidedly positive spin. Although Paper Money cannot match Hard Money in material value, he is, as a printed text, kin to the progeny of great authors: "If a *Printing-office* was the place of *my nativity*," he declares in one sketch, "so has it been of the noblest productions that ever blessed or adorned the world" ("Answer of Continental Currency" 1779: 113). He boasts in the second sketch that he is "by the mother's side of the family of *Paper*; a family that has been of more service to the commonwealth of letters than all of the name of Hard-Money that ever have existed" ("Reply of Continental Currency" 1779: 77). Paper Money acts without the backing of material wealth and so is a testament to the power of legal language. In a political culture that has enshrined documents like the Constitution and Declaration of Independence, his lineage is something to be celebrated.

This version of Paper Money lacks wealth and status but for this reason also fits nicely into a story of self-making. A similar story unfolds in "The Adventures of a Continental Dollar," a serial narrative of which two installments appeared in the *United States Magazine* before the periodical folded in December 1779. In this tale, Paper Money admits he has neither the capital nor prestige that Hard Money enjoys, but he insists nevertheless that readers not overlook his potential. His mother was a printer and his father was Liberty himself. An "enterprizing genius," he was born "in the centre of the vast continent of North-America" where "boundless and unexplored regions" are fit for such "free and uncountrouled souls" as his ("Adventures" 1779: 265). Although a product of European monetary practice and theory, paper money meshed particularly well with an American ethos of enterprise and social mobility: the quixotic quest for quick riches associated with credit schemes was reconfigured in positive terms as the pursuit of the American dream.

DEBT AND COMMUNAL BONDS

In addition to touting its economic benefits, advocates of paper money and national banknotes insisted that currencies could bind communities and motivate the support necessary to keep credit structures afloat. Advocates, however, understood the source of that motivation differently over time. In the colonial and revolutionary eras, promoters imagined that buyers and sellers would suppress their own interests in order to uphold paper money out of communal allegiance and patriotism. In the post-war era, the rhetoric tended to imagine that personal interest—not its suppression—would motivate buyers and sellers to sustain the national bank and credit structures on which their own fortunes might depend.

Writing about Massachusetts money in 1721, John Wise called upon colonists to do their part in sustaining currency values: "Out of Love to your Country, and the Civil Well-being of it. Ponder these things Wisely; and be perswaded to keep up your noble Fund." Through civic-minded deliberation—not solipsistic flights of fancy—people could render bills "as good as Money" (Wise 1721: 203). Similarly, Cotton Mather considered each issue of paper money to be a collective obligation for which "*All the Inhabitants* of the Land, taken as one Body [were] the *Principals*, who Reap the *Benefits*, and must bear the *Burdens*, and are the Security in the *Publick Bonds*" (Mather 1690: 190).

For Mather, moreover, such financial faith was not unlike Christian faith in the face of uncertainty. In a 1714 pamphlet, Mather drew a telling analogy between God's promise and a bill of credit, urging readers to accept the promise until it can be realized: "The *Promise* of GOD is a *Bill of Credit*, not inferior to any Coin of *Silver or Gold*; and it will do for us when we must say with him of old, *Silver & Gold have I none*." Tellingly, the header on each page of the pamphlet read, "How to Live in Hard Times," and Mather's essay was also specifically concerned with the dangerous despair that might plague those suffering economically in Massachusetts. Such despair, he warned, becomes self-fulfilling prophecy, for "A *Fearful* Apprehension, that God cannot or will not *Provide* for us, is the most likely Way to be Left *Unprovided* for" (Mather 1714: 11–12, 7).

During the Revolutionary War, supporters believed that paper money revealed a popular sovereignty at work. Praising the war debt, one anonymous writer declared in 1787 that the "faith of the people" themselves had "impressed" the bills with their value. According to Paine, the colonists could choose to credit the monetary symbols of their own making rather than the empty symbols of monarchical power. At first glance, this rhetoric of volition might seem inconsistent with the fact that currency fluctuations could make the consequences of one's actions impalpable and apparently beyond the reach of individual estimation or control; after all, in such a volatile credit system, one's destiny would seem a function not of agency but of impersonal economic forces. Rhetoric and reality might be easily reconciled, however, if one saw this volition as necessarily *collective*. Otherwise powerless people, that is, could effect change by acting in concert with one another.

One revolutionary-era magazine story, titled "The Adventures of a Continental Dollar," featured a personified Paper Money who similarly emphasizes that such faith figures as a valuable expression of public commitment. Speaking of men who publicly endorsed him shortly after his birth in America, he recalls, "They were the first men that owned me, and stood up for me in the infancy of my affairs, entered into a league with me, and stood firm to it in despite of all the hazards of an uncertain fortune." In this and other instances, the speaking bill describes financial faith but also, in so doing, attempts to solicit faith from the reader as well. When Paper Money speaks, he has in mind a reader who might extend his or her credit to the nation's money ("Adventures" 1779: 266).

As the rhetoric and images on wartime bills made clear, public debt invested each buyer and seller with the power and obligation to help support currency values in the face of uncertainty. When Franklin and other printers designed the mottos for currency, they took full advantage of the fact that bills were not only a source of revenue but also a medium on which patriotic rhetoric might circulate and favorably influence public opinion of the war. A series of ten denominations designed by Franklin, each bearing a distinct image and Latin text, all speak, in one way or another, to the importance of the colonial cause and the promise of the American future: *DEPRESSA RESURGIT* (Tho' oppressed it rises) predicts American victory; *PERSEVERANDO* (by perseverance) features a busy beaver that emblematizes American industry (see Figure 6.6); and *MAJORA MINORIBUS CONSONANT* (the greater and smaller ones sound together) envisions an American consensus akin to musical harmony. Combining optimism with candid acknowledgment that war is costly, a two-dollar note reminds colonists that their endurance will yield reward. This note, which featured the engraving of a hand threshing wheat and the phrase *TRIBULATIO DITAT* (tribulation improves), emphasized that strength will come only with struggle (see Figure 6.7). The rhetoric of Continental dollars worked to foster confidence by implicitly linking financial venture to collective risk-taking and commitment. One particularly memorable bill, which bore the motto "We are One" and the image of thirteen interlocking rings—one for each colony—suggested that the fates of all colonies would be intertwined through the political and economic venture of rebellion (see Figure 6.8).

Portraying the American Revolution years later in his 1789 *History of the American Revolution*, David Ramsey stressed that the collective faith and sacrifice of the people had helped ensure success. Taking pride in the communal cooperation that made paper money possible, he noted that it was a "point of

FIGURE 6.6: A six-dollar Continental bill, issued on November 29, 1775, bears the image of a beaver and the word *PERSEVERANDO* (By Perseverance). The Hesburgh Libraries of Notre Dame.

FIGURE 6.7: A two-dollar Continental bill, issued on May 20, 1777, bears the image of a hand threshing wheat and the words *TRIBULATIO DITAT* (Tribulation Improves). The Hesburgh Libraries of Notre Dame.

FIGURE 6.8: A one-third-dollar Continental bill, issued in 1776, bears the image of thirteen interlocking rings—each representing a colony—and the words WE ARE ONE. The Hesburgh Libraries of Notre Dame.

honor and considered as a part of duty, to take the bills freely at their full value" even when confidence was waning. He added that "[p]rivate gain was then so little regarded, that the whig citizens were willing to run all the hazards incidental to bills of credit, rather than injure the cause of their country by under valuing its money." Ramsey failed to mention the widespread profiteering that took place during the war, and perhaps most telling, when he did describe the bills' depreciation, he attributed it to larger intractable forces rather than to individual decisions of buyers and sellers. Obscuring the human agency that brought about depreciation, he wrote, "Repeated emissions begat that natural depreciation, which results from an excess of quantity" (Ramsey 1789: 459).

Writing shortly before the passage of Hamilton's bank plan, Ramsey's recollection of civic sacrifice might have been, in part, a reaction to the emerging redefinition of money as an investment opportunity and Hamilton's willingness to appeal to self-interest as much as to patriotism. Although Hamilton envisioned a small, elite class of leaders who would make sacrifices to support the new nation, his plans for national banking were aimed at strengthening the nation by entangling private and public interests: people who invested financially in the national bank as subscribers, he argued controversially, would feel more of a stake in the new nation's success precisely because their assets were on the line. This was the thinking behind his decision after the war to exchange all state paper monies for shares in the newly created Bank of the United States. If the federal government assumed each state's debts, Hamilton reasoned, a single national debt would shift people's allegiances from the state to the nation: state creditors would become federal creditors, and their loyalties realigned. A centralized debt was Hamilton's key to transforming a loose confederation of states into a politically unified and economically creditable nation. He praised this debt as a "blessing" and "powerful cement" of the union (Hamilton 1781:

635), arguing that it would create a body politic in which each locality's economy would have consequences for the whole. "Credit is an *entire* thing," he declared. "Every part of it has the nicest sympathy with every other part; wound one limb, and the whole tree shrinks and decays" (Hamilton 1795: 298).

As part of his financial plan, Hamilton also wanted wealthy Americans to invest in the Bank of the United States, making their interests inseparable from those of the new nation. He identified a "certain fermentation of mind, a certain activity of speculation and enterprise," which if "properly directed" could be "made subservient to useful purposes" (but which, if "left entirely to itself," would have "pernicious effects") (Hamilton 1791b: 696). His government-chartered bank was to have 20 percent of its holdings government-funded and the remaining 80 percent privately funded, but because three-quarters of that 80 percent would take the form of government securities, those private investors would have a stake in the government's success.[7] Modeled on the older Bank of England, Hamilton's bank was designed to corrupt wealthy and influential subscribers, turning them into speculators whose assets would motivate them to care about the nation's future. National banknotes, he argued, would be less susceptible to over-emission because they would be issued by individuals whose own assets would be affected by depreciation—unlike government-issued paper money, which was legislated by politicians whose personal assets were not as directly involved in the outcome. As the architect of the new nation's economy, Hamilton sought to curtail self-interest through institutional checks and balances but without ever eliminating this all-important "fermentation of mind." Members of the political elite who believed the nation's leaders should be guided by civic virtue were scandalized by Hamilton's efforts to make patriotism and financial investment mutually reinforcing.

Opposition came from other fronts as well, for those who supported widely available credit for farmers, artisans, and small-scale producers argued that the bank compromised the republic by exacerbating disparities of wealth. These opponents also advanced the increasingly common argument that civic disinterest—long claimed as the special prerogative of gentry leadership—was itself a fallacy, and the men assumed most likely to govern with integrity, it turned out, had assets tied up in national bank shares. At the turn of the nineteenth century, as the classical tradition of virtuous leadership waned, political representation was reimagined accordingly: although legislative representatives were expected to transcend their own interests, they were also increasingly expected to keep their constituents' needs and desires in mind. The model of direct representation that replaced virtual representation—and led to modern interest-group politics—now raises problems of a different sort: whether senators and congressional representatives should vote *only* with their own constituents in mind, rather than national considerations or private conscience, is subject to ongoing debate.

According to detractors, the problem with the classical tradition was not simply that it was illusory, for even if disinterest were possible, they argued, such emotional detachment would hinder a political leader's capacity to understand the wants of a people. The eighteenth-century "economic man" that J.G.A. Pocock describes is insubstantial, impetuous, and emasculated (Pocock 1985), but the erosion of a man's autonomy was also thought to enable a feminized sympathy. This sympathy appealed to post-revolutionary Americans who felt increasingly that the concept of disinterested virtue was morally limited and devoid of emotion. As historian Gordon S. Wood writes, it was the investment in—rather than transcendence of—others' concerns that emerged in the wake of the Revolution as the means to bind the union. Historian Andrew Burstein also notes that a new language of feeling entered political discourse after the war, providing a "decisive vocabulary by which political leaders could claim true representation" of others by identifying intimately with their constituents' needs (Burstein 2001: 629). As the early feminist Judith Sargent Murray argued, dependence—financial and otherwise—was not simply a feminine state but a *human* state.

In *Federalist* 35, Hamilton argued that legislators would identify with those they represented if they stood to gain or lose as their constituents did: "Common interest may always be reckoned upon as the surest bond of sympathy" (Hamilton 1788: 319).[8] The sympathy Hamilton described, however, was not so much a moral sensibility or emotional response as it was a shared vulnerability: in Hamilton's sense, one has sympathy with, rather than sympathy for, another. In the early US novels, by contrast, sympathy *for* another person was commonly the fortuitous by-product of financial interdependence. Such novels used financial scenarios to stress the impossibility of republican disinterest and, more important, its tendency to promote apathy where the suffering of others was concerned. Literary historian Julia Stern detects in novels of the Federalist era especially a "feminized zone of imagination" that criticized republican philosophy as cold, dispassionate, and "unmoored from fellow feeling" (Stern 1997: 6–7). In these narratives, financial vulnerability counters that dispassionate outlook and promotes a character's sympathy. Charles Brockden Brown's *Arthur Mervyn*, for example, depicts a protagonist whose susceptibility to the influence of his own interests actually makes him more capable of imagining the distresses of a "brother in calamity" (C.B. Brown 1799–1800: 398). In William Hill Brown's 1789 novel, *The Power of Sympathy*, those who pride themselves on the virtues of affluence and independence "make but an indifferent figure" (W. Brown 1789: 58). In novels populated with fallen heroes and heroines who have experienced financial downturn in a volatile economy, disinterested characters are apathetic bystanders who refuse to involve themselves in the affairs of others.[9]

The American monetary experiments of the long eighteenth century shaped, and were shaped by, colonial and national thinking about independence and dependence—or, in eighteenth-century parlance, freedom and necessity. In the American narrative of monetary development, paper currencies were devised in the spirit of New World enterprise to reduce the constraints of British trade regulations. They were instrumental in the birth of the nation and, like the Declaration of Independence and Constitution, were understood to showcase the human capacity to use language and print media resourcefully to bring about progress. The fact that indebtedness was the very tool of independence, however, meant that the line between the two conditions was not always clearly drawn, and advocates of paper money had, from its inception, identified the benefits of interdependence and also challenged the enshrinement of autonomy in the classical tradition of republicanism. With public debt permanently established in the post-war era, disputes over national banking focused on the funding and regulation of a nation's debt, which, in turn, raised questions still very much debated today: questions about the gauge of a nation's wealth and economic wellbeing, the distribution of wealth and access to opportunity, and the role of private gain in civic life and the operations of government.

Today's bitcoin, a currency tied to no nation, government, or institution, throws into relief the mechanisms of trust that enabled eighteenth-century government-backed currency as well as that currency's powers to define a community. Bitcoin's peer-to-peer transaction, unmediated by a government or federally insured bank, is ensured by cryptographic proof rather than trust in a third party. For this reason, it has appealed heavily to libertarians, who by definition have no faith in government regulation; in particular, its preset rates of issue and capped quantities promise to limit the kind of depreciation that results when the Federal Reserve prints paper money to stimulate the economy—although being free from government interference has not guaranteed bitcoin's stability, for it has been as prone to hoarding, wild speculation, and drastic fluctuations as the notorious Continental dollars issued during the American Revolution.[10] If, as early American monetary debates indicate, monetary thinking is often a proxy for thinking about community—the government that regulates it, the ties that bind it, and the social relations that inhere within it—the rise of bitcoin indicates that new ways of organizing exchange are mutually involved with new ways of imagining communities. Bitcoin would not have been conceivable without the internet, not simply for the obvious reason that the internet provides the mechanisms for its exchange and ledgers but also because the internet makes conceivable the notion of an exchange community no longer defined in territorial or national terms.

CHAPTER SEVEN

Money and the Issues of the Age

Thinking about Money in the Eighteenth Century

DANIEL CAREY

The obligation to understand money, to interpret it philosophically, and to recognize its practical implications, risks, and opportunities, represents one of the great preoccupations of eighteenth-century Britain and Ireland, apparent in the consolidation of political economy as a major intellectual endeavor. Attention to the topic occurred in the midst of specific crises that punctuated the period, often in order to influence policy and public opinion, as well as in more abstract, philosophical deliberations that tackled a difficult subject of growing concern.

During the period, a number of important debates took place. While the foundation of the monetary system came in the form of silver coin at the start of the period (gold would later assume this role), the currency came under attack from clippers intent on removing silver to melt down as bullion. As commentators explored the issue, they debated whether the Mint's stamp provided a source of value (given that lightweight coins continued to circulate), or whether the value resided only in the intrinsic metal content. The existence of two precious metals in circulation—gold and silver—added further complications to the situation. What was the best way to manage the fact that both of them served as a store of value, yet they fluctuated in price relative to each other and traded as commodities in bullion form? At the same time, proposals emerged for paper money substitutes that offered a means of augmenting the money stock and providing an alternative circulating medium. The question was how to regulate paper, to control its emission, and give it substantial backing that would ensure its value. The debate hinged, to some extent, on tensions between monetary discipline and the desire to support economic development (expanding or constricting the monetary supply), and equally the struggle over prioritizing domestic needs *vs.* international trade (with paper at home and precious metals abroad). Banking likewise became a major focus of discussion, in conjunction with the establishment of the Bank of England (1694), designed to fund the national debt. The Bank promised to pay hard money in exchange for notes as a form of guarantee, but rival schemes appeared that used land as the stock on which to generate funds. The appearance of various new "species" of money required careful consideration of what was real and what was illusory, including the apparatus of credit that supported financial networks and transactions. An integrated account of this history must take into consideration not just metropolitan "discourse" but the locations and issues attending economic debate in Ireland and Scotland.

However confident the voice of participants, the sense still comes across that the "system," such as it was, remained provisional, the choices not fully clear in their implications or justifications. Nor is there a consensus that we can point to—some territory of agreement that constitutes an "Enlightenment" attitude to money in the way that we might say that reason or scientific method enjoyed a particularly wide backing that unifies an important group of commentators. The same openness or indeterminacy appears in the variety of generic forms used to disseminate positions, from pamphlets to treatises, broadsheets, satires, discourses, and other interventions, including Bishop Berkeley's innovative format in *The Querist* (1735–7), consisting solely of pointed questions. Sir James Steuart's *Inquiry into the Principles of Political Oeconomy* (1767) and Adam Smith's *The Wealth of Nations* (1776), with their systematic treatment of economic issues, arguably represent outliers in the century.

Looking across the period as a whole, one cannot fail to be impressed by the degree to which specific crises generated some of the most significant theorizing; the articulation of key principles tended to take place in the midst of traumatic events with huge political and economic implications rather than in more settled circumstances, emerging from abstract contemplation. The defining financial crises start with the need to implement a total recoinage of English silver money in the 1690s, followed in the 1720s by the bubbles associated with the collapse of the Mississippi Company and the South Sea Company, and, near the end of the century, by the Bank of England's suspension of cash payments in 1797 caused by the strain of war with France. The flow of contributions that these episodes generated, from leading lights to minor but optimistic and opinionated projectors, is remarkable. No simple way exists to navigate this terrain. While attention should be given, of course, to the most influential and original figures in the

THE RECOINAGE

We can begin with John Locke and the moment of the Recoinage in the mid-1690s. His viewpoint became a lasting touchstone for commentators across the century. Early in his career, Locke had given some attention to economic questions without publishing the results, specifically in relation to setting the rate of interest; later, in the famous chapter "Of Property" in the *Second Treatise of Government* (1690), he reflected on the implications of the introduction of money in the state of nature and the capacity it furnished to store value and represent labor, thus opening the door to accumulation beyond use-value alone. But his most extended contribution came in the acute circumstances of deteriorating English coinage during the Nine Years' War with France (1688–97) which eventually forced a total reminting of English silver currency (achieved over an extended period from 1696 to 1697). Locke published two significant works that addressed this calamity: *Some Considerations of the Consequences of the Lowering of Interest, and Raising the Value of Money* (1692) and *Further Considerations Concerning Raising the Value of Money* (1695). The presentation of these texts as "Considerations" suggests that his thoughts remained, up to a point, provisional rather than decisive, but this belies Locke's commitment to outlining rigorous principles, even while doing so allowed him to range across a series of issues and, in *Further Considerations*, devote considerable attention to quoting and refuting his opponent William Lowndes, a key government official who set out a rival solution on behalf of the Treasury. Locke's writings on this subject are topical and at times polemical, but they enjoyed widespread influence in Britain and beyond.

The Recoinage came about due to a rapidly deteriorating silver coinage in the 1690s, fueled by the demand for bullion to fund King William's armies on the continent.[1] Currency in different denominations came under attack from clippers who sheared or filed off portions of coin to melt down while the coins themselves continued to circulate and retained their face value and purchasing power despite the loss. Figures recorded by the Treasury indicate that in 1690, silver coins were only 81 percent of their proper weight (partly due to wear and tear, it must be said, rather than illegal clipping); the next year they were down to 79 percent; in 1692 the figure dipped to 73 percent; in 1693, 68 percent; in 1694, 60 percent; in 1695 it had dropped again to just over 50 percent, and the following year, prior to the Recoinage, it came in at an astonishing 45 percent of the required, legal weight.[2] Something had to be done. Locke remarked in *Further Considerations*, without exaggeration, that clipping represented "the great Leak, which for some time past has contributed more to Sink us, than all the Force of our Enemies could do. 'Tis like a Breach in the Sea-bank, which widens every moment till it be stop'd" (Locke 1991b: 472). The question was what to do about the situation.

Two rival solutions presented themselves.[3] The first was to engage in a devaluation, recognizing the loss and attempting to find a new value for the currency which would calibrate the Mint's rating with the market price for silver. One of the major causes of the crisis was precisely the higher market rate of silver than the Mint's, which further incentivized clipping.[4] Lowndes's famous *Report Containing an Essay for the Amendment of the Silver Coins* (1695) advocated a devaluation of 25 percent. Locke took the opposite position, insisting that the existing monetary standard was sacrosanct and that the only remedy was to remint the coinage at the standing rate. How did he arrive at this conclusion?

Locke's principles start with the key claim that money takes its value from the quantity of silver contained in the coin, defined as its intrinsic value (Locke 1991b: 410). The amount of silver also enables it to serve as the medium of exchange, measuring the relative value of different commodities like wheat, lead, or linen. But unlike other measures (for example, quarts or yards), silver is not an arbitrary unit: silver "is the thing bargain'd for, as well as the measure of the bargain; and in commerce passes from the buyer to the seller, as being in such a quantity equivalent to the thing sold" (412). In other words, Locke regards the exchange function of money as dependent on its quantity by weight. He acknowledges that this role came about through "common consent," that is, as a result of a shared decision to place an "imaginary" value on silver (the rarity, durability, and divisibility of which makes it particularly suitable for carrying out the role of medium of exchange and store of value). As for the stamp on the coin, this adds no additional value but merely serves as a "publick voucher" indicating the amount of silver in the coin in terms of weight and fineness (that is, the alloy) (413). Furthermore, according to Locke, when people make contracts, they do so not on the basis of the denomination of coins but rather in reference to their silver content. A devaluation would defraud landlords and creditors by the amount proposed, constituting "a publick failure of Justice, thus arbitrarily to give one Man's Right and Possession to another, without any fault on the suffering Man's side" (416). Money is property, and the role of the state is to defend property, not arbitrarily to intervene and seize, destroy or diminish it. It is worth noting, however, that Locke was at odds with English legal tradition which defended a nominalist interpretation of money as it related to contracts: the face value of coin and not weight or intrinsic value was what mattered in discharging debts (see Fox 2011).

Locke's position depended on his view that once the standard had been settled by "publick Authority," it should remain invariable, unless a change becomes absolutely necessary. But Locke believed that no such situation of necessity could ever occur (415). Even though alterations of the standard had taken place from time to time historically—rising most recently near the end of Elizabeth I's reign in 1601—he argued that the existing standard was now well established in everyone's minds, enabling them to make bargains, reckon accounts, and conduct their affairs. In short, the combination of law and custom made it, for all intents and purposes, inviolable.

Locke presents his principles as intuitive, logical, and effectively incontestable. Nonetheless, there is much to question not merely about their validity but also how well they describe actual practice. For example, regular usage depleted the amount of silver in coins, suggesting that a completely full weight currency was an illusion; thus to restore the missing silver would potentially have penalized debtors (assuming that rent and other contracts had already priced in the loss). Locke's critic Nicholas Barbon made this very point. He observed that if Locke's assertion about contracts being made in silver grains were true, then people should have made their agreements according to the date of the year in which the money was actually coined since, by virtue of wear and tear alone, "the old Unclipp'd Broad Money of England is worn Ten percent. lighter than the new-Mill'd Money" (Barbon 1696: 30).[5] Locke's Scottish critic, James Hodges, weighed in in a similar vein. He dismissed the notion of intrinsic value on which Locke relied as a fallacy. For Hodges, value only came from the estimate placed on money by common consent, which was far from invariable. Indeed, the routine acceptance of lightweight coin demonstrated that the opposite conclusion to Locke's was true (Hodges 1697: 175–6, 195). "Raising" the coin (in other words, devaluing it) could occur by consent and was thus far from difficult to defend.

But perhaps Locke's biggest failure was his inability to provide an answer to the dilemma of a bimetallic system, with silver and gold in circulation, not that the solution was straightforward.[6] Locke's definitional approach led him to maintain that there should only be one measure of value: "it is in the Interest of every country, that all the current money of it should be of one and the same Metal; That the several Species should be all of the same Alloy, and none of a baser mixture: And that the Standard once thus settled, should be Inviolably and Immutably kept to perpetuity" (Locke 1991a: 1:329).

Locke's position did have a number of strengths. He insisted, persuasively, that foreign traders would expose arbitrary manipulations of value and raise their prices accordingly, calculating according to international not domestic valuations of silver.[7] The question was how much emphasis to place on the international versus the domestic economy. Locke's focus on the former led him to comment effectively on the risk of creating arbitrage opportunities, inviting outsiders to bring over lightweight coin of their own or to pay in overvalued gold. Gold was the extreme case during the currency crisis when it spiked as a store of value by 40 percent in June 1695.[8] Locke also made a challenging point by asking where it all would end. If money was a creature of whim, then why not keep raising its value, week on week, month on month?[9] He may have parodied his opponents' intentions in the process, but it was a difficult objection to answer. The bottom line was that Locke favored a tangible monetary system, anchored in a standard as much as a substance, not something subject to mere fantasy or expedient manipulation. His views—however specific the occasion for enunciating them—enjoyed enduring influence.

Although Locke presented his principles as axiomatic, not all of his contemporaries accepted them. Barbon was especially acerbic in his reply. In answer to the view that the value of money consists solely of the silver content of coin by weight, he asserted flatly that "Mr. Lock is mistaken in his supposition." Barbon operated with a very different set of assumptions about the nature of money. He reconceptualized it abstractly as what he called "the Instrument and Measure of Commerce," rather than treating silver as the measure. Intrinsic value was not a meaningful notion; instead, money fulfilled its role as a commercial instrument by virtue of "the Authority of that Government where it is Coined . . . by the Stamp and Size of each piece the value is known" (Barbon 1696: sig. A7v). In other words, contra Locke, names *did* have the power to give or enhance value. Barbon wrote in support of "raising" the coinage, that is, for a devaluation which would "raise" the rating of the currency.

Locke's position prevailed in Parliament in 1696 (though not all the key provisions of his plan were adopted) and the Recoinage proceeded on the basis of the existing monetary standard (see Figures 7.1 and 7.2). The political victory itself, coupled with avoidance of defeat to France in the war, ensured that the Recoinage remained a key point of reference for sound monetary thinking. Certainly this was how Defoe remembered things in *The Complete English Tradesman* (1725), praising William III for the wisdom of this policy (William

FIGURES 7.1 and 7.2: William III crown, 1696, obverse and reverse. This was the milled replacement for the worn and clipped crowns in circulation before the Recoinage. Images reproduced with kind permission of Governing Body of Christ Church, Oxford (owner) and Ashmolean Museum, University of Oxford. Photographs by Daniel Carey.

was actually far from sure how to handle the crisis).[10] As Locke's contemporaries came to grips with the challenges, the notion of intrinsic value provided an especially secure footing for a number of commentators.[11] Two examples will suffice. The first is from John Briscoe's *A Discourse of Money* (1696). In order to explain key concepts, he adopted the dialog form later in the work. The point was made that proclamations alone had no bearing on value, which derived from the intrinsic metal content of the money. The state or the prince could do what they liked; sellers would set their own price on commodities if manipulations took place by decree. But why exactly could a people not decide, of their own accord, "*to make their Money current on what Tearms they please*"? The answer was interesting: such a strategy might work somewhere "secluded from the rest of the world," having no trade beyond its own frontiers, in which case it would be possible to "make Nuts and Shells pass for money as they do at this day in some Countries" (Briscoe 1696: 105).[12] Locke himself had made a similar point in *Some Considerations* (Locke 1991a: 264). As Briscoe's interlocutor confirmed, the domestic had to give way to the international, since "we must swim with the Tide of the World": "in the Calculations of our Measures about Money, we cannot wisely determine therein, but by borrowing many Arguments from abroad, where our chief Intercourse lies" (108; in italics in the original).

If there is a slight note of resignation here, it was not shared by John Evelyn in his deliberations over currency in 1697. Writing as the Recoinage took place, he expressed the view, in his wonted formal diction, that "'tis not *Vultus Imperatoris, Figura & Impressio*; no, nor *Proba Materia* alone; but PONDUS and Weight which renders Money truly valuable to all intents and purposes. This effected, and Money reduced to its Primitive Institution (when Mankind dealt *honestly* and *sincerely* with one another) we may hope for a *Blessing* from *Almighty God*" (Evelyn 1697: 237). In other words, the image of the emperor did not represent the source of value; value came from the weight of the metal out of which the coin was formed. The original purpose of money was consistent with this policy, and it promised to receive divine reward in the implementation of the Recoinage.

To gain some sense of alternatives that came up at this time we can turn briefly to Charles Davenant (1656–1714), the Tory political economist who produced two manuscript deliberations over coinage and credit, the first composed in November 1695 (before the Recoinage) and the second in July 1696 (during it). Davenant shared a number of assumptions with Locke. He preferred to maintain the current monetary standard rather than opt for a devaluation, and he noted, among other things, that foreign merchants would be unswayed by such a move, evaluating the currency based on its intrinsic value. But the needs of the domestic economy in wartime led him to advocate taking an experimental approach with credit. Inability to sustain the wearying financial effects of the long conflict with France made it essential to find new monetary resources. He gave more play to the role of banks in issuing paper but he also suggested an excise tax to raise £800,000, on the basis of which £6 million in tallies could be struck and become in time like cash. Placement of a "false or more than Intrinsick Value" on this sum—in other words a state-authorized overvaluation—would enable it to achieve the urgent goal of circulating (Davenant 1942: 102). Davenant was prepared to deal in probabilities, rather than following Locke's notably definitional and axiomatic lead (in this context Locke's method was not particularly "empirical'). Ultimately, Davenant was prepared to live, domestically, with a fictional or artificial economy. As he boldly remarked, "nothing is more ffantasticall, and Nice than Credit," yet this was not a prelude to condemning it, even though it "hangs upon opinion" and "depends on passions of hope and fear" (75).

The tendency of later critics has been to criticize Locke, sometimes dismissively, for failing to see the deflationary consequences of his proposals, and to uphold William Lowndes as the more incisive thinker in these matters, capable of taking a flexible and pragmatic approach. The complexity of the challenges faced in the period require a more nuanced analysis (see Carey 2014), but it is worth noting that the critical inclination in the eighteenth century and beyond was the opposite. Locke was the hero of the piece. He provided the intellectual ammunition to defend a standard, which, as the eighteenth century progressed, settled on gold. His defense of intrinsic value provided an intuitive criterion for assessing complex debates and uncertain choices, not least in the midst of war when maintaining confidence in currency, investment, and financial institutions was at a premium. He recognized the possibility of a semi-fiduciary currency system (lightweight coin circulating at home), but claimed it was unsustainable and would have its faults exposed in international trade. Locke also gave voice to misgivings about economies run on credit and unhinged imagination, fears that came to fruition in the bubbles that awaited. In reply to his terms, one could argue that the distinction between intrinsic and extrinsic value is questionable at best—an intellectual illusion—and equally that coined money amounts, effectively, to credit, with a collateral of metal content.[13] For that matter, coin, due to wear and tear alone, was never full weight, making his system just as much of a fiction. But this would miss the lasting appeal of his intuitions, rooted in firm common sense. To counter them was no easy task.

SWIFT, BERKELEY, AND LAW: MONEY FORM AND BUBBLE CRISES

Intrinsic value remained a key reference point in later monetary debates as the eighteenth century progressed, even as new possibilities emerged in discussion taking place beyond the metropolitan center of London and the struggles over the definition of money in Parliament. Jonathan Swift (1667–1745) drew support from the concept in the controversy over the infamous patent awarded in July 1722 to the English ironmonger William Wood to produce copper halfpence and farthing coins for Ireland (see Figure 7.3). In his attack on the scheme, Swift composed a series of seven letters between 1724 and 1725 in the guise of a Dublin trader in textiles, "M.B. Drapier." He made an array of objections, employing *ad hominem* attacks against Wood and offering satirical observations on the political machinations behind the patent, but his reply was not without an economic foundation. He complained, for example, about the excessive quantity of the issue. Swift estimated this at £90,000 in copper coins. (In fact, the patent made provisions for a total issue of £100,800.) Using a number of calculations characteristic of political arithmetic (associated with Sir William Petty), Swift maintained that only £25,000 worth of such small coins was needed in order to drive trade (Swift 1965: 20). In other words, he was not unaware that Ireland required such a currency, only that the excessive volume would, presumably, cause inflation. Swift does not always spell out his assumptions, so a certain amount of expansion of the argument is required. Furthermore, he objected to the poor fabrication of the coins which varied considerably in weight (he dismissed reassurances from Sir Isaac Newton, as Master of the Mint, about their conforming to the required standard) (21). But perhaps his most fundamental point of principle came in his objection to the fact that the intrinsic value of the metal in the coin (that is, its market price as a metal) was drastically below its face value (Swift 1965: 19, 23, 24, 30).[14] A surplus of some amount between the face value and market price was obviously essential in order to discourage people from melting down coins and realizing

FIGURE 7.3: Examples of William Wood's copper coinage for Ireland. Far left (top and bottom): obverse and reverse of a 1722 copper halfpenny (type I); center (top and bottom): observe and reverse of a 1723 copper farthing (type III), counter-stamped with an annulet device on the obverse legend; far right (top and bottom): observe and reverse of a 1723 copper halfpenny (type II), with Hibernia seated holding a palm frond. Reproduced courtesy of Sovereign Rarities Ltd of London, UK.

a market price premium, but the copper coinage proffered by Wood constituted something else altogether.

Swift offered an ingenious if not unproblematic answer to further his agenda of political opposition. He insisted that the English Crown and Parliament could not impose the currency on Ireland precisely because copper did not constitute money: only the precious metals of silver and gold enjoyed this status. In short, it was not legal tender (Swift 1965: 10–13). This is a technical legal point but one that gained force when coupled with the criterion of intrinsic value. Thus the Irish people had a legitimate right to resist and refuse Wood's debased currency. Issues of sovereignty and Ireland's status inform the discussion in ways that make the *Drapier's Letters* a dangerous intervention.[15]

George Berkeley (1685–1753)—Swift's contemporary, fellow graduate of Trinity College Dublin, and like him a Church of Ireland cleric—developed a very different understanding of money in *The Querist* (1735–7) in his attempt to create a viable circulating medium and to address Ireland's impoverished economic condition. *The Querist* is innovative, not just intellectually but in literary form: he constructed the work entirely on the basis of questions, hence the title—sometimes searching and paradoxical, on other occasions more obviously rhetorical and polemical in force. In relation to money specifically, he invited his readers to consider that if the circulating medium could be reconceived as a kind of credit, then the precise form that money took became open to discussion. He asks in §426, "Whether all circulation be not alike a circulation of credit, whatsoever medium (metal or paper) is employed, and whether gold be any more than credit for so much power?"[16] He proposed an alternative view according to which money served as a ticket or counter—a placeholder rather than a thing of substance requiring a metallic content to make it valuable, as Locke (with his international focus) had deemed essential. Berkeley famously remarked in §23, "Whether money is to be considered as having an intrinsic value, or as being a commodity, a standard, a measure, or a pledge, as is variously suggested by writers? And whether the true idea of money, as such, be not altogether that of a ticket or counter?"[17]

The potential of this reconceptualization was considerable, but Berkeley still regarded money as a key factor in production and he wanted the notes issued by his proposed national bank to be backed by a promise to pay specie on demand, despite being guaranteed against the stock of the nation (Kelly 2014: 179). Joseph Schumpeter regarded him as a secret metallist, in fact, insofar as Berkeley required land to support the circulation of these counters or tickets through the ministrations of a national bank (Schumpeter 1954: 288). But there was still something important about his proposals, in part because he found a coherent way to privilege domestic interests above international exchange. Land was at least something in possession of the country itself, not varying—to that extent—according to systems of value obtaining elsewhere and capable of being "extracted" and shipped abroad. The trick for Berkeley, in a certain strand of *The Querist*, was to create a money economy and what goes with it—namely the desire to accumulate—and at the same time to do so in isolation, by creating internal markets rather than international ones, predicated on developing a money form not acceptable in international exchange, in other words, paper. As Berkeley says in §316: "Whether we are sufficiently sensible of the peculiar security there is in having a bank that consists of land and paper, one of which cannot be exported [land], and the other is in no danger of being exported [that is, paper]?" Thus there is much more to his philosophy than simply freeing himself from precious metals, and seeing money's role as creating a system of signs facilitating exchange, consistent with the anti-materialist orientation of his wider philosophical commitments.

Berkeley may have learned a certain amount from paper experiments in the American colonies during his residence in Rhode Island (1728–31), although the example of that colony was not exactly salutary. (He referenced the American scene at various stages in *The Querist*.)[18] The land bank model that he developed to support his currency had an important precedent nearer to home, both as a guide and cautionary tale, in the thought and career of the Scottish financial innovator John Law (1671–1729). Law would become notorious for his role in the Mississippi System which finally collapsed in 1720, yet the origins of his rethinking of money began in Scotland where he published *Money and Trade Considered* (1705). While Berkeley had no success in advancing his schemes, Law had essentially too much. Adam Smith would later remark in *The Wealth of Nations* that Law became the "dupe" of his own scheme (Smith 1978: 519). Berkeley shared with Law the experience of living in a country with a chronic "scarcity" of money, a paradoxical problem from the point of view of later monetary theory but a very real one in the eighteenth century when so much depended on access to precious metals to facilitate transactions, in spite of different forms of credit and the use of bills of exchange. Berkeley focused to some extent on the endemic absence of small change which inhibited transactions and trade (§469, 470, 473–6, 482, 485, 486, 487, 571), and on creating a solution that worked for an island nation depending on its own resources; Law maintained a much greater interest in supporting Scotland as a trading nation but he nonetheless required a remedy to address the lack of available specie.

His solution came in the form of land, using it as security (or "pledge") for a paper currency whose note issue would be regulated by a group of forty commissioners appointed by the Scottish Parliament (freeing the enterprise from a problematic dependency on shareholders (Law 1705: 94).[19] The existing stock of silver in the country was insufficient to do the job (in answer to the Bank of Scotland, founded in 1695, as an existing, note-issuing entity, and basing its model on a fractional reserve of coin). To arrive at his proposal, Law engaged in some extended argumentation about the nature of money. He began with a number of

Lockean assumptions set out in a definitional fashion, partly to forestall the suggestion that Scotland's difficulties might be addressed by simply "raising" the value of the limited coinage that the country possessed in order to make it go further (43). He shared with Locke the view that the stamp on the coin merely guarantees silver content and confers no value in itself; silver is the measure and the basis on which contracts are made (7, 9, 11).[20] Nonetheless, silver had a number of defects as a circulating medium. He declared it to be of uncertain value, insofar as magistrates enjoyed the power to manipulate it (despite his definitional admonitions to the contrary). Furthermore, the quantity theory of money (on which, see below) explained how the growth in the supply of silver caused prices to rise over time, diminishing the value of silver, as attention to the historical record made abundantly clear (62, 65–7).[21] It was not until the seventh chapter, almost three-quarters of the way into the book, that Law embarked on his proposal proper. He wanted to create a form of money equal in value to silver but not liable to fall as silver was inclined to do (with inflation). The underpinning argument was that something possessing the same qualities as money—based on his definitions—could serve as money and thereby become a new "species" (11, 60, 89).[22] But unlike silver, land would keep its value because it does not increase in quantity. In answer to standing objections, Law maintained that paper would not depreciate because the commissioners would (somehow)[23] ensure that the note issue remained equal to demand. He also regarded paper money as less liable to counterfeiting and observed that its "consumption" (presumably in the form of wear and tear) represented a loss to the issuer and not to the holder, as in the case of coin (91, 93, 117). The major concern related to the acceptability of the notes, within Scotland and beyond. Law was untroubled on the matter. Paper at home would constitute a preferable medium for payment, conditioned by the rules established by the commission, while, internationally, bills of exchange would mitigate any difficulties in settling accounts. One of the interesting sidelights of his project was the parallel proposal to use the note issue to facilitate a recoinage in Scotland, reducing Scottish and foreign coins in circulation to the English standard (88).[24]

Law is now remembered less for his innovative outlook on money and trade in a Scottish context than for his role as the leading figure in the Mississippi Scheme in France and its demise in 1720. One of the key differences from his 1705 conception was the construction of Law's *Banque Générale Privée*, founded in 1716, as a joint-stock concern (with the French king and Law himself as significant shareholders). The bank's note issue did not initially have the status of legal tender and it contained the provision of convertibility for coin (based on a healthy reserve). When the bank made the transition to a royal bank owned by the state, Law complicated the latter arrangement, with the notes constituting a form of semi-fiduciary or even fiat currency. The architecture became more complex still with the creation of a second company, the Compagnie des Indes Orientales, which took on huge amounts of government debt and acquired various other companies that gave it effective control over the extensive French colonial system. The company eventually moved to buy out the national debt which led to a spike in the share price. The "System" involved the merging of the bank and the company, with important implications for the banknotes which supplanted precious metals as the unit of account. The share price began to collapse, placing huge pressure on the notes which were used to support it. Law had to reduce their face value in May 1720, and they were demonetized by August as the system imploded.[25] Whether the whole thing was an elaborate manipulation by Law or a visionary contribution remains a matter of debate.

In fact Law had partly modeled his system on innovations in England connected with the South Sea Company, which began absorbing increasing amounts of the national debt after its foundation in 1711. The South Sea Company assumed costly liabilities from the Treasury in exchange for a charter guaranteeing its trading monopoly (especially in connection with the supply of slaves to the South American continent); in exchange, the Treasury made an annual interest payment to the Company of 6 percent, reduced to 5 percent in 1717. The government's creditors (that is, those who invested in various government-backed financial instruments) received stock in the company in a debt for equity arrangement. The symbiotic relationship with the Mississippi Scheme and the South Sea Company continued with Law following the debt for equity model in creating the Compagnie des Indes Orientales. As Law moved to take on the entire French national debt, the South Sea Company followed suit, increasing its position from a 23 percent share of British debt by the summer of 1719 to an almost complete ownership of it in April 1720. South Sea Company shares continued to rise spectacularly through the summer of 1720, but the bubble had burst by September (see Figures 7.4 and 7.5).[26]

FIGURES 7.4 and 7.5: George I South Sea Company shilling of 1723, obverse and reverse. The South Sea Company sold silver to the Mint derived from Indonesia, offsetting losses incurred in the collapse of the share price in 1720. Images reproduced with kind permission of Ashmolean Museum, University of Oxford. Photographs by Daniel Carey.

Although the story of these events can be placed, narrowly, in the history of financial speculation and joint stock companies, it forms part of a wider Financial Revolution in which new money forms, public credit, and banking played an integral role (see Wennerlind 2011; Murphy 2009; Kleer 2015; Derringer 2018: ch. 5).[27]

GENERAL PRINCIPLES

The spike in contributions to monetary thinking in the eighteenth century caused by moments of crisis should not lead us to overlook more general articulations of principle in the period. The intervention by David Hume (1711–76) in mid-century shows us once again the variety of literary forms in which such discussion took place—his chosen mode was not the treatise but rather the essay, a polite, deliberative rhetorical occasion, accommodating of observation in a suggestive rather than systematic vein. Nor was he pressed by immediate circumstance to advocate for a particular political solution or proposal, as pamphleteers or promoters were given to doing. Hume's essay "Of Money" appeared in his *Political Discourses* in 1752 (later subsumed into *Essays, Moral and Political*) and displays a distinctive freedom of mind— an openness to paradox and unorthodox conclusions. He questions received wisdom through a mixture of pronouncement and citation of historical example, both ancient and modern, while remaining a dispassionate observer.

Hume begins by emphasizing the exchange function of money in which it serves to facilitate commerce rather than having any decisive role in production. As he famously remarks, "[Money] is none of the wheels of trade. It is the oil which renders the motion of the wheels more smooth and easy" (Hume 1987: 281). The volume of money available to a country is of no particular note since prices depend on the relative amounts in circulation. In making this claim, he articulated the so-called quantity theory, an important position associated with Locke among others that became widely accepted. According to this theory, price levels are determined by the amount of money in circulation; they go up or down in direct proportion to variations in money supply. (It was one of John Maynard Keynes's innovations in the twentieth century to challenge the grip of the theory.)[28]

Hume observes that, in fact, a greater "plenty" of money in a country may lead to undesirable effects. The competitive advantage that one country gains from its industry will drive up wages, creating an offsetting advantage to those countries without an abundance of gold and silver that enjoy a lower price for labor. In a remark that resonates today in a global era of production, he observes that "Manufacturers, therefore gradually shift their places, leaving those countries and provinces which they have already enriched, and flying to others, whither they are allured by the cheapness of provisions and labour" (283).[29] A kind of equilibration takes place (although he does not pursue whether the profits gleaned from sourcing a cheaper labor supply remain abroad or are repatriated).

Hume does, however, acknowledge three areas in which an increase in money represents an advantage. The first is in the conduct of war and the capacity that hard money creates to fund an army. The second is the stimulus function of money—its role in stirring up economic activity (a point that Berkeley had earlier emphasized). The third advantage comes about from the delay between an influx of money and a corresponding rise in prices (predicted by the quantity theory). In fact it takes time for the effects to work their way through the system, during which a benefit is realized. Evidence from France, where the king's frequent intervention to increase the value of money did not (at least for an interval) lead to matching price rises, confirmed his point. For this reason, Hume advocated "a gradual and universal increase of the denomination of money" (287n). Removal of an amount of silver from the coin would not reduce its purchasing power, and he questioned the wisdom (associated with Locke) of dealing with clipped money in the reign of William III by recoining it at the old standard (288n).[30]

For Hume, as he discusses in his essay "Of the Balance of Trade," a natural level exists for money, in which it remains proportional to a country's "commodities, labour, industry, and skill" (315n). This maxim gives him the confidence to address a number of erroneous assumptions, in particular the notion that a country could deplete itself of money or experience a true scarcity of it, a much repeated refrain in seventeenth- and eighteenth-century economic discourse. The equilibrating effects of the specie-flow-mechanism themselves militate against such a predicament. (This argument, credited to Hume, countered the mercantilist assumption that it was in the interest of a country to accumulate precious metals and thereby beggar its competitors. Hume noted, on the contrary, that an influx of money would raise prices and make exports uncompetitive and imports attractive, thus transferring balances to the competitor, a pattern that would naturally equilibrate.)[31]

There is a shadow cast over this reassuring scenario by paper money, which Hume regards as a counterfeit form (284). Several problems attend it, most notably its capacity to disturb the natural proportion of labor and commodities. The quantity theory dispatches the idea that paper money on its own can augment wealth. How does he square this with his observation about the beneficial interval that occurs before price rises kick in? Hume considers the point in a note and reaffirms the potential for such a benefit; but in the case of paper, "it is dangerous to precipitate matters, at the risk of losing all by the failing of that credit, as must happen upon any violent shock in public affairs" (317n). What is more, paper credit drives out precious metals, which remain a valuable resource. He cites as an example, interestingly, the American colonies where the introduction of paper currency led to a "total banishment of the precious metals," in his view, a situation that would reverse itself if paper were abolished (318).[32] A more familiar account, at least in the colonies, regarded paper money as an innovation necessitated precisely by the absence of a hard money medium of exchange.

Hume, for all of his caution, nonetheless entertains a "right use" of paper (318), and he commended the Edinburgh innovation of bank credit which facilitated loans secured against goods, real estate, and various other kinds of property (including foreign debt), generating a form of "ready money." With this, merchants effectively turned their holdings into "coin" (319). We find in Hume, then, an intriguing mixture of argument from principle and empirical observation, combining a characteristic independence of mind in the midst of conservative reticence about the path ahead.

Hume's conservative tendencies appear again in his essay "Of Public Credit," where he dubbed this modern phenomenon "ruinous" (350). He conceded that investment in public debt did have some advantages, enjoying greater liquidity than land that made it attractive for those with funds. But for Hume, these "stocks" constituted a form of paper credit, possessing "all the disadvantages attending that species of money" (355). They too served to banish precious metals and raise prices (while also occasioning additional taxes to cover interest payments, driving up the cost of labor).[33]

Hume's freedom of thought on these topics was matched in a number of respects by Joseph Harris, assay master at the Mint in the 1750s and author of a two-part *Essay upon Money and Coins* (1757–8). In his attempt to provide a systematic account, Harris was similarly unburdened by conventional thinking on the balance of trade; he shared a belief in a natural standard of value, arguing that money finds its level through natural processes, which called into question the "common cry" about a lack of money (1757: 103). He objected on the same grounds as Hume to paper bills as an "artificial" means of increasing the amount of money in circulation if they had no "bullion locked up in their stead" (1757: 96). The quantity theory showed that the effects would be nullified, but the risk was also that proper cash would be drained away in amounts corresponding to the paper put into circulation. Banks he approved of, provided that they issued paper while holding an equivalent "in real treasure" (1757: 100). But there was a limit to the convergence between Harris and Hume. Harris devoted his second volume to a lengthy demonstration of the perniciousness of debasing or devaluing coinage. Where Hume was willing to acknowledge the French Crown's gains from such interventions, Harris referred to the same source of evidence as Hume cited (Du Tot's *Réflexions politiques sur les finances et le commerce* (1738)) to draw an opposite conclusion, leading him to condemn "the pranks that had been played with coins, by *Lewis* XIV" (1758: 111).[34] The two parts of Harris's *Essay* demonstrate the considerable grip of Lockean principles as the century progressed.

The aspiration to provide a systematic treatment of money (in the wider setting of political economy) is abundantly clear in the work of the Scottish theorist Sir James Steuart (1713–80) (see Figure 7.6). His *Inquiry into the Principles of Political Oeconomy* (1767) covers a great deal of ground in its two lengthy volumes, predicated throughout—as the title suggests—on referring to principles from which he makes deductions, punctuated by illustrative hypothetical scenarios and citation of historical precedent. His analysis leads him to arrive at some forceful conclusions, parting company with Hume on a number of important occasions. For example, he rejected the quantity theory as articulated by Locke, Hume, and others. Contrary to the standard view, Steuart maintained that increases in the quantity of money do not drive price rises; rather, demand or "the desire of spending it" (2: 79) has this effect (in concert with competition among different groups of buyers and sellers).[35] He similarly took issue with Hume on the balance of trade and the metaphor of money as a fluid that finds its balance even after a disruption. Hume had given a sanguine response to a supposed situation in which the money of Britain found itself annihilated overnight by four-fifths, on the grounds that the loss would be resupplied by the foreign demand for British goods once their price plummeted (as per the quantity theory).[36] Steuart argued that such a catastrophic event

FIGURE 7.6: Portrait of Sir James Steuart by Wolfgang Dietrich Mayer (1761). Reproduced by permission of National Galleries Scotland.

would lead Britain's inhabitants to abandon selling the "necessaries of life" to their countrymen (who would lack the funds to buy them) in favor of export markets where they could get the best price (2: 95).

When he turned formally to the subject of "Money and Coin" in Book III of his *Inquiry*, Steuart made a number of significant discriminations, starting with the difference between ("pure ideal") money of account and money in the form of coin. He stressed the mensuration function of money, an arbitrary division into a scale that allowed for the measurement of value and determination of proportion, similar to those used for weight, volume, or distance. Keeping these units consistent was of course crucial, but in the case of money it did not follow that doing so required attaching them to metals.[37] Gold and silver did not constitute the scale; rather, they registered price. The confusion between the two frames of reference had a long history (2: 217). His discussion of the limitations of coin mounted up a series of difficulties that demonstrated the problem of assigning it the task of measuring value (including the disruptive effect of bimetallism).[38]

Steuart's reservations about coin complement his views elsewhere in the work about the utility of paper money, another theme on which he took a different line to Hume.[39] The crucial need to maintain circulation and to avoid stagnation, at all costs, dictated that the statesman (Steuart's rhetorical addressee) facilitate the introduction of what he called "symbolical money" (1: 56). Like his countryman John Law, Steuart proposed backing paper with land (1: 58). Some difficulties remained about clearing title to land used as security, but as long as the lands "subsist," he said, "this paper-money must retain its value" (1: 60). In essence, it constituted a species of credit, and its function was to encourage consumption and demand (2: 62). Certainly it was bad policy for a country to pay interest in order to borrow coin overseas if the supply was depleted at home when paper money could circulate in its stead, backed by the same securities pledged for the loan (2: 110–11). In his formal treatment in Book III on money, Steuart appeared to retrench by stating that "Paper credit or symbolical money . . . is an obligation to pay the intrinsic value of certain denominations of money contained in the paper," but he went on to add that "Some intrinsic value or other"—presumably land—"must be found out to form the basis of paper money" (2: 212–13), thus making his position consistent with Law and Berkeley.

In Book IV on credit and debts, Steuart clarified the key role of banks, "that branch of credit which best deserves the attention of a statesman" (3: 168), again placing him in the company of Berkeley and Law (the latter he praised for his "superior genius" in transforming France by establishing his bank (3: 169)). The standard model, even in Law's case, was to back banknotes with a promise to pay in coin on demand. Steuart devoted a separate chapter to examining the consequences of this convention which arose initially from the weak state of credit and persisted among those who considered all money aside from coin to be "false and fictitious" (3: 177). The main difficulty for an institution like the Bank of England was how to manage a fractional reserve, in place to serve domestic needs, when an adverse foreign balance came into play that required settlement in specie. But he also pointed out that the bank's position suffered due to the requirement to accept lightweight coin at face value since the bank was then obligated to provide new coin at full weight (3: 180).

Something of a middle ground on the subject of paper money emerged in Adam Smith's discussion in *The Wealth of Nations* (1776) (see Figure 7.7). He began by reviewing the historical adoption of precious metals as the medium of exchange, in which he indicated problems of debasement as well as the persistent issue of wear and tear that diminished value. When he turned to paper in II.ii, he commented that the substitution of this form for gold and silver "replaces a very expensive instrument of commerce with one much less costly, and sometimes equally convenient" (292). If banks operated on a fractional reserve of 20 percent, then it could be said that £20,000 in gold and silver discharged the functions that would have required £100,000 without the use of paper. Transferring this model to the needs of an economy as a whole, which required,

FIGURE 7.7: Engraved portrait of Adam Smith by Robert Graves. Published in *An Inquiry into the Nature and Causes of the Wealth of Nations* (London: J.F. Dove, 1826). Courtesy of the James Hardiman Library, National University of Ireland Galway.

for the sake of argument, £1 million sterling to run its affairs, the introduction of paper would create a kind of surplus of £800,000. What would become of this sum? The domestic economy having covered its needs, the value would be "sent abroad," as he put it. Should the amount be employed in acquiring foreign goods for domestic consumption (for example, wines and silks), then the development would be "hurtful" in his view, promoting "prodigality" (294). On the other hand, if the money was put to purchasing materials, tools, and provisions that set people to work, then it was a positive development. He alluded to the growth in the Scottish economy supported by banks and their issuance of paper to confirm this assessment. The amount of specie in the country did not exceed a quarter of the total circulation (297–8). Nevertheless, unlike Steuart, Smith remained tied to a model defined by gold and silver. Partly this was defined by the strict premise of convertibility. If the value of the paper in circulation exceeded "the value of the gold and silver, of which it supplies the place", then it would return to the bank that issued it in exchange for gold and silver since notes could not be sent abroad. A superfluous issue would therefore end up causing a run on the bank (300–1). The lesson of prudence was clear, but it did not mean that individual banks acted in their own interests in the matter. In fact the Bank of England itself had fallen into this trap (302).

A FINAL CRISIS: PAPER AGAINST GOLD

Smith died in 1790. Within a decade, a state of affairs he would have found dismaying had emerged. In 1797, in the midst of war with France and fears of an invasion, the Bank Restriction Act came into force (originally an Act of Council on February 26, confirmed by the legislation enacted on May 3), suspending the obligation of the Bank of England to exchange its notes for gold on demand.[40] The crisis represents the final major episode productive of monetary thinking of the period. During the Restriction, at least 800 pamphlets appeared on the subject (Dick 2013: 36).

The Act, originally intended as a temporary measure, remained in place as war escalated with the advent of Napoleon and well after his defeat, ending only in 1821. It defined a new stage of public argument about the nature of money, banking, and the need or otherwise for a determinate mechanism to regulate the issuance of paper notes. The prospect of a run on the bank prompted the move, but the suspension was not unprecedented: the Bank of England had been forced to take this step during the Recoinage crisis in 1696 amid similar concerns about a run (an event remembered long afterwards by Adam Smith),[41] but this lasted for days not years. What made the Restriction of 1797 so significant was its duration, the outpouring of responses, and the cultural and intellectual impact of this "revolution in the whole system of our paper currency," as Lord King described it (1803: 10).[42]

One of the first major contributions to public discussion came in Henry Thornton's *An Enquiry into the Nature and Effects of the Paper Credit of Great Britain* (1802) (see Figure 7.8), which had morphed unexpectedly into a "general treatise," he said, as he responded to what he called "popular errors" associated with thinking about the suspension. Thornton, a former banker and MP, attempted to navigate the crisis with a measured analysis, recognizing the danger of an overissue of notes but also the risk of reducing their emission unduly (124). To reproach paper, he remarked, "with being a merely fictitious thing, because it possesses not the intrinsic value of gold, is to quarrel with it on account of that quality which is the very ground of its merit" (178). He objected to the "absurdities" of "democratic pamphlets" that condemned paper not just as excessive but as a government connivance and form of public fraud (171n). No doubt William Cobbett's later *Paper against Gold and Glory against Prosperity* (1815) would have struck him as an especially vocal example. Thornton accepted that it was true that a restriction in the volume of banknotes tended to support their value, but he argued that the Bank of England had not fallen into the mistake of overindulging itself; in fact it had maintained an appropriate rather than "extraordinary" amount in circulation, even if the precise quantity that suited the country's needs was inevitably difficult to judge (223, 225; see also 108). The real challenge seemed to be the note-issuing capacity of country banks, and he was sympathetic to the predicament of the Bank of England as the de facto lender of last resort (123–4). His father and grandfather had served as directors of the Bank, and his elder brother Samuel was deputy governor at the time of the Restriction and governor from 1799 to 1801, so he was no doubt predisposed to give it a favorable hearing.

Others were less sure of the Bank's probity. Lord King—a familial descendant of John Locke and member of the House of Lords—published his important contribution a year after Thornton. He too was no enemy of paper, but its function was to represent coin exactly, which it did by being convertible for coin on demand. Without this limitation, excessive issue would take place and inevitably depreciate the value of the currency. David Ricardo commended King and regretted that his sound policy went unheeded. Ricardo gathered his newspaper commentary in the *Morning Chronicle* into the book *The High Price of Bullion, A Proof of the Depreciation of Bank Notes* (1810). He pointed to two "unerring tests" that demonstrated the pernicious effects of excessive note issue by the Bank (27–8), namely the high price of bullion and the falling exchange rate. He argued that the depreciation against gold would continue at the same pace as the overissue of notes. The effect was the same, in fact, as that produced by the clipping of coins (32). In answer, Ricardo proposed a gradual reduction of the bank's notes until they reached a level with the coin that they represented (50–1). The parallel with the era of the Recoinage is suggestive, given that a depreciated currency needed to be reduced to an agreed, existing

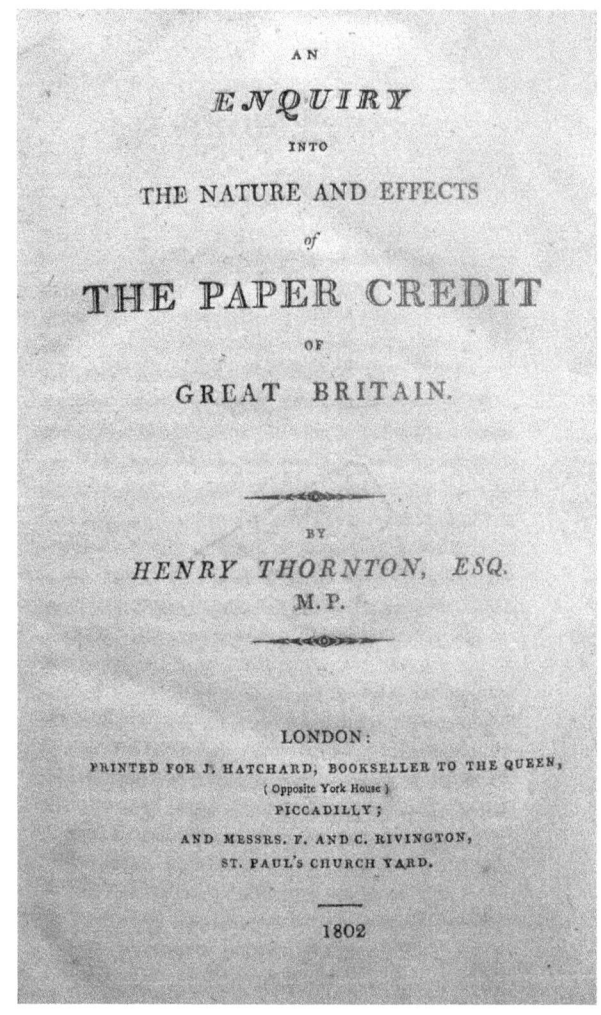

FIGURE 7.8: Title page, Henry Thornton, *An Enquiry into the Nature and Effects of the Paper Credit of Great Britain* (1802). Courtesy of the James Hardiman Library, National University of Ireland Galway.

standard. This connection becomes more clear when Ricardo quoted Adam Smith at length on the evils of "raising" the coinage, extending a line of thought we can trace back to Locke (52–4).

In 1809, the spike in the market price of gold bullion (well in excess of the Mint's price), together with a steep decline in the exchange rate of the pound in Hamburg, Amsterdam, and Paris (Fetter 1959: 104), led to the creation of a House of Commons select committee, better known as the Bullion Committee. The committee prepared the famous Bullion Report of June 1810 (composed by

Thornton, Francis Horner, and William Huskisson), indicating a hardening of positions. The committee maintained that the rising price of gold did not result from scarcity, even as it affirmed the disappearance from circulation of guineas (Cannan 1919: 9). The fact that silver had also climbed by a similar amount, without being scarce, confirmed the point. The major cause was the excessive issuing of paper by the Bank of England and secondarily by country banks,[43] without the provision of converting it into gold, so much so that the committee doubted whether gold in fact continued to serve as the true measure of value (reminding us of Steuart's strictures on the need for a rigorous standard). They proposed a proper return to the gold standard ensured by convertibility, "as speedily as circumstances will permit" (16; see also 68). An excessive note issue, not being exportable to other countries, would (following the quantity theory) lead to a rise in prices. Bullion, on this account, became another mere commodity like other commodities, subject to parallel increases in price. The same price-driven scenario was responsible for the decline in the exchange value of the pound, since no corresponding price rise had occurred in other countries to offset it (17)—the exchange being governed by a simple comparison of the cost of goods measured by the intrinsic value of precious metal.

The Bullion Committee advanced its case through principled argument, testimony, and analysis of some historical precedents. The Recoinage of 1696–8 remained a point of reference, but the committee also saw excessive note issue as the cause behind the depreciation against specie of Scottish notes during the Seven Years War (supported by a citation of Adam Smith, 37–8). The other great and more recent example came from Ireland, and the depreciation in the Irish exchange rate with England in 1804. The committee dismissed the statements of a number of witnesses to the Irish Currency Committee who blamed trade imbalances while attending to the Edinburgh banker James Mansfield, who, more accurately in their view, saw the real reason as overissue (40). According to the Bullion Committee, the Bank of England's system, prior to the Restriction, was, after a fashion, self-regulating, in the sense that a spike in the value of gold and an adverse exchange rate would draw paper back to the Bank from those who wanted to redeem it for the extra value: "In this manner the evil soon cured itself" (43–4) by prompting the directors to restrict note issue in response. With this check no longer in operation, no natural stop on undue note issue came into play. The long and the short of it was that the legislature had entrusted the directors of the Bank of England with the unreasonable responsibility of determining "that quantity of circulating medium which is exactly proportioned to the wants and occasions of the Public" (52). The only remedy was a recommitment to a currency system consisting solely of coin fabricated from precious metals or notes convertible "at will" into coin. No proper alternative existed to this "natural system" underpinning commerce and exchange rates. This dogma of the gold standard remained in place, of course, until the major challenge to it issued by John Maynard Keynes after World War I (in response to Winston Churchill's restoration of the gold standard in 1925).[44] For all of its earnestness, the Bullion Report was rejected by Parliament in May 1811, following a pamphlet war between advocates and detractors. The motives for rejecting it ranged from concern over the wartime effort, defense of the Tory government (despite dissenting voices among party members), and support for the Bank of England (Fetter 1959). Consensus on money, it seems, remained an elusive quarry.

The Restriction period established money and political economy as crucial concerns and matters of public debate. The expectation that intellectual authorities would intervene with articulate and reasoned positions built on a century of prior reflection in which money, banking, and trade captured the attention of a wide range of commentators and philosophers. Crises of various kinds often defined the parameters of discussion, but influential principles still emerged in these contested circumstances. The search for monetary standards, providing an anchor in the midst of financial shocks and war, maintained an enduring appeal, even as experience began to show that a free-floating alternative was evidently viable, not just in the periphery but at the center of what Thornton called "the trading metropolis of Europe, and, indeed, of the whole world" (104).

NOTES

Introduction

1. John Broughton, "A Letter to a Member of the Present Honourable House of Commons, Relating to the Credit of Our Government, and of the Nation in General" (London: printed by A.R. and sold by J. Nutt, 1705), 3, 4, 5–6. John Broughton's authorship is contested; I follow the determination made by those sourcing the Making of the Modern World database. See Gale, Document Number U108966337.
2. See William Paterson, *A Brief Account of the Intended Bank of England* (n.p.p.: Randal Taylor, 1694); Christine Desan, *Making Money: Coin, Currency, and the Coming of Capitalism* (Oxford: Oxford University Press, 2014), 295–329. The first paper instruments issued by the Bank for the purpose of the government loan were actually sealed bills. For discussion of bills, notes, and the shift between them, see Desan, *Making Money*, 308–11, 322–7.
3. "The Case of Mixed Money," *Cobbett's complete collection of state trials and proceedings for high treason and other crimes and misdemeanors from the earliest period to the present time*, ed. T.B. Howell (London: n.p., 1812 (1605)), 114, 118 (*Monetandi jus principum ossibus inhaeret*). See generally Peter Spufford, *Money and its Use in Medieval Europe* (Cambridge: Cambridge University Press, 1988); Thomas N. Bisson, *Conservation of Coinage: Monetary Exploitation and its Restraint in France, Catalonia, and Aragon (c. AD1000–c. 1225)* (Oxford: Clarendon Press, 1979); Peter Spufford, "Assemblies of Estates, Taxation and Control of Coinage in Medieval Europe," in *XII Congrès International des Sciences Historiques* (Louvain-Paris: Études Présentée à la Commission Internationale pour l'Histoire des Assémblées d'États, XXXI, 1966).
4. See Desan, *Making Money*, 108–50. For the complex medieval system of free minting, see Desan, *Making Money*, 70–107; Thomas J. Sargent and François R. Velde, *The Big Problem of Small Change*, Princeton Economic History of the Western World Indexes (Princeton, NJ: Princeton University Press, 2002).

5. Edward Misselden, *Free Trade or, the Meanses to Make Trade Flourish* (London: John Legatt, for Simon Waterson, 1622), Chap. II; see generally Carl Wennerlind, *Casualties of Credit: The English Financial Revolution, 1620–1720* (Cambridge, MA: Harvard University Press, 2011), 17–43. For the contribution of credit to the early modern exchange, see Craig Muldrew, *The Economy of Obligation: The Culture of Credit and Social Relations in Early Modern England* (Basingstoke: Palgrave Macmillan, 1998).
6. See, *e.g.*, Ryan Patrick Hanley and Maria Pia Paganelli, "Adam Smith on Money, Mercantilism and the System of Natural Liberty," in Daniel Carey (ed.), *Money and Political Economy in the Enlightenment* (Oxford: Voltaire Foundation, 2014), 186–188; Wennerlind, *Casualties of Credit*, 42–79.
7. See Desan, *Making Money*, 231–54, 296–304; Steven Pincus, *1688: The First Modern Revolution* (New Haven, CT: Yale University Press, 2009), 366–93; Bruce G. Carruthers, *City of Capital: Politics and Markets in the English Financial Revolution* (Princeton, NJ: Princeton University Press, 1996), 76–7, 139–46.
8. Exchequer bills were, however, interest-bearing. See the National Land Bank Act of 1696 (7 & 8 Will 3 c 31 ss 67, 69; 8 & 9 Will 3 c 20 ss 63, 64, 66 (1696–7)).
9. Bank of England Act 1694 (5 & 6 W & M c 20). Examples of the continued effort to improve the Bank notes' circulation abound. Thus the Bank experimented with paying or withholding interest on its issues. The Bank and government also worked to reinforce the public's willingness to hold Bank notes by moving to take those notes for taxes. Desan, *Making Money*, 311–27.
10. 7 Anne c 7 (1708); see also 6 Anne c 21 (1707) (temporary measure); see generally 12 Anne c 11 (1713); 15 Geo. II c 13 (1742); 4 Geo. III c 25 (1764); 21 Geo. III c 60 (1781); 40 Geo. III c 28 (1800); 3 & 4 Will. IV c 19 (1833); 7 & 8 Vict. c 32 (1844). After 1844, the British government optionally continued the Bank without going through the charter renewal process. See J. Lawrence Broz and Richard S. Grossman, "Paying for Privilege: The Political Economy of Bank of England Charters, 1694–1844," *Explorations in Economic History* 41, no. 1 (2004): 50.
11. Tontines were annuities in which survivors benefited from the death of other participants. For medieval precedents, see John H. Munro, "The Medieval Origins of the Financial Revolution: Usury, Rentes, and Negotiability," *International History Review* 25, no. 3 (2003): 505–62; David Stasavage, *States of Credit: Size, Power, and the Development of European Polities* (Princeton, NJ: Princeton University Press, 2011).
12. For Downing's background, see "Downing, Sir George," in *Encyclopaedia Britannica*, ed. Hugh Chisholm (Cambridge: Cambridge University Press, 1911). Charles faced a Parliament increasingly unwilling to grant him funds given his affinity for Catholicism and his efforts to explore an alliance with France. His wars against the Dutch drove his immediate need for money. See Carruthers, *City of Capital*, 32–4, 54, 56. The next paragraphs draw on material in Desan, *Making Money*, 245–66.
13. On earlier lending patterns, see Robert Ashton, "Revenue Farming Under the Early Stuarts," *Economic History Review* (New Series) 8, no. 3 (1956): 310–22; C.D. Chandaman, *The English Public Revenue, 1660–1688* (Oxford: Clarendon Press, 1975), 22–31. For the limits inherent to the much-vaunted Dutch model, see Anne

L. Murphy, *The Origins of English Financial Markets: Investment and Speculation Before the South Sea Bubble* (Cambridge: Cambridge University Press, 2009), 443–4, 47; and Marjolein 't Hart, "'The Devil or the Dutch': Holland's Impact on the Financial Revolution in England, 1643–1694," *Parliaments, Estates and Representation* 11, no. 1 (1991): 50–1. For the complex French tontines, see David R. Weir, "Tontines, Public Finance, and Revolution in France and England, 1688–1789," *Journal of Economic History* 49, no. 1: 95–124.

14. See Henry Roseveare, *The Treasury, 1660–1870: The Foundations of Control*, Historical Problems, Studies and Documents, 22 (London: Allen and Unwin, 1973), 23–5; *A State of the Case, between Furnishing His Majesty with Money by Way of Loan, or by Way of Advance of the Tax of Any Particular Place, Upon the Act for the £1250000* (1666).

15. Dutch public debt instruments, although backed by specific revenues, were issued only at the provincial level. As Larry Neal notes, "In short, the Netherlands, due to the fragmented character of its political structure, never issued during this period a truly national debt backed by a national taxing authority." Larry Neal, "How It All Began: The Monetary and Financial Architecture of Europe from 1648 to 1815," *Financial History Review* 7, no. 2 (October 2000): 122–3.

16. On Catholic prohibitions of money interest and the complex impact of the Reformation, see, *e.g.*, Max Weber, *The Protestant Ethic and the Spirit of Capitalism*, trans. Talcott Parsons (London: Routledge, 2001 (1930)); Christopher Hill, *The World Turned Upside Down: Radical Ideas During the English Revolution* (London: Temple Smith, 1972); John Thomas Noonan, *The Scholastic Analysis of Usury* (Cambridge, MA: Harvard University Press, 1957), 105–32; Barry J. Gordon, *Economic Analysis before Adam Smith: Hesiod to Lessius* (London: Macmillan, 1975), 187–217, 244–72; André Biéler, *Calvin's Economic and Social Thought*, trans. James Greig and Edward Dommen (Geneva: World Alliance of Reformed Churches, 2005 (1961)), 145–8. On interest in statecraft, see Albert O. Hirschman, *The Passions and the Interests: Political Arguments for Capitalism Before its Triumph*, 20th anniversary edn. (Princeton, NJ: Princeton University Press, 1997), 12–14, 32–4; Istvan Hont, *Jealousy of Trade: International Competition and the Nation-State in Historical Perspective* (Cambridge: Belknap Press, 2005), 8–17. On the importance of interest during the English Civil War, see J.A.W. Gunn, *Politics and the Public Interest in the Seventeenth Century*, Studies in Political History (London: Routledge & Kegan Paul, 1969), 3–41; C.B. Macpherson, *The Political Theory of Possessive Individualism: Hobbes to Locke* (Oxford: Clarendon Press, 1969), 263–71. See also, *e.g.*, Thomas Hobbes, *Leviathan, or the Matter, Forme, and Power of a Common-wealth, Ecclesiasticall and Civill* ([London]: Andrew Crooke, 1651); Richard Tuck, *The Sleeping Sovereign: The Invention of Modern Democracy* (Cambridge: Cambridge University Press, 2016).

17. Sir William Killigrew, *An Humble Proposal Shewing How This Nation May Be Vast Gainers by All Sums of Money Given to the Crown without Lessening the Prerogative* (1663, republished 1690, 1696), 9; Anon., *Reasons for Encouraging the Bank of England* (London: n.p., 1695), 3, as quoted in Murphy, *The Origins of English Financial Markets*, 36.

18. "The Case of the Bankers," in *Cobbett's complete collection of state trials and proceedings for high treason and other crimes and misdemeanors from the earliest period to the present time*, ed. T.B. Howell (London: n.p., 1812 (1696, 1700)); see generally J.K. Horsefield, "The 'Stop of the Exchequer' Revisited," *Economic History Review* (2nd Series) 35, no. 4 (1982): 511–28.
19. For the breadth of sovereign prerogative over money, see "The Case of Mixed Money."
20. The fallout consumed the next decades: Parliament would expand its authority as the monarchy declined. See Horsefield, "The 'Stop of the Exchequer' Revisited," 522–3; Richard David Richards, *The Early History of Banking in England* (London: P. S. King & Son, 1929), 66–7. The fate of the litigants in the *Bankers' Case* undermines the argument that the Glorious Revolution transformed financial practice (and market activity more generally) because the English government "credibly committed" to protect private rights at that junction. See Douglass C. North and Barry R. Weingast, "Constitutions and Commitment: The Evolution of Institutions Governing Public Choice in Seventeenth-Century England," *Journal of Economic History* XLIX, no. 4 (1989): 803–32. As I have argued elsewhere, the government effectively defaulted on the bankers' payment and on other debt held in the decades following the Glorious Revolution. In addition, the government prioritized the rights of creditors in part by degrading the private rights of others, including taxpayers aggressively hounded for revenue. Desan, *Making Money*, 287–94. The ascendance of creditors' rights at the end of the seventeenth century was an important change—but not because it represented the triumph of rights as an abstract property or the insulation of private rights from public authority. Rather, creditors and their rights were organizing elements of the modern market order that the government was itself making.
21. For the revolution in public debt and its roots more generally, see P.G.M. Dickson, *The Financial Revolution in England: A Study in the Development of Public Credit, 1688–1756*, Modern Revivals in History (London: Macmillan, 1967); Roseveare, *The Treasury*.
22. For discussion of these indicators, as well as economic and empirical approaches to money scarcity, see Desan, *Making Money*, 254–65. For a recent estimate of the rising "velocity" of the coin supply, suggesting that people had to move coin quickly between themselves, see Nuno Palma, "Reconstruction of Money Supply over the Long Run: the Case of England, 1270–1870," *Economic History Review* 71, no. 2 (2017): 12 (Figure 4).
23. The British did, in fact, experiment with both methods. For Exchequer bills, see National Land Bank Act 1696 (7 & 8 Will 3 c 31 ss 69, 70); 8 & 9 Will 3 c 20 s 63 (1696–1697); Desan, *Making Money*, 340–1. The loan from the Bank was longer-term; its authorizing legislation specified the revenue source for repaying interest on the loan. See Bank of England Act 1694 (5 & 6 W & M c 20 s 19). For the gradual movement by the government to take Bank of England notes in taxes, see Desan, *Making Money*, 313–17. The basic logic seemed to be that a public authority had to recognize the value of a mode of payment it used itself.
24. For a study demonstrating the fragility of goldsmith banks that operated without the support of government revenue, see Peter Temin and Hans-Joachim Voth, *Prometheus*

Shackled: Goldsmith Banks and England's Financial Revolution After 1700 (Oxford: Oxford University Press, 2012).

25. While the Bank drew supporters and opponents from all parties, prominent Whigs promoted the Bank, subscribed to it, and dominated its directorate. See Carruthers, *City of Capital*, 76–7, 139–46; Desan, *Making Money*, 301–4, 361–70.
26. The position was also at odds with technical expertise, as debates over how best to reform and rebalance coin supplies in the 1690s demonstrated. Those most expert in the matter, including William Lowndes and Isaac Newton, favored depreciating coin's content. Their arguments lost out to Locke's insistence that coin be strengthened to restore its pre-existing content. For the argument and its impact on the 1690s, see Desan, *Making Money*, 341–70.
27. See also Robert C. Hockett and Saule T. Omarova, "The Finance Franchise," *Cornell Law Review* 102 (2017): 1169–75 (reviewing recent scholarship).
28. By 1698, England carried some £32 million in short-term debt and another £6.9 million in longer-term obligations. Dickson, *The Financial Revolution*, 343. From 1702 to 1712, public expenses averaged £7.8 million a year, while revenues brought in £5.3 million a year; the gap was closed by increasing amounts of public debt. Richard Kleer, "'A New Species of Money': British Exchequer Bills, 1701–1711," *Financial History Review* 22, no. 2 (2015): 180. While short-term amounts are difficult to total, long-term debt for the second war amounted to almost £29 million. Anne M. Carlos et al., "Financing and Refinancing the War of the Spanish Succession, and then Refinancing the South Sea Company," in D'Maris Coffman, Adrian Leonard and Larry Neal (eds), *Questioning Credible Commitment: Perspectives on the Rise of Financial Capitalism* (New York: Cambridge University Press, 2013), 153.
29. See, *e.g.*, Carlos et al., "Financing and Refinancing," 151 (describing the borrowing accomplished by Exchequer bills before 1697); Kleer, "A New Species of Money" (describing the borrowing accomplished by tallies between 1702 and 1712).
30. *An Excellent New Song, call'd, An End to our Sorrows* (1711), quoted in Wennerlind, *Casualties of Credit*, 207.
31. The Bank gained a monopoly over note issue as a joint-stock company in 1708; other banks could contain no more than six partners. 7 Anne c 30 ss 66 (1708).
32. In effect, the government in the guise of its tax collectors was taking local notes, then returning them to the commercial banks to cancel. The government was thereby allowing those banks to monetize credit in local notes for producers who could eventually pay off the credit in the metropol, using earnings in the official unit of account. For other variations, see L.S. Pressnell, *Country Banking in the Industrial Revolution* (Oxford: Oxford University Press, 1956), 162–79.
33. Pressnell, *Country Banking*, 80 (quoting Lewis Loyd).
34. *The Mint and Exchequer United: Being a Method to Furnish His Majesty with Two, Three, Or Four Millions Immediately, at the Present Charge But of One Million Or Less, and Supply the Want of Coin, Till New Money Can be Had* (1695), 2. The Bank of Amsterdam was thus, consistent with seventeenth-century norms, a full reserve bank.
35. See, *e.g.*, "The Case of Mixed Money," 116 (portraying money as "the just medium and measure of all exchangeable things, for it is through the medium of money that a just and fitting price for all things that exist in the world may come about").

Chapter 1

1. Edmund Burke, *Speech of Edmund Burke, Esq. member of Parliament for the city of Bristol: on presenting to the House of Commons (on the 11th of February, 1780) a plan for the better security of the independence of Parliament, and the oeconomical reformation of the civil and other establishments* (London: Printed for J. Dodsley, 1780), 47.
2. *Oxford English Dictionary*, "technology," 4.a. "The branch of knowledge dealing with the mechanical arts and applied sciences; the study of this." The introduction to Diderot and d'Alembert's *Encyclopédie* notes that in compiling the project, they were "eager above all for useful knowledge." Jean-Baptiste le Rond d'Alembert, "Preliminary Discourse," *The Encyclopedia of Diderot & d'Alembert Collaborate Translation Project*, trans. Richard N. Schwab and Walter E. Rex (Ann Arbor: University of Michigan Library, 2009), http://quod.lib.umich.edu/cgi/t/text/text-idx?c=did;rgn=main;view=text;idno=did2222.0001.083 (accessed May 17, 2017).
3. For classic works on credit, finance, and banking in Britain, see Anne Murphy, *The Origins of English Financial Markets: Investment and Speculation before the South Sea Bubble* (Cambridge: Cambridge University Press, 2009); and P.G.M. Dickson, *The Financial Revolution in England: A Study in the Development of Public Credit, 1688–1756*, Modern Revivals in History (London: Macmillan, 1967). Some extraordinary works have indeed examined the technological process of minting, and they will be cited throughout this chapter. They include C.E. Challis, *A New History of the Royal Mint* (Cambridge: Cambridge University Press, 1992); George Selgin, *Good Money: Birmingham Button Makers, the Royal Mint, and the Beginnings of Modern Coinage, 1775–1821* (Ann Arbor: University of Michigan Press, 2008); Guy Rowlands, *The Financial Decline of a Great Power: War, Influence, and Money in Louis XIV's France* (Oxford: Oxford University Press, 2012); and Rebecca L. Spang, *Stuff and Money in the Time of the French Revolution* (Cambridge, MA: Harvard University Press, 2015).
4. See N.J. Mayhew, "Population, money supply, and the velocity of circulation in England, 1300–1700," *Economic History Review* (New Series) 48, no. 2 (May 1995): 238–57, esp. 253–4. For an eighteenth-century theorist who made a similar observation, see David Bindon, *Some Reasons Shewing the Necessity the People of Ireland are under, for continuing to refuse Mr. Wood's Coinage, By the Author of the Considerations* (Dublin, 1724), 12.
5. For an in-depth discussion of the extraordinary instability that ensued from the efforts of states to reconcile the commodity value of coins with their nominal value, see Christine Desan, *Making Money: Coin, Currency and the Coming of Capitalism* (Oxford: Oxford University Press, 2014), 110–20. See also Angela Redish, *Bimetallism: An Economic and Historical Analysis* (Cambridge: Cambridge University Press, 2000).
6. For counterfeiting and capital punishment, see Carl Wennerlind, *Casualties of Credit: The English Financial Revolution, 1620–1720* (Cambridge, MA: Harvard University Press, 2011), 123–60.

7. Louis, chevalier de Jaucourt, "Money," *Encyclopedia of Diderot & d'Alembert Collaborative Translation Project*, trans. Thomas M. Luckett, http://hdl.handle.net/2027/spo.did2222.0001.707 (accessed October 24, 2016).
8. See also Charles Goodhart, "The Two Concepts of Money: Implications for the Analysis of Optimal Currency Areas," *European Journal of Political Economy* 14, no. 3 (1998): 407–32.
9. For a detailed description of English medieval coinage by hammer, which was substantially similar to hammered coinage elsewhere, see Ian Stewart, "The English and Norman Mints, *c.* 600–1158," in C.E. Challis (ed.), *A New History of the Royal Mint* (Cambridge: Cambridge University Press, 1992), 76–82.
10. For a comprehensive and gripping treatment of the changing role and status of the Cour des Monnaies in the sixteenth century, see Jotham Parsons, *Making Money in Sixteenth-Century France: Currency, Culture, and the State* (Ithaca, NY: Cornell University Press, 2015), 17–59. For an illustration of coinage by hammer, see Redish, *Bimetallism*, 56.
11. Proceedings and orders of the Privy Council Board on Mint affairs, the National Archives Mint 1/1, ff. 142–6. Hocking believed that Blondeau's new edging method probably involved replacing the heavy segmented collar with a thin strip of steel that would sit inside a fixed collar and mark the edges of coins as they were struck in the screw press. However, more recent numismatic research has revealed that Blondeau's "secret" method for marking the edges of coins involved a separate device in a separate stage of the production process. Furthermore, contemporary observers of the mechanical process noted that the coins were edged before they entered the screw press. See C.E. Challis, "Lord Hastings to the Great Silver Recoinage, 1464–1699," in C.E. Challis (ed.), *A New History of the Royal Mint* (Cambridge: Cambridge University Press, 1992), 346, and *The Diary of Samuel Pepys*, May 19, 1663, ed. Robert Latham and William Matthews (London: Bell, 1970–83).
12. See, for example, the case of Gerrard Bovey, button-maker of London, whose press was seized by the Royal Mint in the aftermath of the Great Recoinage, when a new act made it treasonous to have a press that could be used for coining. The National Archives (TNA) T1/60, f. 132.
13. See, for example, TNA T1/38, ff. 75–6; TNA Mint 10/2; *Journal of the House of Commons*, Vol. 11, 1693–1697 (1803), April 23, 1696.
14. *Report of the Commissioners Appointed to Inquire into the Constitution, Management, and Expense of the Royal Mint* (London: William Clowes and Sons, 1849), vii.
15. On the seventeenth-century decline in the output of Mexican mines and the correlation between the availability of mercury and the output of silver, see P.J. Bakewell, *Silver Mining and Society in Colonial Mexico: Zacatecas 1546–1700* (Cambridge: Cambridge University Press, 1971), 187–9, 194–5. See also David Brading, *Miners and Merchants in Bourbon Mexico, 1763–1810* (Cambridge: Cambridge University Press, 1971), 140–6.
16. For descriptions and specimens of these coins, see Humberto F. Burzio, "The Colonial Monetary System," in Theodore V. Buttery, Jr. (ed.), *Coinage of the Americas* (New York: American Numismatic Society, 1973), 8–29.

17. Anthony Zachariah Helms, quoted in Lewis Hanke, *The Imperial City of Potosí: An Unwritten Chapter in the History of Spanish America* (The Hague: Martinus Nijhoff, 1956), 23.
18. For Portuguese goldmining in Brazil, see Manoel Cardozo, "The Brazilian Gold Rush," *The Americas* 3, no. 3 (October 1946): 137–60.

Chapter 3

1. For an account of the immanent frame, see Taylor 2007: 539–93.
2. Swedborg observes that for Weber, "The economic sphere *clashes* ... with the religious sphere in capitalist society because it is very difficult to regulate rational economic actions through religious rules" (my emphasis, Swedborg 1999: 133). Swedborg, further, shows that Weber believed the "economic sphere" to be an exclusively modern idea (8).
3. According to Swedborg's account of Weber, "[t]he ascetic Protestants, however, succeeded in bringing the two together because they believed that systematic work and honest profit-making were legitimate ways of honoring God and that all human beings should be treated in the same way. The result was that profit-making was freed from the old disapproval of the Church and that foreigners and members of one's own community were treated alike in economic matters" (Swedborg 1999: 20).
4. That history is a movement from a religious worldview to a less- or differently- or non-religious worldview has been the emphasis of writers since at least the seventeenth century, and most such writers weave a theory of economic history into their larger pattern. The eighteenth-century French economist Turgot advanced a theory of history as a process of secularization in *On the Historical Progress of the Human Mind*. Another salient instance in this tradition is Saint-Simon's *New Christianity*, which presents a religion of industry and art displacing a corrupted Christianity. Equally significant is Comte's "religion of humanity," which he unfolded over the six volumes of his work on positivist philosophy (like Saint-Simon, Comte saw industrialization and secularization as intimately and productively linked).

   Marx's infamous repudiation of religion as an "opiate for the masses," which combines a thoroughly materialistic perspective with hostility toward transcendental entities, was part of an assault on Hegel, whom Marx thought had failed to appreciate the importance of economic life in the movement of history. "Religion," Marx writes, "is the sigh of the oppressed creature, the heart of a heartless world and the soul of soulless conditions" (1970: 131). Hegel nevertheless had already prepared the ground for Marx's more intense secularizing move by assuming the ideal would emerge in this world rather than the next.

   British writers since Hume told versions of this history, but it reached its high point in the work of Lecky, whose eight-volume Whig history of Britain is as notable for its condemnation of strictures concerning profit as it is for such rhapsodic moments as this praise of the Enlightenment: "The empire of superstition seemed passing away like the shadows of night before the rising sun" (1891: 396). Equally notable in the British tradition was Bentham—who was particularly loud concerning religious strictures on lending—as well as his acolyte, J.S. Mill.

Regarding the status of such views today, Pecora writes "the developmental perspective that has shaped much of the political and philosophical discourse of the West since the Enlightenment has assumed the inexorability of the process by which religious beliefs are subordinated to nominally secular ones, such as a desire for individual self-determination, affiliation with one's occupational identity, and political allegiance to the nation-state" and that modernization, among other things, entails a combination of social differentiation (in which the economic is split apart from the religious and other spheres) as well as disenchantment at every level (2006: 7).

5. Marx perceived a common faith element in religion and economics: "It is *faith* [Marx's emphasis] that brings salvation. Faith in money value as the immanent spirit of commodities, faith in the mode of production and its predestined disposition, faith in the individual agents of production as mere personifications of self-valorizing capital. But the credit system is no more emancipated from the monetary system as its basis than Protestantism is from the foundations of Catholicism" (1981: 727). Marx's "predestined disposition" must surely reference Smith's invisible hand or some other quasi-spiritual commercial mover, given its hinting at "predestination" and the idea of God as the "great disposer of all human events." For an assessment of faith and early modern credit, see de Goede.

6. Carlyle described Smith as "only second to David Hume in learning and ingenuity" and considered him a man of "unbounded benevolence" (279, 281).

7. Although during his presidency George Bush was strongly associated with Judeo-Christian communities and values, he, along with Dick Cheney, hoped to encourage secularizing of the Middle East through the promotion of free trade (Brown 2010: 84).

8. Two useful resources concerning the religious lives of Protestant merchants include the astrological diary of Samuel Jeake and Kadan's *The Watchful Clothier*. An historical reconstruction of the religious lives of merchants appears in Bailyn (1979). Updating Bailyn's account are Baker (2005) and Valeri (2010).

9. For more on the relation between Misselden and Smith's "invisible hand," see Finkelstein 2000: 70–3. For a "religious" reading of Smith's hand, as well as a summary of this debate, see Oslington 2012: 429–38.

10. The secularity of the invisible hand was already at issue in Leslie's critique of Thomas Buckle (Leslie 1870: 553). Leslie later developed the "theological" reading of Smith (1879: 172–4).

11. For a discussion of the semantic transformation of prudence from practical wisdom into what economists now think of as economic rationality, see Codr (2016: 145–50).

12. Much has been said on the noble savage, but there isn't space to develop the theme here. Muthu situates Lahontan's noble savage in the context of Enlightenment thought and empire (2003: 24–30). For more on Lahontan and deism/religion in the Enlightenment, see Betts (1984: 129–36).

13. Similarly, Millar would write of an indiscriminate savage who "arrives at the end of his wishes, before they have sufficiently occupied his thoughts, or engaged him in those delightful anticipations of happiness which the imagination is apt to display in the most flattering colours" (1771: 3).

Chapter 4

1. Money (2010: 550). Because of the great length of the manuscript, this edition has had to summarize some of the material. Here all references to the *Chronicles* use Cannon's original pagination. Where quotations are given they have been taken from Money's transcription where available, and from the original manuscript where Money has only been able to provide a summary. The manuscript is in the Somerset Record Office, DD/SAS/1193/4: *John Cannon's Chronicles*.
2. Bell was a mercer or tailor.
3. To date these are the only published trial accounts which can be used to access such incidental information which would otherwise require years of reading in the archives of other state legal records.
4. This is based on Peter Laslett's estimation of an average household size of 4.75, and a national population of 4,000,000 (Laslett and Wall 1972: 125–58; Wrigley and Schofield 1989: 531).
5. For the English undervaluation of silver to gold compared to their prices in the rest of Europe, see Sargent and Velde (2003: 296–8).
6. Rice Vaughan claimed that it was very difficult to get a 20s. piece of gold changed into silver (Vaughan 1675: 71; Supple 1964: 173).
7. Smith (1978: 504). Using sealed money bags was one way of overcoming this problem, as long as those doing the sealing were trusted, but this is an obvious example of how large numbers of coins were kept out of circulation.
8. Henry Best also cancelled debts owed to him by his servants and other laborers by paying their debts with local shopkeepers (Woodward 1984: 146, 168–9, 172, 175).
9. The very extensive use of bills of exchange drawn on London and other north-east towns by the wealthy mercer, Joseph Symson of Kendal between 1711 and 1720, including 33.9% of local bills with endorsements, has been well documented and discussed by Smith (2001: lxvi–lxxii, 787–8).
10. I would like to thank Mr. Alex Waklam for pointing out the huge extent of detail to be found on coins in these records.
11. These have all been digitalized and are available at the Old Bailey online. Tim Hitchcock, Robert Shoemaker, Clive Emsley, Sharon Howard, Jamie McLaughlin, et al., *The Old Bailey Proceedings Online, 1674–1913*, www.oldbaileyonline.org, version 7.0 (March 24, 2012) (accessed March 17, 2018), hereafter referred to as POB.
12. https://www.oldbaileyonline.org/static/Crimes.jsp#theft (accessed March 17, 2018).
13. POB, Case of John Mason, Theft, 6th September 1716.
14. POB, Case of Thomas Bowers, James Newman, John Kellyhorn, Violent Theft, 25th April 1770.
15. POB, Case of William Wager, Edward Baker, Violent Theft, 8th December 1736.
16. POB, Case of Anne Keys, Theft, 3rd December 1729.

17. POB, Case of Maria Ann Doon, Theft, 18th October 1780.
18. POB, Case of Anne Newman, Theft, 25th February 1736.
19. POB, Case of Theft, 28th August 1678.
20. POB, Case of Elizabeth Stanmore, Alice Calvert, Theft, 18th September 1765.
21. POB, Case of William Dawson Pilkington, Theft, 10th September 1760.
22. POB, Case of Elizabeth Halbin, Theft, 8th April 1752.
23. POB, Case of Phillis Noble, Theft, 14th January 1726.
24. POB, Case of Joseph Gill and Thomas Mayo, Violent Theft, 16th January 1754.
25. POB, Case of Rachel Allison, Theft, 17th May 1716.
26. POB, Case of Elizabeth Jones, Theft, 25th April 1726.
27. POB, Case of Thomas Devenish, Deception, 15th October 1735.
28. POB, Case of Dorothy Taylor, Theft, 26th February 1755; Case of Robert Bignal, Mary Fitzgerald, Theft 11th December 1765.
29. POB, Case of Elizabeth Burton, Theft, 7th September 1715.
30. 1,106 shillings have also been subtracted from the shilling column for cases in which the defendant was "fined one shilling." All of these cases were from the period after 1770, reflecting a change in the law. The measurement for promissory notes and notes of hand includes some cases where the note mentioned is a message rather than a financial instrument or bill, but these were relatively uncommon. It should also be noted that cases in which both the singular and plural form of money are mentioned are counted in each category. Furthermore, Crowns have not been counted owing to the proliferation of alehouses called "The Crown."
31. £4,457,649 worth of these coins was introduced between 1804 and 1815 (Muldrew and King 2003: 159).

Chapter 5

1. For introductions to "visual culture" (as distinct from art history), see Mitchell (1986) and Mirzoeff (1999). On eighteenth-century "audio-visual" culture, see Loughridge (2016).
2. Good studies of gambling's place in eighteenth-century culture include Kavanagh (1993, 2005) and Molesworth (2010).
3. This "Westphalian" model of money (one territory, one currency) is, in historical terms, a recent development (Cohen 1998; Helleiner 2003). An outcome of the past 200 or so years, it today shows signs of being superseded by transnational, centrally issued currencies such as the euro and/or by decentralized, private cryptocurrencies like bitcoin.
4. Important works in this vein include Brantlinger (1996), Valenze (2006), and Poovey (2008). For a welcome corrective to this tendency, see Craig Muldrew's chapter in this volume.
5. "In the Scottish law, there is a peculiar word, fungible, used to designate such articles as may be subject of contracts of mutuum" (Story 1840: 195).
6. At least, according to David Hume in his letter to Marie Charlotte Hippolyte Boufflers-Rouverel (January 19, 1766); www.e-enlightenment.com (accessed March 17, 2018).

7. Key texts on credit in the early-modern era include Muldrew (1998), Crowston (2013), and Fontaine (2014).
8. The joint liability rule—in brief, that the transfer of a bill of exchange was not final and that responsibility for payment therefore belonged to all who endorsed it—had been codified in the French Ordonnance de Commerce of 1673 and in England by the judge's decision in the common law case of *William v. Field* (1694); it was also enforced in German trading cities (Aoki Santarosa 2015).
9. A ledger kept by one shopkeeper (William Ramsay of Alexandria, Virginia) is available online: http://amhistory.si.edu/american-enterprise/merchant-ledger/ (accessed June 20, 2017). For an excellent, accessible introduction to accounting practices in this period, with references for further reading, see McCusker (2017).
10. See also the scarlet-bound, gold-embossed ledgers on which Nicholas Boylston rests his left arm in Copley's 1767 portrait (Harvard Art Museums).
11. See Jennifer Baker's chapter in this volume.

Chapter 6

1. Much of the elite class of American Revolutionaries, as J.G.A. Pocock, Bernard Bailyn, and Gordon S. Wood have detailed, took inspiration from the Country tradition in English politics, which grounded civic personality in property ownership and a putative transcendence of market involvement.
2. According to the *Oxford English Dictionary*, this use of the word "tenor" to refer to a bill's value in relation to metal coin was unique to Massachusetts and Rhode Island. The modern, more familiar use of "tenor" in financial lexicon, which refers to the length of time before a bill matures, dates only to 1866. For information on tenor revaluation, see Colonial Currency, University of Notre Dame, Department of Special Collections, http://www.coins.nd.edu/ColCurrency/CurrencyText/MA-1690-1750.html (accessed March 17, 2018).
3. Speaking on behalf of the US Congress in 1779, a writer for the *United States Magazine* advanced a similar argument about Continental dollars: "Let it also be remembered that paper money is the only kind of money which cannot 'make to itself wings and fly away.' It remains with us, it will not forsake us, it is always ready and at hand for the purpose of commerce or of taxes, and every industrious man can find it" ("Circular Letter" 1779: 438).
4. Trumbull draws an analogy between defunct paper money and the disabled veteran, suggesting that both were necessary sacrifices for the war effort. In fact, the Revolutionary War soldier sacrificed life and limb but also felt more keenly than anyone the effects of currency depreciation. Continental dollars entered circulation through the hands of soldiers when the government printed money to pay their salaries. Many soldiers sold them out of desperation to speculators when they became severely depreciated, and under Hamilton's debt plan, those bills were redeemed at near-face value, bringing profits to speculators at the expense of soldiers.
5. A self-made man himself, Hamilton did envision private banks as a tool for funding individual enterprise: "If banks, in spite of every precaution, are sometimes betrayed into giving a false credit to the persons described," he had written in his *Report on*

a National Bank, "they more frequently enable honest and industrious men of small or perhaps of no capital to undertake and prosecute business with advantage to themselves and to the community" (Hamilton 1790a: 585).

6. Speaking of public credit in 1787, a Massachusetts politician proclaimed that states "become respectable on the same principles by which the character of individuals is maintained" ("Speech of a Member" 1787: 412–13).
7. The potentially disastrous public issue of national banknotes in 1791 made clear to Hamilton that wealthy, elite investors were not necessarily looking for civic-minded investment. Bond-holders did not always see themselves as custodians of public credit and did not hesitate to use short-term speculation to profit off margins (in one incident, wealthy speculators staged fake purchases to drive up the price). See the chapter "Avarice and Enterprise" in Chernow (2004).
8. Hamilton stands as a transitional figure in the dismantling of the classical tradition, for although he held his own conduct as a statesman to standards of classical virtue (divesting from business interests that might raise conflicts once he was Secretary of the Treasury and forbidding Treasury employees from dealing in governmental securities), he was perfectly willing to exploit investors' interests to create national cohesion (Chernow 2004: 293–4).
9. For a discussion of sympathy and financial self-interest in Federalist literature, see Part III of Baker (2005).
10. The causes of bitcoin's fluctuation have varied. The anonymity of its transactions, which makes it desirable to those carrying out illegal exchange, has driven up its price. On the other hand, questions about security—and rumors of its susceptibility to theft, hacking, and viruses—have also caused the value to plummet.

Chapter 7

1. See Li (1963), Jones (1988), Rose (1999), Gaskill (2000), and Kleer (2017).
2. See the table in Kelly (1991, 1: 116).
3. See Li (1963), Horsefield (1960), and Kleer (2017).
4. The market rate had risen to 6s. 5d. per ounce, compared to the Mint's value of 5s. 2d.
5. Traditionally, coins were fabricated by "hammering". In 1662, machine-struck "milled" coins were introduced, more standard in weight (and with fluted edges designed to thwart clippers) (Kleer 2017: 9).
6. For a contemporary assessment of the difficulty, see Hill (1690: 2). In the eighteenth century, Joseph Harris (1758) pointed out limitations in Locke's perspective and drew out some of the challenges facing a bimetallic system.
7. R. Ford disputed this point (1696: 9–10), noting that although silver in the coinage had been depleted by 50 percent, prices had not gone up by the same amount; nor had the exchange rate fallen by a commensurate amount.
8. Horsefield (1960: 77, 73) (the price in 1690 was 21s. 6d.; at the height of the crisis it reached 30s.).
9. Interestingly, given his innovative proposals on paper credit and banking, John Law (1705: 44) shared Locke's position on these matters.

10. Defoe (2007: 190); for William III's position in support of maintaining the standard and his later regret over not adopting a devaluation, see Kelly (1991, 1: 27–8, 29–30, 37, 64–5).
11. For a discussion of the importance of this concept for Thomas Mun in the earlier seventeenth century, see Finkelstein (2000: 85, 88); and in relation to Rice Vaughan in 1675, see Valenze (2006: 39–40).
12. It is notable that this statement came from Briscoe, who had initiated a failed land bank scheme in 1694, later joining forces with John Asgill and Nicholas Barbon. He proposed in this context to issue bills of credit, "being a new Species of Money, and to all Intents and Purposes as useful as Money" (Briscoe 1694: 30; quoted in Glaisyer 2004).
13. I am grateful to Christine Desan for suggesting these points.
14. It is worth noting that Swift, in his lament over disallowing an Irish mint, argued that a copper currency could have been coined in Dublin "of only one Fifth below the Intrinsick Value" (20), so he was not such a strict adherent to his principle as it might at first seem.
15. Swift composed these writings in the aftermath of the Declaratory Act of 1720 which settled the question of the right to legislate decisively in favor of the British Crown. This explains why he cannot arrogate the entitlement to the Irish Parliament but instead adopts a definitional approach which enables him to make his case without (ostensibly) offending the law or British authority.
16. *The Querist* is reprinted in Johnston and Berkeley (1970). I have quoted from this edition.
17. See also §35.
18. For example, §240, 251, 253, 449.
19. Law (1705: 118) succinctly explains how the system would work.
20. At the same time, Law rejected Locke's understanding of "vent" and the notion that money has only an "imaginary value" (Murphy 1997: 85–7).
21. "In *England* 20 times the Quantity of Money is given for Goods, that was given 200 years ago" (Law 1705: 69).
22. For land bank exponents who adopted the same line of argument about creating a new "species" prior to Law, see Asgill (1696: 5) and Chamberlen (1696: 2). See also note 12 above. On land bank schemes, see Kleer (2017: 95–114).
23. "It cannot well be known what Sum will serve the Occasions of the Nation, for as Manufacture and Trade advance, the demand for Money will increase; but the many Poor we have always had, is a great Presumption we have never had Money enough" (Law 1705: 117).
24. Antoin Murphy observes that Law later used the technique of reducing the value of silver coins in France in 1720 in order to make the Royal Bank's notes more attractive (Murphy 1997: 82).
25. For valuable discussions of Law's Mississippi Scheme, see Murphy (1997) and Velde (2009).
26. For the financial history of the South Sea Bubble, see Carswell (1993) and Dickson (1967). On connections with Law's activities, see Kleer (2012).
27. For example, Kleer (2015) tells this story in relation to the Bank's support for a new issue of Exchequer bills in 1707, with the Bank offering to pay specie on demand to

holders, as required (185); for eighteenth-century observers who recognized the relationship in conjunction with public debt, see Steuart (1767) and Paine (1796).

28. On the quantity theory, see Blaug et al. (1995) and Rassekh (2017: ch. 4). Eltis (1995) credits Locke with giving the first coherent version of the theory. On Keynes and the quantity theory, see Skidelsky (1995) and Dostaler (2007: 166–9).

29. Hume makes this point again in "Of the Balance of Trade" (311).

30. Carl Wennerlind (2005) argues that Hume was not an inflationist: "he considered only endogenous increases in the money stock to be favourable" and "did not advocate for the state to increase the money supply" (224). Endogenous increases resulted from enhanced domestic industry and productiveness, resulting in more exports and an inflow of gold. This resulting impact on prices was therefore not to be regretted. Rather than seeing this as a contradiction in the application of the quantity theory by Hume, Wennerlind proposes that Hume distinguished analytically between endogenous and exogenous money.

31. The Irish economist and emigré to France, Richard Cantillon, author of *Essai sur la Nature du Commerce en Générale* (composed *c.* 1730 but not published until 1755), independently developed a more elaborate theory (Murphy 1986: 270–4).

32. Scotland experienced a less dramatic but nonetheless significant loss of its stock of precious metals, despite a healthy growth in trade after the Act of Union (Hume 320).

33. There is an extensive secondary literature on Hume's political economy; for valuable discussions, see Wennerlind (2005, 2008), Schabas (2008), Caffentzis (2000), and Finlay (2011).

34. See Hume 287.

35. Steuart spells this out more fully in his remark that "whatever be the quantity of money in any nation, in correspondence with the rest of the world, there never can remain in circulation, but a quantity nearly proportional to the consumption of the rich, and to the labour and industry of the poor inhabitants. The value of each particular species of which consumption is determined by a complication of circumstances at home and abroad; consequently, the proportion is not determined by the quantity of money actually in the country" (2: 85–6).

36. Hume 311.

37. On money of account as a pure ideal, see 2: 228, 236. Steuart made a conceptual connection with bank money, as conceived in the Bank of Amsterdam, while also noting the discovery of this principle among the "savages" of Angola (2: 219). For Keynes's emphasis on money of account, see the opening of *A Treatise on Money* (1930) (Keynes 2013).

38. For Steuart's account of endemic problems with bimetallism, see 2: 222–3, 228–31, 233–7. The problem was only addressed with the formal adoption of the gold standard in 1816, which introduced small value fiduciary silver coins. See Redish (1990, 2000).

39. See 2: 86 for his direct reply to Hume on the subject of paper money.

40. On the early stages of the suspension, following the French arrival in Bantry Bay in Ireland and in Wales, see Shin (2015).

41. On May 6, 1696, during the Recoinage, a partial suspension of cash payments took place. Two days earlier, clipped coins had ceased to be accepted by law but the Bank

of England had insufficient stores of reminted money to answer demand. See Clapham (1970: 1: 32, 35–6). For Adam Smith's recollection of this moment in his critique of paper credit, see Smith (1976: II.ii.80). In turn, Thomas Paine referenced Smith's information on this subject when noting in 1796, prophetically, that the bank could again stop payment (Paine 1796: 23–4). Clapham (1970: 2: 4) points out that in 1797, "Though broken in to paper, Scotland at the start had suffered more inconvenience than England. This was because, when the news of the suspension had reached Edinburgh, the Scottish banks, without any legal authority, had refused to cash their notes."

42. On the cultural and intellectual impact, see Dick (2013), Poovey (2008), and Clery (2017). The failure of the *assignats* circulated by the French National Assembly did not encourage confidence in unbacked notes.

43. "[S]o long as the Cash payments of the Bank are suspended, the whole paper of the Country Bankers is a superstructure raised upon the foundation of the paper raised by the Bank of England" (Cannan 1919: 61).

44. In *The Economic Consequences of Mr Churchill* (1925), Keynes correctly predicted the economic effects of re-establishing the gold standard (in terms of unemployment, wage depression, and deflation). The gold standard, suspended during World War I, was restored at the pre-war levels by Churchill as Chancellor of the Exchequer. Britain abandoned the standard again in 1931. For discussion of Keynes's views, see Dostaler (2007: 207–14).

BIBLIOGRAPHY

Adams, John (1809). Letter to F.A. Vanderkemp, February 16. In Charles Francis Adams (ed.), *Works of John Adams*, Vol. 9. Boston: Little, Brown and Company.
Addison, Joseph (1711). "The Royal Exchange." *The Spectator* 1, no. 69 (May 19). Glasgow: Printed by R. Urie and Company, for A. Stalker, and J. Barry (1745).
"The Adventures of a Continental Dollar" (1779) (chapter one). *United States Magazine* (June).
Alvarez, David (2005). "'Poetical Cash': Joseph Addison, Antiquarianism, and Aesthetic Value." *Eighteenth-Century Studies* 38, no. 3: 509–31.
Anonymous (1707). *A Vindication of the Bank of England from the Misrepresentations, and Groundless Suggestions of a late Pamphlet entitled, "Remarks upon the Bank of England . . . by a Merchant."*
"Answer of Continental Currency to the Representation and Remonstrance of Hard Money" (1779). *United States Magazine* (March).
Aoki Santarosa, Veronica (2015). "Financing Long-Distance Trade: The Joint Liability Rule and Bills of Exchange in Eighteenth-Century France." *Journal of Economic History* 75, no. 3: 690–719.
Asgill, John (1696). *Several Assertions Proved, in Order to Create another Species of Money than Gold and Silver*. London: n.p.
Ashton, Robert (1956). "Revenue Farming Under the Early Stuarts." *Economic History Review* (New Series) 8, no. 3: 310–22.
Bailey, Colin (ed.) (2003). *The Age of Watteau, Chardin, and Fragonard: Masterpieces of French Genre Painting*. New Haven, CT: Yale University Press.
Bailyn, Bernard (1967). *The Ideological Origins of the American Revolution*. Cambridge, MA: Harvard University Press.
Bailyn, Bernard (1979). *The New England Merchants in the Seventeenth Century*. Cambridge, MA: Harvard University Press.
Baker, Jennifer J. (2005). *Securing the Commonwealth: Debt, Speculation, and Writing in the Making of Early America*. Baltimore, MD: Johns Hopkins University Press.
Bakewell, P.J. (1971). *Silver Mining and Society in Colonial Mexico: Zacatecas 1546–1700*. Cambridge: Cambridge University Press.

Bakewell, P.J. (1984). *Miners of the Red Mountain: Indian Labor in Potosí, 1545–1650.* 1st edition. Albuquerque: University of New Mexico Press.

Bakewell, P.J. (1988). *Silver and Entrepreneurship in Seventeenth-Century Potosí: The Life and Times of Antonio López de Quiroga.* Albuquerque: University of New Mexico Press.

Bank Charter Act (1833).

Bank of England Act (1694).

Banner, Stuart (1998). *Anglo-American Securities Regulation, Cultural & Political Roots, 1690–1860.* Cambridge: Cambridge University Press.

Barbon, Nicholas (1696). *A Discourse Concerning Coining the New Money Lighter.* London: Printed for Richard Chiswell.

Barragán, Rossana (2017). "Working Silver for the World: Mining Labor and Popular Economy in Colonial Potosí." *Hispanic American Historical Review* 97, no. 2: 193–222.

Berg, Maxine and Helen Clifford (2007). "Selling Consumption in the Eighteenth Century: Advertising and the Trade Card in Britain and France." *Cultural and Social History* 4, no. 2: 145–70.

Berkeley, George (1735–7). *The Querist, Containing Several Queries, Proposed to the Consideration of the Public.* Dublin: n.p.

Betts, C.J. (1984). *Early Deism in France.* The Hague: Martinus Nijhoff Publishers.

Bickham, Troy (2005). *Savages within the Empire: Representations of American Indians in Eighteenth-Century Britain.* Oxford: Clarendon Press.

Biéler, André (1961 (2005)). *Calvin's Economic and Social Thought.* Translated by James Greig and Edward Dommen. Geneva: World Alliance of Reformed Churches.

Bindon, David (1724). *Some Reasons Shewing the Necessity the People of Ireland are under, for continuing to refuse Mr. Wood's Coinage, By the Author of the Considerations.* Dublin: n.p.

Bisson, Thomas N. (1979). *Conservation of Coinage: Monetary Exploitation and its Restraint in France, Catalonia, and Aragon (c. AD 1000–c. 1225).* Oxford: Clarendon Press.

Blaug, Mark et al. (eds) (1995). *The Quantity Theory of Money: From Locke to Keynes and Friedman.* Aldershot: Edward Elgar.

Borden, William (1746). *An Address to the Inhabitants of North Carolina; Occasioned by the Difficult Circumstances the Government Seems to Labour under, for Want of a Medium, or Something to Answer in Lieu of Money.* Williamsburg, VA: n.p.

Bordo, Michael and Robert Cortés-Conde (2001). *Transferring Wealth and Power from the Old to the New World: Monetary and Fiscal Institutions in the 17th through the 19th Centuries.* Cambridge: Cambridge University Press.

Bouton, Terry (2007). *Taming Democracy: "The People," the Founders, and the Troubled Ending of the American Revolution.* Oxford: Oxford University Press.

Brading, David (1971). *Miners and Merchants in Bourbon Mexico, 1763–1810.* Cambridge: Cambridge University Press.

Brantlinger, Patrick (1996). *Fictions of State: Culture and Credit in Britain, 1694–1994.* Ithaca, NY: Cornell University Press.

Braudel, F.P. and F. Spooner (1967). "Prices in Europe from 1450 to 1750." In E.E. Rich and C.H. Wilson (eds), *Cambridge Economic History of Europe*, 374–486. Cambridge: Cambridge University Press.

Brenner, Y.S. (1962). "The Inflation of Prices in England, 1551–1650." *Economic History Review* 15, no. 2: 266–84.

Briscoe, John (1694). *Discourse on the Late Funds of the Million-Act, Lottery-Act, and Bank of England*. London: n.p.

Briscoe, John (1696). *A Discourse of Money: Being an essay on that subject, historically and politically handled, with reflections on the present evil state of the coin of this kingdom, and proposals of a method for the remedy, in a letter to a nobleman, &c.* London: Printed for Sam. Briscoe.

Broughton, John (1705). *A Letter to a Member of the Present Honourable House of Commons, Relating to the Credit of Our Government, and of the Nation in General.* London: printed by A.R. and sold by J. Nutt.

Brown, Charles Brockden (1799–1800 (1998)). *Arthur Mervyn; or Memoirs of the Year 1793. Three Gothic Novels.* Edited by Sydney J. Krause, 229–637. New York: Library of America.

Brown, Kendall W. (2012). *A History of Mining in Latin America from the Colonial Era to the Present*. Albuquerque: University of New Mexico Press.

Brown, Wendy (2010). "The Sacred, the Secular, and the Profane: Charles Taylor and Karl Marx." In Michael Warner, Jonathan VanAntwerpen, and Craig Calhoun (eds), *Varieties of Secularism in a Secular Age*. Cambridge, MA: Harvard University Press.

Brown, William Hill (1789 (1996)). *The Power of Sympathy*. In Carla Mulford (ed.), *The Power of Sympathy and The Coquette*, 1–103. New York: Penguin.

Broz, J. Lawrence and Richard S. Grossman (2004). "Paying for Privilege: The Political Economy of Bank of England Charters, 1694–1844." *Explorations in Economic History* 41, no. 1: 48–72. doi: http://dx.doi.org/10.1016/j.eeh.2003.08.002.

Bullion Committee (Select Committee on the High Price of Gold) (1810). Report. Edited by House of Commons. London: Richard Taylor and Co.

Burke, Edmund (1780). *Speech of Edmund Burke, Esq. member of Parliament for the city of Bristol: on presenting to the House of Commons (on the 11th of February, 1780) a plan for the better security of the independence of Parliament, and the oeconomical reformation of the civil and other establishments*. London: Printed for J. Dodsley.

Burstein, Andrew (2001). "The Political Character of Sympathy." *Journal of the Early Republic* 21, no. 4 (Winter): 601–32.

Burton, Richard (1860 (2010)). *The Lake Regions of Central Africa*. New York: Cosimo Classics.

Burzio, Humberto F. (1973). "The Colonial Monetary System." In Theodore V. Buttery, Jr. (ed.), *Coinage of the Americas*. New York: American Numismatic Society.

Caffentzis, George (1989). *Clipped Coins, Abused Words & Civil Government: John Locke's Philosophy of Money*. New York: Autonomedia.

Caffentzis, George (2000). *Exciting the Industry of Mankind: George Berkeley's Philosophy of Money*. Amsterdam: Springer.

Caffentzis, George (2008). "Fiction or Counterfeit?: David Hume's Interpretation of Paper and Metallic Money." In Carl Wennerlind and Margaret Schabas (eds), *David Hume's Political Economy*, 146–67. London: Routledge.

Cameron, Angus, blog post, "The First Money Devil?" https://xenotopia.wordpress.com/2012/01/24/the-first-money-devil/ (accessed March 17, 2018).

Cannan, Edward (ed.) (1919). *The Paper Pound of 1797–1821: A Reprint of the Bullion Report*. London: P.S. King & Son.

Cannon, John and John Money (2010). *The Chronicles of John Cannon, Excise Officer and Writing Master I–II*. Oxford: Oxford University Press.

Carboni, Mauro (2012). "Converting Goods into Cash: An Ethical Approach to Pawnbroking in Early Modern Bologna." *Renaissance and Reformation / Renaissance et Réforme* 35, no. 3: 63–83.

Cardozo, Manoel (1946). "The Brazilian Gold Rush." *The Americas* 3, no. 3 (October): 137–60.

Carey, Daniel (2011). "John Locke, Money, and Credit." In Daniel Carey and Christopher Finlay (eds), *The Empire of Credit: The Financial Revolution in Britain, Ireland, and America, 1688–1815*, 25–51. Dublin: Irish Academic Press.

Carey, Daniel (2014). "John Locke's Philosophy of Money." In Daniel Carey (ed.), *Money and Political Economy in the Enlightenment*, 57–81. Oxford: Voltaire Foundation.

Carlos, Ann M., Erin K. Fletcher, Larry Neal, and Kirsten Wandschneider (2013). "Financing and Refinancing the War of the Spanish Succession, and then Refinancing the South Sea Company." In D'Maris Coffman, Adrian Leonard, and Larry Neal (eds), *Questioning Credible Commitment: Perspectives on the Rise of Financial Capitalism*. New York: Cambridge University Press.

Carlyle, Alexander (1861). *Autobiography of the Rev. Dr. Alexander Carlyle, Minister of Inveresk*. 3rd edition. Edinburgh: n.p.

Carruthers, Bruce G. (1996). *City of Capital: Politics and Markets in the English Financial Revolution*. Princeton, NJ: Princeton University Press.

Carswell, John (1993). *The South Sea Bubble*. Revised edition. Sutton: Stroud.

"The Case of the Bankers" (1696, 1700 (1812)). In *Cobbett's complete collection of state trials and proceedings for high treason and other crimes and misdemeanors from the earliest period to the present time*. Edited by T.B. Howell. London: n.p.

"The Case of Mixed Money" (1605 (1812)). In *Cobbett's complete collection of state trials and proceedings for high treason and other crimes and misdemeanors from the earliest period to the present time*. Edited by T.B. Howell. London: n.p.

Challis, C.E. (1978). *The Tudor Coinage*. Manchester: Manchester University Press.

Challis, C.E. (1992). "Lord Hastings to the Great Silver Recoinage, 1464–1699." In C. E. Challis (ed.), *A New History of the Royal Mint*, 179–397. Cambridge and New York: Cambridge University Press.

Challis, C.E. (1992). *A New History of the Royal Mint*. Cambridge and New York: Cambridge University Press.

Chalmers, Robert (1893). *A History of Currency in the British Colonies*. London: H.M.S.O.

Chamberlen, Hugh (1696). *The Constitution of the Office of Land-Credit*. London: T. Sowle.

Chandaman, C.D. (1975). *The English Public Revenue, 1660–1688*. Oxford: Clarendon Press.

Charles II (1667). *His Majesties Declaration to All His Loving Subjects to Preserve Inviolable the Securities by Him Given for Moneys: and the Due Course of Payments Thereupon in the Receipt of the Exchequer*. London: John Bill & Christopher Barker.

Chernow, Ron (2004). *Alexander Hamilton*. New York: Penguin.

"A Circular Letter from the Congress of the United States of America to Their Constituents" (1779). *United States Magazine* (October).

Clapham, Sir John (1944, reprinted 1970). *The Bank of England: A History*. Cambridge: Cambridge University Press.

Clark, T.J. (1994). "Painting in the Year Two." *Representations* 47: 13–63.

Clery, E.J. (2017). *Eighteen Hundred and Eleven: Poetry, Protest and Economic Crisis*. Cambridge: Cambridge University Press.

Codr, Dwight (2016). *Raving at Usurers: Anti-Finance and the Ethics of Uncertainty in England, 1690–1750*. Charlottesville: University of Virginia Press.

Cohen, Benjamin J. (1998). *The Geography of Money*. Ithaca, NY: Cornell University Press.

Cohen, Patricia Cline (1993). "Reckoning with Commerce: Numeracy in Eighteenth-Century America." In John Brewer and Roy Porter (eds), *Consumption and the World of Goods*. London: Routledge.

Commissioners Appointed to Inquire into the Constitution . . . of the Royal Mint (1849). *Report of the Commissioners Appointed to Inquire into the Constitution, Management, and Expense of the Royal Mint*. London: William Clowes and Sons.

"Considerations on the use and abuse of Mottos" (1775). *Supplement to the Pennsylvania Magazine*.

Cooke, Ebenezer (1730 (1900)). *Sotweed Redivivus: Or the Planters Looking-Glass*. In Bernard C. Steiner (ed.), *Early Maryland Poetry: The Works of Ebenezer Cook, Gent, Laureat of Maryland, with an Appendix Containing The Mousetrap*. Baltimore: Maryland Historical Society.

Corporation of Moneyers (1653). *The Answer of the Corporation of Moniers in the Mint, at the Tower of London, to two false and scandalous libells printed at London, and lately come forth without date : the first intituled, The humble representation of Peter Blondeau. . ., the second intituled, A most humble memorandum from Peter Blondeau. . . : set forth to undeceive all the good people that have seen or read the said Peter Blondeau's false and scandalous libells*. [London: n.p.].

Craig, John (1953). *The Mint: A History of the London Mint from AD 287 to 1948*. Cambridge: Cambridge University Press.

Crowston, Clare (2013). *Credit, Fashion, Sex: Economies of Regard in Old Regime France*. Durham, NC: Duke University Press.

Cullen, Karen J. (2010). *Famine in Scotland: the "Ill Years" of the 1690s*. Edinburgh: Edinburgh University Press.

d'Alembert, Jean-Baptiste le Rond (2009). "Preliminary Discourse." In *Encyclopedia of Diderot & d'Alembert Collaborate Translation Project*. Translated by Richard N. Schwab and Walter E. Rex. Ann Arbor: University of Michigan Library.

Davenant, Charles (1696 (1942)). "A memoriall concerning creditt." In Abbott Payson Usher (ed.), *Two Manuscripts*. Baltimore, MD: Johns Hopkins University Press.

Davenant, Charles (1698). *Discourses on the Publick Revenues, and on the Trade of England*. London: James Knapton.

Davis, Kathleen (2008). *Periodization and Sovereignty: How Ideas of Feudalism and Secularization Govern the Politics of Time*. Philadelphia: University of Pennsylvania Press.

de Goede, Marieke (2005). *Virtue Fortune and Faith: A Genealogy of Finance*. Minneapolis: University of Minnesota Press.

de Vries, Jan (2001). "The Netherlands in the New World: The Legacy of European Fiscal, Monetary and Trading Institutions on New World Development from the Seventeenth to the Nineteenth Century." In Michael Bordo and Roberto Cortés-Conde (eds), *Transferring Wealth and Power from the Old to the New World: Monetary and Fiscal Institutions in the 17th through the 19th Centuries*. Cambridge: Cambridge University Press.

Defoe, Daniel (1710). *An essay upon publick credit: being an enquiry how the publick credit comes to depend upon the change of the ministry, or the dissolutions of Parliaments; and whether it does so or no. With an argument, proving that the publick credit may be upheld and maintain'd in this nation; and perhaps brought to a greater height than it ever yet arriv'd at; tho' all the changes or dissolutions already made, pretended to, and now discours'd of, shou'd come to pass in the world*. London: n.p.

Defoe, Daniel (1725 (2007)). *The Complete English Tradesman*. In John McVeagh (ed.), *Religious and Didactic Writings of Daniel Defoe*. London: Pickering & Chatto.

Denzel, Markus (2002). "Die Geschäftsbeziehungen des Schaffhauser Handels- und Bankhauses Amman 1748–1779: ein mikroökonomisches Fallbeispiel." *Vierteljahrschrift für Sozial- und Wirtschaftsgeschichte* 89, no. 1: 1–40.

Dermigny, Louis (1955). "La France à la fin de l'ancien régime: une carte monétaire." *Annales. Histoires, Sciences Sociales* 10, no. 4: 480–93.

Derringer, William (2018). *Calculated Values: Finance, Politics, and the Quantitative Age*. Cambridge, MA: Harvard University Press.

Desan, Christine (2008). "From Blood to Profit: Making Money in the Practice and Imagery of Early America." *Journal of Policy History* 20, no. 1: 26–46.

Desan, Christine (2014). *Making Money: Coin, Currency, and the Coming of Capitalism*. Oxford: Oxford University Press.

Desan, Christine (2016). "Money as a Legal Institution." In Wolfgang Ernst and David Fox (eds), *Money in the Western Legal Tradition*. Oxford: Oxford University Press.

Dick, Alexander (2013). *Romanticism and the Gold Standard: Money, Literature, and Economic Debate in Britain 1790–1830*. Basingstoke: Palgrave Macmillan.

Dickson, P.G.M. (1967). *The Financial Revolution in England: A Study in the Development of Public Credit, 1688–1756*. Modern Revivals in History. London: Macmillan.

Dostaler, Gilles (2007). *Keynes and his Battles*. Translated by Niall B. Mann. Cheltenham: Edward Elgar.

"Downing, Sir George" (1911). In *Encyclopaedia Britannica*. Edited by Hugh Chisholm. Cambridge: Cambridge University Press.

Dubin, Nina (2010). *Futures and Ruins: Eighteenth-Century Paris and the Art of Hubert Robert*. Los Angeles: Getty Research Institute.

Dyer, G.P. and P.P. Gaspar (1992). "Reform, the New Technology and Tower Hill, 1700–1966." In C.E. Challis (ed.), *A New History of the Royal Mint*, 398–606. Cambridge: Cambridge University Press.

Eagleton, Catherine and Artemis Manolopoulou. "Paper Money of England and Wales." British Museum Online Research Catalogue. http://www.britishmuseum. org/research/publications/online_research_catalogues/paper_money/paper_money_ of_england_ wales.aspx (accessed January 20, 2018).

Earle, Peter (1989). *The Making of the English Middle Class: Business, Society and Family Life in London, 1660–1730*. London: Methuen.

Eldem, Edhem (2005). "Ottoman Financial Integration with Europe: Foreign Loans, the Ottoman Bank and the Ottoman Public Debt." *European Review of Economic History* 13, no. 3: 431–45.

Eltis, Walter (1995). "John Locke, the Quantity Theory of Money and the Establishment of a Sound Currency." In Mark Blaug et al. (eds), *The Quantity Theory of Money: From Locke to Keynes and Friedman*, 4–26. Aldershot: Edward Elgar.

Erickson, Amy Louise (1990). "An Introduction to Probate Accounts." In G.H. Martin and Peter Spufford (eds), *The Records of the Nation: The Public Record Society 1838–1988*, 273–86. London: British Record Society.
Evelyn, John (1697). *Numismata: A Discourse of Medals, Antient and Modern*. London: Benj. Tooke.
Fabian, Johannes (2002). *Time and the Other: How Anthropology Makes its Object*. New York: Columbia University Press.
Feavearyear, Albert Edgar (1931). *The Pound Sterling: A History of English Money*. Oxford: Oxford University Press.
Ferguson, Adam (1782). *Essay on the History of Civil Society*. 5th edition. London. http://oll.libertyfund.org/titles/ferguson-an-essay-on-the-history-of-civil-society (accessed March 17, 2018).
Fetter, Frank Whitson (1959). "The Politics of the Bullion Report." *Economica* (new series) 26, no. 102: 99–120.
Finkelstein, Andrea (2000). *Harmony and the Balance: An Intellectual History of Seventeenth-Century English Economic Thought*. Ann Arbor: University of Michigan Press.
Finlay, Christopher J. (2011). "Commerce and the Law of Nations in Hume's Theory of Money." In Daniel Carey and Christopher J. Finlay (eds), *The Empire of Credit: The Financial Revolution in the British Atlantic World, 1688–1815*, 53–72. Dublin: Irish Academic Press.
Fiske, Jane (ed.) (1990). *The Oakes Diaries: Business, Politics and the Family in Bury St Edmunds 1778–1827*, Vols I–II, Vol. 32. Woodbridge: Boydell Press for the Suffolk Records Society.
Fontaine, Laurence (2014). *The Moral Economy: Poverty, Credit, and Trust in Early Modern Europe*. Cambridge: Cambridge University Press.
Force, Pierre (2003). *Self-Interest Before Adam Smith: A Genealogy of Economic Science*. Cambridge: Cambridge University Press.
Ford, R. (1696). *A Further Attempt towards the Reformation of the Coin*. London: n.p.
Fox, D. (2011). "The *Case of Mixt Monies* : Confirming Nominalism in the Common Law of Monetary Obligations." *Cambridge Law Journal* 70, no. 1: 144–74.
Frank, Jason and Isaac Kramnick (2016). "What 'Hamilton' Forgets About Hamilton." *New York Times*, June 10.
Franklin, Benjamin (1729 (1971)). *A Modest Enquiry into the Nature and Necessity of a Paper Currency*. Philadelphia: New Printing Office. In Andrew McFarland Davis (ed.), *Colonial Currency Reprints, 1682–1751*. New York: B. Franklin.
Franklin, Benjamin (1765 (1968)). "Scheme for Supplying the Colonies with a Paper Currency." In Leonard Labaree (ed.), *Papers of Benjamin Franklin*, Vol. 12. New Haven, CT: Yale University Press.
Franklin, Benjamin (1767 (1970)). "The Legal Tender of Paper Money in America." In Leonard Labaree (ed.), *Papers of Benjamin Franklin*, Vol. 14. New Haven, CT: Yale University Press.
Franklin, Benjamin (1771–90 (1986)). *Autobiography: An Authoritative Text*. Edited by J.A. Leo Lemay and P.M. Zall. New York: Norton.
Gaskill, Malcolm (2000). *Crime and Mentalities in Early Modern England*. Cambridge: Cambridge University Press.
Gaspar, Peter (1976). "Simon's Cromwell Crown Dies in the Royal Mint Museum and Blondeau's Method for the Production of Lettered Edges." *British Numismatic Journal* 46: 55–63.

Glaisyer, Natasha (2004). "Briscoe, John (d. 1697), Merchant and Projector." In *Oxford Dictionary of National Biography*. Oxford: Oxford University Press.
The Glass; or Speculation: A Poem (1791). New York: n.p.
The Gleaner (1798 (1992)). Introduction by Nina Baym. Schenectady, NY: Union College Press.
Goetzmann, William (ed.) (2013). *The Great Mirror of Folly: Finance, Culture, and the Crash of 1720*. New Haven, CT: Yale University Press.
Goldberg, Dror (2009). "The Massachusetts Paper Money of 1690." *Journal of Economic History* 69, no. 4: 1092–106.
Goodhart, Charles (1988). *The Evolution of Central Banks*. Cambridge, MA: MIT Press.
Goodhart, Charles (1998). "The Two Concepts of Money: Implications for the Analysis of Optimal Currency Areas." *European Journal of Political Economy* 14, no. 3: 407–32.
Goodhart, Charles (2008). "Foreword." In George Selgin (ed.), *Good Money: Birmingham Button Makers, the Royal Mint, and the Beginnings of Modern Coinage, 1775–1821*. Ann Arbor: University of Michigan Press.
Gordon, Barry J. (1975). *Economic Analysis before Adam Smith: Hesiod to Lessius*. London: Macmillan.
Goux, Jean-Joseph (1984 (1994)). *The Coiners of Language*. Translated by Jennifer Curtiss Gage. Norman: University of Oklahoma Press.
Graeber, David (2011). *Debt: The First 5,000 Years*. New York: Melville House.
Grassby, Richard (1995). *The Business Community of Seventeenth-Century England*. Cambridge and New York: Cambridge University Press.
Green, Joseph (1750). *The Dying Speech of Old Tenor*. Boston: n.p.
Green, Joseph (1781). *A Mournful Lamentation On the Untimely Death of Paper Money*. Wilmington, DE: n.p.
Grubb, Farley (2006). *Benjamin Franklin and the Birth of a Paper Money Economy*. Philadelphia: Library Company of Philadelphia.
Grubb, Farley (2008). "Money Supply in the American Colonies." In Steven N. Durlauf and Lawrence E. Blume (eds), *New Palgrave Dictionary of Economics*. Basingstoke and New York: Palgrave Macmillan.
Grubb, Farley (2016). "Is Paper Money Just Paper Money? Experimentation and Local Variation in the Fiat Monies Issued by the Colonial Governments of British North America, 1690–1775." *Research in Economic History* 32: 147–224.
Gunn, J.A.W. (1969). *Politics and the Public Interest in the Seventeenth Century*. Studies in Political History. London: Routledge & Kegan Paul.
Hamilton, Alexander (1781 (1961)). Letter to Robert Morris, April 30. In Harold C. Syrett (ed.), *The Papers of Alexander Hamilton*, Vol. 2. New York: Columbia University Press.
Hamilton, Alexander (1788 (2001)). *Federalist 35*. In Joanne Freeman (ed.), *Writings*. New York: Library of America.
Hamilton, Alexander (1790a (2001)). *Report on a National Bank*. In Joanne Freeman (ed.), *Writings*. New York: Library of America.
Hamilton, Alexander (1790b (2001)). *Report on Public Credit*. In Joanne Freeman (ed.), *Writings*. New York: Library of America.
Hamilton, Alexander (1791a (1965)). Letter to Rufus King. In Harold C. Syrett (ed.), *The Papers of Alexander Hamilton*, Vol. 9. New York: Columbia University Press.
Hamilton, Alexander (1791b (2001)). *Report on Manufacturers*. In Joanne Freeman (ed.), *Writings*. New York: Library of America.

Hamilton, Alexander (1795). "Public Credit, Communicated to the Senate, 16 and 21 January, 1795."

Hanke, Lewis (1956). *The Imperial City of Potosí: An Unwritten Chapter in the History of Spanish America*. The Hague: Martinus Nijhoff.

Hanley, Ryan Patrick and Maria Pia Paganelli (2014). "Adam Smith on Money, Mercantilism and the System of Natural Liberty." In Daniel Carey (ed.), *Money and Political Economy in the Enlightenment*, 185–99. Oxford: Voltaire Foundation.

Hardwick, Julie (2009). *Family Business: Litigation and the Political Economies of Daily Life in Early Modern France*. Oxford and New York: Oxford University Press.

Haskill, Francis (1993). *History and its Images: Art and the Interpretation of the Past*. New Haven, CT: Yale University Press.

Helleiner, Eric (2003). *The Making of National Money: Territorial Currencies in Historical Perspective*. Ithaca, NY: Cornell University Press.

Hill, Abraham (1690). *A Letter about Raising the Value of Coin*. London: n.p.

Hill, Christopher (1972). *The World Turned Upside Down: Radical Ideas During the English Revolution*. London: Temple Smith.

Hindmarsh, D. Bruce (2018). "Newton, John (1725–1807), slave trader and Church of England clergyman." *Oxford Dictionary of National Biography*. http://www.oxforddnb.com/view/10.1093/ref:odnb/9780198614128.001.0001/odnb-9780198614128-e-20062 (accessed January 16, 2018).

Hirschman, Albert O. (1997). *The Passions and the Interests: Political Arguments for Capitalism Before its Triumph*. 20th anniversary edition. Princeton, NJ: Princeton University Press.

Hitchcock, Tim, Robert Shoemaker, Clive Emsley, Sharon Howard, Jamie McLaughlin et al. (2012). *The Old Bailey Proceedings Online, 1674–1913*. http://www.oldbaileyonline.org, Version 7.0 (March 24, 2012) (accessed March 17, 2018).

Hobbes, Thomas (1651). *Leviathan, or the Matter, Forme, and Power of a Commonwealth, Ecclesiasticall and Civill*. [London]: Andrew Crooke.

Hobbes, Thomas (1651 (1991)). *Leviathan*. Edited by Richard Tuck. Cambridge: Cambridge University Press.

Hockett, Robert C. and Saule T. Omarova (2017). "The Finance Franchise." *Cornell Law Review* 102: 1143–218.

Hocking, W.J. (1909). "Simon's Dies in the Royal Mint Museum, With Some Notes on the Early History of Coinage by Machinery." *Numismatic Chronicle and Journal of the Royal Numismatic Society* 9: 56–118.

Hodges, James (1697). *The Present State of England, as to Coin and Publick Charges*. London: Andr. Bell.

Hoffman, Philip T., Gilles Postel-Vinay, and Jean-Laurent Rosenthal (2001). *Priceless Markets: The Political Economy of Credit in Paris, 1660–1870*. Chicago: University of Chicago Press.

Hogendorn, Jan and Marion Johnson (1986). *The Shell Money of the Slave Trade*. Cambridge: Cambridge University Press.

Hont, Istvan (1993). "The 'Rich Country–Poor Country' Debate in Scottish Classical Political Economy." In I. Hont and M. Ignatieff (eds), *Wealth and Virtue: The Shaping of Political Economy in the Scottish Enlightenment*. Cambridge: Cambridge University Press.

Hont, Istvan (2005). *Jealousy of Trade: International Competition and the Nation-State in Historical Perspective*. Cambridge: Belknap Press.

Hont, Istvan (2008). "The 'Rich Country–Poor Country Debate' Revisited: The Irish Origins and French Reception of the Hume Paradox." In C. Wennerlind and M. Schabas (eds), *David Hume's Political Economy*. London: Routledge.

Hont, Istvan (2015). *Politics in Commercial Societies: Jean-Jacques Rousseau and Adam Smith*. Edited by Béla Kapossy and Michael Sonenscher. Cambridge, MA: Harvard University Press.

Hoppit, Julian (2002). *A Land of Liberty? England 1689–1727*. Oxford History of England. Oxford: Oxford University Press.

Horsefield, J.K. (1960). *British Monetary Experiments, 1650–1710*. Cambridge, MA: Harvard University Press.

Horsefield, J.K. (1982). "The 'Stop of the Exchequer' Revisited." *Economic History Review* (Second Series) 35, no. 4: 511–28.

House of Commons (1803). *Journal of the House of Commons*. Volume 11: 1693–1697.

Hume, David (1739–40 (1978)). *A Treatise of Human Nature*. Edited by L.A. Selby-Bigge. Oxford: Oxford University Press.

Hume, David (1777 (1987)). "Of Public Credit." In Eugene F. Miller (ed.), *David Hume: Essays Moral, Political, and Literary*. Indianapolis: Liberty Fund.

Hume, David (1777 (1987)). "Superstition and Enthusiasm." In Eugene F. Miller (ed.), *David Hume: Essays Moral, Political, and Literary*. Indianapolis: Liberty Fund.

Hume, David (1987). *Essays Moral, Political, and Literary*. Edited by Eugene F. Miller. Revised edition. Indianapolis: Liberty Fund.

Humphreys, David, Joel Barlow, John Trumbull, and Lemuel Hopkins (1786–7 (1967)). *The Anarchiad: A New England Poem*. Edited by Luther G. Riggs. Gainesville, FL: Scholars' Facsimiles and Reprints.

Ince, Onur Ulas (2018). "Between Commerce and Empire: David Hume, Colonial Slavery, and Commercial Incivility." Research Collection School of Social Sciences. *History of Political Thought* 39, no. 1: 107–34.

Irving, Washington (1809 (2008)). *A History of New York*. Introduction and notes by Elizabeth L. Bradley. London: Penguin.

Jaucourt, Louis (1765 (2011)). "Money." In *The Encyclopedia of Diderot & d'Alembert Collaborative Translation Project*. Translated by Thomas M. Luckett. Ann Arbor: Michigan Publishing, University of Michigan Library. Available online: http://hdl.handle.net/2027/spo.did2222.0001.707 (accessed October 24, 2016). Originally published as "Monnoie." In *Encyclopédie ou Dictionnaire raisonné des sciences, des arts et des métiers* 10: 644–8 (Paris: n.p., 1765).

Jeake, Samuel (1988). *An Astrological Diary of the Seventeenth Century: Samuel Jeake of Rye, 1652–1699*. Edited by Annabel Gregory and Michael Hunter. Oxford: Clarendon Press.

Jefferson, Thomas (1791 (1986)). Letter to Edward Rutledge, August 25. In Charles T. Cullen et al. (eds), *The Papers of Thomas Jefferson*, Vol. 22. Princeton, NJ: Princeton University Press.

Johnston, Joseph and George Berkeley (1970). *Bishop Berkeley's Querist in Historical Perspective*. Dundalk: Dundalgan Press.

Jones, D.W. (1988). *War and Economy in the Age of William III and Marlborough*. Oxford and New York: Blackwell.

Kadane, Matthew (2013). *The Watchful Clothier: The Life of an Eighteenth-Century Protestant Capitalist*. New Haven, CT: Yale University Press.

Kant, Immanuel (2005). "An Answer to the Question: What is Enlightenment?" In Lara Denis (ed.) and Thomas K. Abbott (trans.), *Groundwork for the Metaphysics of Morals*. Peterborough: Broadview.

Kaplan, Steven L. (1996). *The Bakers of Paris and the Bread Question, 1700–1775*. Durham, NC: Duke University Press.

Kavanagh, Thomas (1993). *Enlightenment and the Shadows of Chance: The Novel and the Culture of Gambling in Eighteenth-Century France*. Baltimore, MD: Johns Hopkins University Press.

Kavanagh, Thomas (2005). *Dice, Cards, Wheels: A Different History of French Culture*. Philadelphia: University of Pennsylvania Press.

Kaye, Joel (1998). *Economy and Nature in the Fourteenth Century: Money, Market Exchange, and the Emergence of Scientific Thought*. Cambridge Studies in Medieval Life and Thought, Fourth series, 35. New York: Cambridge University Press.

Kelly, Patrick Hyde (1991). "General Introduction: Locke on Money." In Patrick Hyde Kelly (ed.), *Locke on Money*, 1–121. Oxford: Clarendon Press.

Kelly, Patrick Hyde (2014). "Berkeley and the Idea of a National Bank." In Daniel Carey (ed.), *Money and Political Economy in the Enlightenment*, 163–84. Oxford: Voltaire Foundation.

Kelly, Patrick Hyde (ed.) (1991). *Locke on Money*. 2 vols. Oxford: Oxford University Press.

Kerridge, Eric (1988). *Trade and Banking in Early Modern England*. Manchester: Manchester University Press.

Keynes, John Maynard (1930 (1963)). "Economic Possibilities for our Grandchildren." In *Essays in Persuasion*. New York: Norton.

Keynes, John Maynard (1930 (2013)). *A Treatise on Money 1: The Pure Theory of Money*. In *The Collected Writings of John Maynard Keynes*. Cambridge: Cambridge University Press.

Kibbie, Ann Louise (2006). "Object Narratives." In David Scott Kastan (ed.), *Oxford Encyclopedia of British Literature*, Vol. 4, 113–16. Oxford: Oxford University Press.

Killigrew, Sir William (1663, republished 1690, 1696). *An Humble Proposal Shewing How This Nation May Be Vast Gainers by All Sums of Mony Given to the Crown without Lessening the Prerogative*.

King, Peter (Lord) (1803). *Thoughts on the Restriction of Payments in Specie at the Banks of England and Ireland*. London: Printed for Cadell and Davies, Strand; and J. Debrett, Piccadilly.

King, Rufus (1791 (1965)). Letter to Alexander Hamilton, August 15. In Harold C. Syrett (ed.), *The Papers of Alexander Hamilton*, Vol. 9. New York: Columbia University Press.

Kleer, Richard A. (2012). "'The Folly of Particulars': The Political Economy of the South Sea Bubble." *Financial History Review* 19, no. 2: 175–97.

Kleer, Richard A. (2015). "'A New Species of Money': British Exchequer Bills, 1701–1711." *Financial History Review* 22, no. 2: 179–203.

Kleer, Richard A. (2017). *Money, Politics and Power: Banking and Public Finance in Wartime England, 1694–96*. London: Routledge.

Knafo, Samuel (2013). *The Making of Modern Finance: Liberal Governance and the Gold Standard*. London: Routledge.

Lahontan, Louis Armand de Lom d'Arce, Baron de (1703). *New Voyages to North-America*. 2 vols. London: n.p.

Lamb, Jonathan (2011). *The Things Things Say*. Princeton, NJ: Princeton University Press.

Laslett, Peter and Richard Wall (1972). "Mean Household Size in England since the Sixteenth Century." In Peter Laslett and Richard Wall (eds), *Household and Family in Past Time Comparative Studies in the Size and Structure of the Domestic Group Over the Last Three Centuries in England, France, Serbia, Japan and Colonial North America, with Further Materials from Western Europe*, 126–58. Cambridge: Cambridge University Press.

Law, John (1705). *Money and Trade Considered, With a Proposal for Supplying the Nation with Money*. Edinburgh: Heirs and Successors of Andrew Anderson.

Lecky, William Edward Hartpole (1891). *A History of England in the Eighteenth Century*. 8 vols. New York: Appleton and Company.

Leslie, Thomas Edward Cliffe (1870). "The Political Economy of Adam Smith." *Fortnightly Review* 8: 549–63.

Leslie, Thomas Edward Cliffe (1888). *Essays in Political Economy*. Dublin: Hodges, Figgis, & Co.

Levy, David (2010). "Pirates, Autographs, and a Bankruptcy: *A Short Treatise on the Game of Whist* by Edmond Hoyle, Gentleman." *Script & Print* 34, no. 3: 133–61.

Li, Ming-Hsun (1963). *The Great Recoinage of 1696 to 1699*. London: Weidenfeld and Nicolson.

Library Company (2006). "Benjamin Franklin: Writer and Printer." Online exhibition. http://www.librarycompany.org/BFWriter/ (accessed May 18, 2017).

Library Company (2014). "Benjamin Franklin Printing Block's Discovered." Press release, December 12, 2014. http://www.librarycompany.org/about/press/141212-FranklinBlocksPR.pdf/ (accessed January 18, 2018).

Locke, John (1689 (1960)). *Two Treatises of Government*. Edited by Peter Laslett. Cambridge: Cambridge University Press.

Locke, John (1692 (1991a)). *Some Considerations of the Consequences of the Lowering of Interest, and Raising the Value of Money*. In Patrick Hyde Kelly (ed.), *Locke on Money*. 2 vols. Oxford: Clarendon Press.

Locke, John (1695 (1991b)). *Further Considerations Concerning Raising the Value of Money*. In Patrick Hyde Kelly (ed.), *Locke on Money*. 2 vols. Oxford: Clarendon Press.

Lockhart, James and Stuart B. Schwartz (1983). *Early Latin America: A History of Colonial Spanish America and Brazil*. Cambridge: Cambridge University Press.

Loughridge, Deirdre (2016). *Haydn's Sunrise, Beethoven's Shadow: Audiovisual Culture and the Emergence of Musical Romanticism*. Chicago: University of Chicago Press.

Lowndes, William (1695). *A Report Containing an Essay for the Amendment of the Silver Coins, Essay for the amendment of silver coins*. London: Printed by Charles Bill, and the executrix of Thomas Newcomb deceas'd.

Lucassen, Jan (2014). "Deep Monetization: The Case of the Netherlands 1200–1940." *Tijdschrift voor Sociale en Economische Geschiedenis* 11, no. 3: 73–121.

Lynch, Deidre (1998). *The Economy of Character: Novels, Market Culture, and the Business of Inner Meaning*. Chicago: University of Chicago Press.

Mackenzie, A.D. (1953). *The Bank of England Note: A History of its Printing*. Cambridge: Cambridge University Press.

Macpherson, C.B. (1969). *The Political Theory of Possessive Individualism: Hobbes to Locke*. Oxford: Clarendon Press.

Madison, James (1787 (1977)). Letter to Thomas Jefferson, July 18. In Robert A. Rutland and William M. E. Rachal (eds), *The Papers of James Madison*, Vol. 10. Chicago: University of Chicago Press.

Mandeville, Bernard (1723). *The fable of the bees: or, private vices, publick benefits. The second edition, enlarged with many additions. As also an essay on charity and charity-schools, and a search into the nature of society*. London: n.p.

Marshall, Richard K. (1999). *The Local Merchants of Prato: Small Entrepreneurs in the Late Medieval Economy*. Baltimore, MD: Johns Hopkins University Press.

Martinez, Mauricio (2013). "From Peruvian Gold to British Guinea: Tropicopolitanism and Myths of Origin in Charles Johnstone's *Chrysal*." In Ileana Baired and Christina Ionescu (eds), *Eighteenth-Century Thing Theory in a Global Context*. Aldershot: Ashgate.

Marx, Karl (1970). *Critique of Hegel's "Philosophy of Right."* Edited by Joseph O'Malley. Translated by Annette Jolin and Joseph O'Malley. London: Cambridge University Press.

Marx, Karl (1981). *Capital: A Critique of Political Economy*, Vol. 3. Translated by David Fernback. London: Penguin.

Mather, Cotton (1690). *Some Considerations on the Bills of Credit Now Passing in New-England*. Boston: n.p. In Andrew McFarland Davis (ed.), *Colonial Currency Reprints, 1682–1751*. New York: B. Franklin.

Mather, Cotton (1714). *Pascentius: A Very Brief Essay upon the Methods of Piety*. Boston: n.p.

Mathias, Peter (1979). "The People's Money in the Eighteenth Century: The Royal Mint, Trade Tokens and the Economy." In Peter Mathias (ed.), *The Transformation of England: Essays in the Economic and Social History of England in the Eighteenth Century*, 190–208. London: Routledge.

Mayhew, N.J. (1995). "Population, Money Supply, and the Velocity of Circulation in England, 1300–1700." *Economic History Review* (New Series) 48, no. 2 (May).

Mayhew, N.J. (2000). *Sterling: The History of a Currency*. London: Penguin.

Mazerolle, Fernand (1907). *L'Hôtel des Monnaies*. Paris: Librarie Renouard.

McCulloch, J.R. (1845). *The Literature of Political Economy: A Classified Catalogue*. London: Longman, Brown, Green, and Longman.

McCurdy, Henry (2007). "Social Incidence and Economic Significance of the Growth in Transferable Paper Instruments in Seventeenth Century England." PhD thesis, University of Cambridge.

McCusker, John (2017). "To 'arrange my accounts'—Fulfilling the Last Wishes of George Washington." *George Washington Financial Papers Project*. http://financial.gwpapers.org/sites/financial.gwpapers.org/files/To%20Arrange%20My%20Accounts.pdf (accessed March 17, 2018).

Meldrum, Tim (2000). *Domestic Service and Gender, 1660–1750: Life and Work in the London Household*. Harlow: Longman.

Melon, Jean François (1738). *A Political Essay upon Commerce*. Dublin: n.p.

Menant, François and Odile Redon (2004). *Notaires et crédit dans l'occident méditerranéen médiéval: [colloques organisés . . . à Nice et Bordighera en octobre 1996 et à Lyon en décembre 1997]*. Rome: Ecole française de Rome.

Michener, Ron (2010). "Money in the American Colonies." https://eh.net/encyclopedia/money-in-the-american-colonies/ (accessed March 17, 2018).

Millar, John (1771). *Observations Concerning the Distinction of Ranks in Society*. London: n.p.

The Mint and Exchequer United: Being a Method to Furnish His Majesty with Two, Three, Or Four Millions Immediately, at the Present Charge But of One Million Or Less, and Supply the Want of Coin, Till New Money Can be Had (1695).

Mirzoeff, Nicholas (1999). *An Introduction to Visual Culture*. New York: Routledge.

Misselden, Edward (1622). *Free Trade or, the Meanses to Make Trade Flourish*. London: John Legatt, for Simon Waterson.

Mitchell, W.J.T. (1986). *Iconology: Image, Text, Ideology*. Chicago: University of Chicago Press.
Molesworth, Jesse (2010). *Chance and the Eighteenth-Century Novel: Realism, Probability, Magic*. Cambridge: Cambridge University Press.
Montesquieu, Charles de Secondat, baron de (1750 (1989)). *The Spirit of the Laws*. Edited by Anne Cohler, Basia Miller, and Harold Stone. Cambridge: Cambridge University Press.
Moore, Giles (1971). *The Journal of Giles Moore*. Edited by Ruth Bird. Lewes: Sussex Record Society.
More, Thomas (1516 (1989)). *Utopia*. London: Penguin.
A Mournful Lamentation on the untimely Death of Paper Money (1781). Wilmington, DE: n.p.
Mueller, Reinhold C. (1997). *The Venetian Money Market: Banks, Panics, and the Public Debt, 1200–1500*. Baltimore, MD: Johns Hopkins University Press.
Muldrew, Craig (1998). *The Economy of Obligation: The Culture of Credit and Social Relations in Early Modern England*. Basingstoke: Palgrave Macmillan.
Muldrew, Craig (2001). "'Hard Food for Midas': Cash and Its Social Value in Early Modern England." *Past & Present* 170: 78–120.
Muldrew, Craig (2007). "Wages and the Problem of Monetary Scarcity in Early Modern England." In Jan Lucassen (ed.), *Wages and Currency: Global Comparisons from Antiquity to the Twentieth Century*, 391–410. Bern: Peter Lang.
Muldrew, Craig (2018a). "Self-Control and Savings: Adam Smith and the Creation of Modern Capital." In Simon Middleton and James E. Shaw (eds), *Market Ethics and Practices, c. 1300–1850*, 63–86. Milton: Routledge.
Muldrew, Craig (2018b). "The Social Acceptance of Paper Credit as Currency in Eighteenth Century England: A Case Study of Glastonbury *c*. 1720–1742." In Marcella Lorenzini, Lorandini Cinzia, and D'Maris Coffman (eds), *Financing in Europe: Evolution, Coexistence and Complementarity of Lending Practices from the Middle Ages to Modern Times*. London: Palgrave Macmillan.
Mun, Thomas (1621). *A Discourse of Trade, from England unto the East-Indies*. London: n.p.
Munro, John H. (2003). "The Medieval Origins of the Financial Revolution: Usury, Rentes, and Negotiability." *International History Review* 25, no. 3: 505–62. doi: 10.2307/40109398.
Murphy, Anne L. (2009). *The Origins of English Financial Markets: Investmentand Speculation Before the South Sea Bubble*. Cambridge: Cambridge University Press.
Murphy, Antoin E. (1986). *Richard Cantillon: Entrepreneur and Economist*. Oxford: Clarendon Press.
Murphy, Antoin E. (1997). *John Law: Economic Theorist and Policy-Maker*. Oxford: Oxford University Press.
Murray, Judith Sargent (1798). *The Gleaner*. "Introduction" by Nina Baym (1992). Schenectady, NY: Union College Press.
Muzzarelli, M.G. (2012). "From the Closet to the Wallet: Pawning Clothes in Renaissance Italy." *Renaissance and Reformation/Renaissance et Réforme* 35, no. 3: 23–38.
National Archives (TNA). Mint Office (Mint).
National Archives (TNA). Treasury Office (T).
National Land Bank Act (1696).
Neal, Larry (2000). "How It All Began: The Monetary and Financial Architecture of Europe from 1648 to 1815." *Financial History Review* 7, no. 2 (October): 117–40.

Newman, Eric (1964). "Nature Printing on Colonial and Continental Currency." *Numismatist* 77, no. 2: 146–54.
Newman, Eric (1990). *The Early Paper Money of America*. 3rd edition. Iola, WI: Krause Publications.
Newman, Eric (2008). *The Early Paper Money of America*. 5th edition. Iola, WI: Krause Publications.
Noonan, John Thomas (1957). *The Scholastic Analysis of Usury*. Cambridge, MA: Harvard University Press.
North, Douglass C. and Barry R. Weingast (1989). "Constitutions and Commitment: The Evolution of Institutions Governing Public Choice in Seventeenth-Century England." *Journal of Economic History* XLIX, no. 4: 803–32.
Oslington, Paul (2012). "God and the Market: Adam Smith's Invisible Hand." *Journal of Business Ethics*: 429–38.
Pabst, Adrian (2011). "From Civil to Political Economy: Adam Smith's Theological Debt." In Paul Oslington (ed.), *Adam Smith as Theologian*, 106–24. London: Routledge.
Pagden, Anthony (2013). *The Enlightenment and Why It Still Matters*. New York: Random House.
Paine, Thomas (1778 (1974)). *American Crisis VII*. In Philip S. Foner (ed.), *The Life and Major Writings of Thomas Paine*. New York: Citadel Press.
Paine, Thomas (1796). *The Decline and Fall of the English System of Finance*. Paris: Hartley, Adlard and Son.
Palma, Nuno (2017). "Reconstruction of Money Supply over the Long Run: The Case of England, 1270–1870." *Economic History Review* 71, no. 2: 373–92.
Parsons, Jotham (2015). *Making Money in Sixteenth-Century France: Currency, Culture, and the State*. Ithaca, NY: Cornell University Press.
Paterson, William (1694). *A Brief Account of the Intended Bank of England*. [London]: Randal Taylor.
Pecora, Vincent (2006). *Secularization and Cultural Criticism: Religion, Nation, and Modernity*. Chicago: University of Chicago Press.
Pepys, Samuel (1970–83). *The Diary of Samuel Pepys*. Vols 1–10. Edited by Robert Latham and William Matthews. London: Bell.
Phelps Brown, E.H. and Sheila V. Hopkins (1962). "Seven Centuries of the Prices of Consumables, Compared with Builders' Wage-Rates." In E.M. Carus-Wilson (ed.), *Essays in Economic History*, 179–97. London: Economic History Society.
Phillipson, N.T. (2010). *Adam Smith: An Enlightened Life*. London: Yale University Press.
Pietz, William (1988). "The Problem of the Fetish, IIIa: Bosman's Guinea and the Enlightenment Theory of Fetishism." *RES: Anthropology and Aesthetics* 16: 105–24.
Piketty, Thomas (2014). *Capital in the Twenty-First Century*. Translated by Arthur Goldhammer. Cambridge, MA: Harvard University Press.
Pincus, Steven (2009). *1688: The First Modern Revolution*. New Haven, CT: Yale University Press.
Pocock, J.G.A. (1975). *The Machiavellian Moment: Florentine Political Thought and the Atlantic Republican Tradition*. Princeton, NJ: Princeton University Press.
Pocock, J.G.A. (1985). *Virtue, Commerce and History: Essays in Political Thought and History, Chiefly in the Eighteenth Century*. Cambridge: Cambridge University Press.

Poovey, Mary (2008). *Genres of the Credit Economy: Mediating Value in Eighteenth- and Nineteenth-Century Britain*. Chicago: University of Chicago Press.

Pope, Alexander (1728–43 (1986)). *The Dunciad*. In M.H. Abrams et al. (eds), *The Norton Anthology of English Literature*. New York: Norton.

Potter, William (1650). *The key of wealth: or, a new way, for improving of trade: lawfull, easie, safe and effectuall: shewing how a few tradesmen agreeing together, may (borrow wherewith to) double their stocks, and the increase thereof*. London: n.p.

Pressnell, L.S. (1956). *Country Banking in the Industrial Revolution*. Oxford: Oxford University Press.

Ramsey, David (1789 (1990)). *The History of the American Revolution*. Edited by Lester Cohen. 2 vols. Indianapolis: Liberty Classics.

Randolph, Peyton (1759). *A Letter to a Gentleman in London, from Virginia*. Williamsburg, VA: n.p.

Rassekh, Farhad (2017). *Four Central Theories of the Market Economy: Conception, Evolution and Application*. London: Routledge.

Rawle, Francis (1721). *Some Remedies Proposed for the Restoring the Sunk Credit of the Province of Pennsylvania, with Some Remarks on its Trade*. Philadelphia: n.p.

Redish, Angela (1990). "The Evolution of the Gold Standard in England." *Journal of Economic History* 50, no. 4: 789–805.

Redish, Angela (2000). *Bimetallism: An Economic and Historical Analysis*. Cambridge: Cambridge University Press.

"Reply of Continental Currency to the Representation and Remonstrance of Hard Money" (1779). *United States Magazine* (February).

"The Representation and Remonstrance of Hard Money. Addressed to the People of America" (1779). *United States Magazine* (January).

Ricardo, David (1810). *The High Price of Bullion, A Proof of the Depreciation of Bank Notes*. London: John Murray.

Richards, Richard David (1929). *The Early History of Banking in England*. London: P.S. King & Son.

Ricks, Morgan (2016). *The Money Problem: Rethinking Financial Regulation*. Chicago: University of Chicago Press.

Robertson, John (2015). *The Enlightenment: A Very Short Introduction*. Oxford: Oxford University Press.

Robertson, William (n.d.). *History of America, Volume I*. London: n.p.

Rogers, James Steven (1995). *The Early History of the Law of Bills and Notes: A Study of the Origins of Anglo-American Commercial Law*. Cambridge Studies in English Legal History Index. Cambridge: Cambridge University Press.

Rose, Craig (1999). *England in the 1690s: Revolution, Religion and War*. Oxford: Blackwell.

Roseveare, Henry (1973). *The Treasury, 1660–1870: The Foundations of Control*, Historical Problems, Studies and Documents, 22. London: Allen and Unwin.

Rothschild, Emma (2001). *Economic Sentiments: Adam Smith, Condorcet, and the Enlightenment*. Cambridge, MA: Harvard University Press.

Rousseau, Jean-Jacques (1772 (1997)). "Considerations on the Government of Poland." In Victor Gourevitch (ed.), *Rousseau: The Social Contract and other later Political Writings*. Cambridge: Cambridge University Press.

Rousseau, Jean-Jacques (1983). "Discourse on the Origin of Inequality." Translated by Donald Cress. In *On the Social Contract*. Indianapolis: Hackett.

Rousseau, Jean-Jacques (2003). "Luxury, Commerce, and the Arts." Translated by Henry C. Clark. In Henry C. Clark (ed.), *Commerce, Culture, and Liberty: Readings on Capitalism Before Adam Smith*. Indianapolis: Liberty Fund.

Rowlands, Guy (2012). *The Financial Decline of a Great Power: War, Influence, and Money in Louis XIV's France*. Oxford: Oxford University Press.

Royal Bank of Scotland (2017). "RBS History in 100 Objects." https://www.rbs.com/heritage/rbs-history-in-100-objects/objects-by-date.html (accessed January 18, 2018).

Saidel, Benjamin Adam and Abed S.K. Barakat (2007). "The Pillars of Hercules as Metaphors for Fertility and Health among Bedouin in the Southern Levant." *Anthropos* 102, no. 1: 220–4.

Saint-Simon, Henri, comte de (1834). *New Christianity*. London: n.p.

Sargent, Thomas J. and François R. Velde (2003). *The Big Problem of Small Change*. Princeton, NJ: Princeton University Press.

Saville, Richard (1996). *Bank of Scotland: A History, 1695–1995*. Edinburgh: Edinburgh University Press.

Schabas, Margaret (2008). "Temporal Dimensions in Hume's Monetary Theory." In Carl Wennerlind and Margaret Schabas (eds), *David Hume's Political Economy*, 127–45. London: Routledge.

Schumpeter, Joseph A. (1954). *History of Economic Analysis*. Edited by Elizabeth Boody Schumpeter. New York: Oxford University Press.

The Second Part of South-Sea Stock. Being an Inquiry into the Original of Province Bills or Bills of Credit (1721 (1971)). In Andrew McFarland Davis (ed.), *Colonial Currency Reprints, 1682–1751*. New York: B. Franklin.

Selgin, George (2008). *Good Money: Birmingham Button Makers, the Royal Mint, and the Beginnings of Modern Coinage, 1775–1821*. Ann Arbor: University of Michigan Press.

Semple, Clara (2005). *A Silver Legend: The Story of the Maria Theresa Thaler*. Gloucester: Barzan.

Shaw, James E. and Evelyn S. Welch (2011). *Making and Marketing Medicine in Renaissance Florence*. Amsterdam and New York: Rodopi.

Sheehan, Jonathan and Dror Wahrman (2015). *Invisible Hands: Self-Organization and the Eighteenth Century*. Chicago: University of Chicago Press.

Shell, Marc (1982). *Money, Language, and Thought: Literary and Philosophical Economies from the Medieval to the Modern Era*. Berkeley: University of California Press.

Sheriff, Mary (2003). "The Portrait of the Queen." In Dena Goodman (ed.), *Marie Antoinette: Writings on the Body of a Queen*, 45–72. London: Routledge.

Sheriff, Mary (ed.) (2006). *Antoine Watteau: Perspectives on the Artist and the Culture of his Time*. Newark: University of Delaware Press.

Shin, Hiroki (2015). "Paper Money, the Nation, and the Suspension of Cash Payments in 1797." *Historical Journal* 58, no. 2: 415–42.

Siegfried, Susan (1992). "Boilly and the Frame Up of 'Trompe l'oeil'." *Oxford Art Journal* 15, no. 2: 27–37.

Simmel, Georg (1907 (1978)). *The Philosophy of Money*. 2nd edition. Translated by Tom Bottomore and David Frisby. London: Routledge.

Skidelsky, Robert (1995). "J. M. Keynes and the Quantity Theory of Money." In Mark Blaug et al. (eds), *The Quantity Theory of Money: From Locke to Keynes and Friedman*, 80–96. Aldershot: Edward Elgar.

Smith, Adam (1776 (1976)). *An Inquiry into the Nature and Causes of the Wealth of Nations*. Edited by Edwin Cannan. Chicago: University of Chicago Press.

Smith, Adam (1776 (1976)). *An Inquiry into the Nature and Causes of the Wealth of Nations*. Edited by R.H. Campbell and A.S. Skinner. Textual editor W.B. Todd. Oxford: Oxford University Press.

Smith, Adam (1978). *Lectures on Jurisprudence*. Edited by Ronald L. Meek, Peter Stein, and D.D. Raphael. Oxford: Oxford University Press.

Solkin, David (1996). *Painting for Money: The Visual Arts and the Public Sphere in Eighteenth-Century England*. New Haven, CT: Yale University Press.

Sonenscher, Michael (1984). "Work and Wages in Paris in the Eighteenth Century." In Maxine Berg, Pat Hudson, and Michael Sonenscher (eds), *Manufacture in Town and Country Before the Factory*, 147–72. Cambridge: Cambridge University Press.

Spang, Rebecca L. (2015). *Stuff and Money in the Time of the French Revolution*. Cambridge, MA: Harvard University Press.

Spector, Céline (2007). "'Il faut éclairer l'histoire par les lois et les lois par l'histoire': statut de la romanité et rationalité des coutumes dans *L'Esprit des lois* de Montesquieu." In M. Xifaras (ed.), *Généalogie des savoirs juridiques: le carrefour des lumières*. Brussels: Bruylant; Edited by R.H. Campbell and A.S. Skinner. Textual editor W.B. Todd. Oxford: Oxford University Press.

"Speech of a Member of the General Court of Massachusetts, on the Question whether the Public Securities should be redeemed at their Current Value" (1787). *American Museum* (May).

Speke, John Hanning (1868). *Journal of the Discovery of the Source of the Nile*. Eugene, OR: Resource Publications.

Spufford, Peter (1966). "Assemblies of Estates, Taxation and Control of Coinage in Medieval Europe." In *XII Congres International des Sciences Historiques*. Louvain-Paris: Etudes Présentée à la Commission Internationale pour L'histoire des Assemblées D'etats, XXXI.

Spufford, Peter (1988). *Money and its Use in Medieval Europe*. Cambridge: Cambridge University Press.

Stasavage, David (2011). *States of Credit: Size, Power, and the Development of European Polities*. Princeton, NJ: Princeton University Press.

A State of the Case, between Furnishing His Majesty with Money by Way of Loan, or by Way of Advance of the Tax of Any Particular Place, Upon the Act for the £1250000 (1666).

Stern, Julia A. (1997). *The Plight of Feeling: Sympathy and Dissent in the Early American Novel*. Chicago: University of Chicago Press.

Stern, Philip and Carl Wennerlind (2013). *Mercantilism Reimagined: Political Economy in Early Modern Britain and its Empire*. Oxford: Oxford University Press.

Steuart, Sir James (1767 (1998)). *An Inquiry into the Principles of Political Oeconomy*. Edited by Andrew S. Skinner with Noboru Kobayashi and Hiroshi Mizuta. 4 vols. London: Pickering & Chatto.

Stewart, Dugald (1866). *Elements of the Philosophy of the Human Mind*. Boston: William H. Dennet.

Stewart, Ian (1992). "The English and Norman Mints, c. 600–1158." In C.E. Challis (ed.), *A New History of the Royal Mint*. Cambridge: Cambridge University Press.

Story, Joseph (1840). *Commentaries on the Law of Bailments, with Illustrations from the Civil and the Foreign Law*. 2nd edition. Boston: Little & Brown.

Styles, John (1980). "'Our Traitorous Moneymakers': The Yorkshire Coiners and the Law, 1760–83." In John A. Styles and John Brewer (eds), *An Ungovernable People: the English and Their Law in the Seventeenth and Eighteenth Centuries*, 172–249. New Brunswick, NJ: Rutgers University Press.

Supple, Barry (1964). *Commercial Crisis and Change in England, 1600–1642*. Cambridge: Cambridge University Press.

Swedborg, Richard (1999). *Marx, Weber and the Idea of Economic Sociology*. Princeton, NJ: Princeton University Press.

Swift, Jonathan (1726). *Travels into Several Remote Nations of the World. In Four Parts. By Lemuel Gulliver, First a Surgeon, and then a Captain of Several Ships*. London: Benj. Motte.

Swift, Jonathan (1729). *A Modest Proposal for Preventing the Children of Poor People in Ireland From Being a Burden to Their Parents, or the Country, and for Making Them Beneficial to the Publick*. Dublin: S. Harding.

Swift, Jonathan (1965). *The Drapier's Letters to the People of Ireland*. Edited by Herbert Davis. Oxford: Clarendon Press.

Symson, Joseph (2002). *An Exact and Industrious Tradesman: The Letter Book of Joseph Symson of Kendal, 1711–1720*. Edited by S.D. Smith. Oxford and New York: Oxford University Press.

Tandeter, Enrique (1993). *Coercion and Market: Silver Mining in Colonial Potosí, 1692–1826*. Translated by Richard Warren. Albuquerque: University of New Mexico Press.

Taylor, Charles (2007). *A Secular Age*. Cambridge, MA: Harvard University Press.

Temin, Peter and Hans-Joachim Voth (2012). *Prometheus Shackled: Goldsmith Banks and England's Financial Revolution After 1700*. Oxford: Oxford University Press.

't Hart, Marjolein (1991). "'The Devil or the Dutch': Holland's Impact on the Financial Revolution in England, 1643–1694." *Parliaments, Estates and Representation* 11, no. 1: 39–52.

Thayer, Theodore (1953). "The Land-Bank System in the American Colonies." *Journal of Economic History* 13, no. 2: 145–59.

Thomson, Erik (2004). "Chancellor Oxenstierna, Cardinal Richelieu, and Commerce: The Problems and Possibilities of Governance in Early-Seventeenth-Century France and Sweden." PhD thesis, Johns Hopkins University.

Thornton, Henry (1965). *An Enquiry into the Nature and Effects of Paper Credit of Great Britain (1802)*. Edited by F.A. von Hayek. New York: Augustus M. Kelley.

Tortella, Gabriel and Francisco Comín (2001). "Fiscal and Monetary Institutions in Spain (1600–1900)." In Michael Bordo and Roberto Cortés-Conde (eds), *Transferring Wealth and Power from the Old to the New World: Monetary and Fiscal Institutions in the 17th through the 19th Centuries*. Cambridge: Cambridge University Press.

Tracy, James D. (1984). *A Financial Revolution in the Hapsburg Netherlands*. Berkeley and Los Angeles: University of California Press.

Trettien, Whitney (2017). "Leaves." In Bill Maurer and Lana Swartz (eds), *Paid: Tales of Dongles, Checks, and Other Money Stuff*. Cambridge, MA: MIT Press.

Trumbull, John (1775–82 (1962)). *M'Fingal*. In Edwin T. Bowden (ed.), *The Satiric Poems of John Trumbull: The Progress of Dullness and M'Fingal*. Austin: University of Texas Press.

Tschoegl, Adrian (2001). "Maria Theresa's Thaler: A Case of International Money." *Eastern Economic Journal* 27, no. 4: 443–62.

Tuck, Richard (2016). *The Sleeping Sovereign: The Invention of Modern Democracy*. Cambridge: Cambridge University Press.
Ullman, Walter (1966). *Principles of Government and Politics in the Middle Ages*. London: Methuen & Co. Ltd. Reprint, Routledge, 2010.
Usher, A.P. (1954–8). "Machines and Mechanisms." In C. Singer, E.J. Holmyard, A.R. Hall and T. Williams (eds), *A History of Technology*, Vol. 3: *From the Renaissance to the Industrial Revolution, c. 1500 – c. 1750*, 324–46. Oxford: Clarendon Press.
Valenze, Deborah (2006). *The Social Life of Money in the English Past*. Cambridge: Cambridge University Press.
Valeri, Mark (2010). *Heavenly Merchandize: How Religion Shaped Commerce in Puritan America*. Princeton, NJ: Princeton University Press.
Vaughan, Rice (1675). *A Discourse of Coin and Coinage: The First Invention, Vse, Matter, Forms, Proportions and Differences, Ancient & Modern: with the Advantages and Disadvantages of the Rise or Fall Thereof, in Our Own or Neighbouring Nations: and the Reasons*. London: Printed by Th. Dawks for Th. Basset.
Veblen, Thorstein (1899). "The Preconceptions of Economic Science [Part II]." *Quarterly Journal of Economics* 13: 396–426.
Velde, François R. (2009). "Was John Law's System a Bubble?: The Mississippi Bubble Revisited." In Jeremy Atack and Larry Neal (eds), *The Origins and Development of Financial Markets and Institutions: From the Seventeenth Century to the Present*, 99–120. Cambridge: Cambridge University Press.
Violet, Thomas (1650). *A true discovery to the Commons of England, how they have been cheated of almost all the gold and silver coyn of this nation, which hath been, and is daily transported into forraign parts: and how the people of this nation are, and have been abused by light and clipped English money, and the means shewed for the prevention thereof*. London: W.B.
Von Glahn, Richard (2016). *The Economic History of China from Antiquity to the Nineteenth Century*. Cambridge: Cambridge University Press.
Vries, Jan de and Ad van der Woude (1997). *The First Modern Economy: Success, Failure, and Perseverance of the Dutch Economy, 1500–1815*. Cambridge: Cambridge University Press.
Waddell, Brodie (2015). "The Politics of Economic Distress in the Aftermath of the Glorious Revolution, 1689–1702." *English Historical Review* 130, no. 543: 318–51.
Walsh, Patrick (2014). *The South Sea Bubble and Ireland: Money, Banking and Investment, 1690–1721*. Woodbridge: Boydell.
Weber, Max (1930 (2001)). *The Protestant Ethic and the Spirit of Capitalism*. Translated by Talcott Parsons. London: Routledge Classics.
Weil, Rachel (2013). *A Plague of Informers: Conspiracy and Trust in William III's England*. New Haven, CT: Yale University Press.
Weir, David R. (1989). "Tontines, Public Finance, and Revolution in France and England, 1688–1789." *Journal of Economic History* 49, no. 1: 95–124.
Weiss Smith, Courtney (2016). *Empiricist Devotions: Science, Religion, and Poetry in Early Eighteenth-Century England*. Charlottesville: University of Virginia Press.
Wennerlind, Carl (2005). "David Hume's Monetary Theory Revisited: Was He Really a Quantity Theorist and an Inflationist?" *Journal of Political Economy* 113, no. 1: 223–37.

Wennerlind, Carl (2008). "An Artificial Virtue and the Oil of Commerce: A Synthetic View of Hume's Theory of Money." In Carl Wennerlind and Margaret Schabas (eds), *David Hume's Political Economy*, 105–26. London: Routledge.

Wennerlind, Carl (2011). *Casualties of Credit: The English Financial Revolution, 1620–1720*. Cambridge, MA: Harvard University Press.

Winstanley, Gerrard (1649a). *A declaration from the poor oppressed people of England, directed to all that call themselves, or are called lords of manors, through this nation; that have begun to cut, or that through fear and covetousness, do intend to cut down the woods and trees that grow upon the commons and waste land.*

Winstanley, Gerrard (1649b). *The true Levellers standard advanced; or, The state of community opened, and presented to the sons of men*. London: n.p.

Winstanley, Gerrard (1652). *The law of freedom in a platform: or, true magistracy restored. Humbly presented to Oliver Cromwel, . . . wherein is declared, what is kingly government, and what is Commonwealths government*. London: printed by J.M. for the author.

Wise, John [as Amicus Patriae] (1721 (1971)). *A Word of Comfort to a Melancholy County. Or the Bank of Credit Erected in the Massachusetts-Bay*. In Andrew McFarland Davis (ed.), *Colonial Currency Reprints, 1682–1751*. New York: B. Franklin.

Wiséhn, Ian (1995). "Sweden's Stockholm Banco and the First European Banknotes." In Virginia Hewitt (ed.), *The Banker's Art: Studies in Paper Money*, 12–19. London: British Museum Press.

Wood, Gordon S. (1991). *The Radicalism of the American Revolution*. New York: Knopf.

Wordie, J.R. (1997). "Deflationary Factors in the Tudor Price Rise." *Past & Present* 154: 32–70.

Wrigley, E.A. and Roger S. Schofield (1989). *The Population History of England, 1541–1871: A Reconstruction*. Cambridge: Cambridge University Press.

INDEX

Italic numbers are used for illustrations. **Bold** numbers are used for tables.

accounts, keeping of 97, 102
Adams, John 144
Addison, Joseph 69, 85, 130–1
Africa, trade in 62
Africans, alleged inferiority of 70, 93
alchemy 5
America, objects as currency 129–30
America, paper money in 136, 139–42, 145–62
    credit and social mobility 153–6
    debt and communal bonds 156–62, *159*
    funding independence 146–53, *147*, *149–51*
    Pennsylvania 48–50, *49*, *142*, 152–3
American Indians 87, *87*, 92
Americas, mines and mints in 38–42
Aristotle 55
art and representation 121–42
    art and money 122–8, *123–4*, *126*, *128*
    coins, designs of 131–6, *132*, *134–5*
    objects as currency 128–31
artistic rights 125
assignats (France) 127, *128–9*, 138
Augsburg Mint 31
Austria 134–5, *134*, 136
Ayr Bank 103

balance of trade 5, 85, 177, **178**, 179
bank failures 103
Bank of Amsterdam 104
Bank of England
    establishment of 1–4, 6, 7, 164
    John Locke and 60
    paper money of 13–16, 47–8, 58–9, 105, 137–8, *137*
Bank of Scotland 103, 138
Bank of the United States 145, 159–60
Bank Restriction Act (1797) 119, 182–3
Bankers' Case 11–12, *13*
banknotes (England)
    origins of 13, *14*, 20–2, *21*, *23*
    use of in London 115–17, **116**, *117–18*, 119, *120*
Barbon, Nicholas 167, 168
barter 24, 62, 146
benefits of money 67–71, **72**
Berkeley, George 61–2, 69, 70
    The Querist 172–3
Best, Henry 102
billon coins 43
bills of exchange 104, 105–6, 129, 136, *137*
bills, personal 96, 105, 106, 114–15
bimetallic ratios **42**
bimetallism 98, 167, 180
bitcoin 162
blanks, coin 29
Blondeau, Pierre 32–3, *37*

Blundell, Nicholas 102
Boliva 39–40, 42
Borden, William 147
Boulton, Matthew 44–6
Bouton, Terry 152–3
Bramante, Donato 29
Briot, Nicholas 32
Briscoe, John, *Discourse of Money* 169
brokers 20
Broughton, John 2–3
Brown, Charles Brockden, *Arthur Mervyn* 161
Brown, William Hill, *The Power of Sympathy* 161
Bullion Report (1810) 184–6
burglary 109, *109*
Burstein, Andrew 161
Burton, Richard 93
Busaglo, Jacob 112
button-making technologies 36, 45

Canada 48, 125–6
Cannon, John 95–6, 106
capital markets 7, 16–18
capitalism 78
Carboni, Mauro 104
card games 126
card money (Canada) 48, 125–6
Carlyle, Alexander 79
Cellini, Benvenuto 30
Chardin, Jean-Baptiste Siméon, *The House of Cards* 125
China 102–3
civic disinterest 160–1
Clark, T. J. 127
clipping of coins
　acceptance of 148–9
　deterrents to 31, 33, 35
　effects of 165–6
　practice of 27–8, 33, *34*, 100–1
Cobbett, William, *Paper against Gold and Glory against Prosperity* 183
coin collectors 130–1
coins
　in art 126–7
　counterfeit 26–7, 33, 35–6, 43, 45–6
　designs of 131–6, *132*, *134–5*
　and interpersonal credit 97–102, **101**
　mechanical production of 28–38, *30*, *34*
　problems with according to Steuart 180
　quality of 26–7
collectors of coins 130–1
colonies, paper money in 48
commercial banking 7, 20–3, *21–2*
commercial culture 122–3
commodity money 4–5, 26–7
Continental dollar (America) 150–2, *150–1*, 158, *158–9*
contracts, discharge of 56–7, 166–7
Cooke, Ebenezer, *Sotweed Redivivus* 147–8
Copley, John Singleton, *John Hancock* 139–40, *139*
copper coins 43, 100
copper plate money (Sweden) 100
Corporation of Moneyers, England 29, 32, 36–7, 38, 46
corruption by money 72–3
costs of coin production 36
counterfeit money
　anti-counterfeiting devices 141–2, *142*
　coins 26–7, 33, 35–6, 43, 45–6
　paper money 48–9, *50*
　punishments for 100
Cour de Monnaies, France 29, 36–7, 38
covenants 57
cowrie shells 129, 130
credit
　covenants 57
　creation of 2–4
　in everyday use 98, 101–2, 104, 105–7
　and progress 144–5
　role of money in 58–9, 62, 64
　and social mobility in America 153–6
creditors' rights 11–12
criminal trial records, money in 107–20, *109*, **116**, *117–18*, **120**, *131*, *133*
crises 34–5, 164, 170–6, *171*, *175*, 182–6, *184*
criticisms of money 71–3

d'Alembert, Jean le Rond, *Encyclopedie* 27
Davenant, Charles 59, 169–70
David, Jacques Louis, *Death of Marat* 127–8, *129*
Davis, Kathleen 88
debased coins 148–9
debt and communal bonds 144–5, 156–62, *159*

definitions of money 27, 55, 97, 159, 168, 169, 170–1, 173–4
Defoe, Daniel 59
  The Complete English Tradesman 168
  Essay upon Projects 79, 147
demand for money 98
Desan, Christine 152
designs of money
  coins 131–6, *132, 134–5*
  paper money 141–2, *142,* 149–50, *149–51,* 158, *158–9*
devaluation of currency 166
Devenish, Thomas 114–15
Diderot, Denis, *Encyclopedie* 27
discounting of notes 115
divination and prudence 88–90
Doon, Maria 110–11
Downing, Sir George 8, 9, 11
ducat (Basel) 133
Dutch East India Company 99

Earle, Peter 108
economic benefits of money 67–8, 70
economic man 161
écu (France) 131–2, *132,* 133
edge-marking of coins 31, 33, 35
England
  capital markets 16–18
  coin supply 98–9
  commercial banking 20–3, 105
  debts in probate accounts 101–2, **101**
  everyday credit 105–6
  mercantilism 5
  minting of coins 31–3, 34, 37, 44–6
  modern money 12–16
  personal use of money in 108–20, *109,* **116,** *117–18, 120*
  public debt 8–12
  See also Bank of England; banknotes (England); Great Recoinage, England
Enlightenment, definitions of 76
Enlightenment ideas about money. *See* ideas of money; issues of the age
Evelyn, John 169
everyday money, new practices 95–120
  coins and interpersonal credit 97–102, **101**
  money in criminal trial records 107–20, *109,* **116,** *117–18, 120*

types of paper money 102–7
exchange function of money 166, 176
extrinsic value 55

Fabian, Johannes 87–8
faith in money 157
farthing (England) 116–17, *116, 117*
farthing (Ireland) 171, *171*
Fear, George 95
feminism 161
Ferguson, Adam 88–9
fobs 109
fractional reserve lending 103, 104, 149, 181, 182
France
  bimetallic ratios 42
  credit in 104
  minting of coins 29, 31, 32, 36–7, 38, 129
  paper money 136, 138, 174–5
  playing cards 48, 125–6
  political crises 34, 35
  variety of money 130
Franklin, Benjamin 49, 50, 141, *142,* 146–8, 153–4, 158
  A Modest Inquiry into the . . . Necessity of a Paper-Currency 148
  Poor Richard's Almanac 147

gambling 124–5
Gathney, Mary 133
Gildon, Charles, *The Golden Spy* 121
Girodet, Anne-Louis, *Portrait of Mlle Lange as Danae* 126–7, *126*
globalization of trade 70
gold 99, 119, 167, 184–6
  See also bimetallism
Goodale, Leonard 102
Goodhart, Charles 27
Goux, Jean-Joseph 148
Graham, James 114–15
grand larceny 108–9, *109*
Grassby, Richard 108
Great Debasement, England 34
Great Mirror of Folly 127
Great Recoinage, England 33–4, 35, 38, 60, 68, 99, 165–70, *168*
Green, Joseph
  The Dying Speech of Old Tenor 146–7

A Mournful Lamentation On the untimely Death of Paper Money 151
Green, Thomas 114–15
Gresham's law 33
guilds of moneyers 29, 36–7, 38, 46
guinea (England) 99, 116–17, **116**, *117–18*, 119, *120*
Guy, Joseph 131

Hall, Benjamin 109–10
Hall, David 50
Hamilton, Alexander 145, 152, 155, 159–60
  Federalist 35 161
  Report on the Public Credit 150
hammered coinage 28–9
Hancock, John 139–40, *139*
Hardwick, Julie 104
Harris, Joseph, *Essay upon Money and Coins* 178
Hartlib Circle 57
Het groote tafereel der dwaasheid (The Great Mirror of Folly) 127
high-powered money 6–7
highway robberies 106–7, 109, 110
Hirschman, Albert O. 9
Hobbes, Thomas 55–7, *56*
  Leviathan 85
Hodges, James 167
Hogarth, William, *The Rake's Progress* 123–5, *124*
housebreaking 109, *109*
Howard, Mary 102
Hoyle, Edmond, *A Short Treatise on the Game of Whist* 126
Hume, David 64–6, *65*, 69–70, 92, 176–8
  Of the Balance of Trade 177
  Of Money 176–7
  Of National Character 70
  Of Public Credit 89–90, 178

ideas of money 53–74
  benefits of money 67–73, *72*
  sociability of money 54–67, *56*, *61*, *63*, *65*
"In God We Trust" 83–4, *84*
indented bills 141, *141*
intelligence and money 130
interests in England 9, 11, 17–18
intrinsic value 26–7, 59, 166, 168–9, 170–2
"invisible hand" allusion of Adam Smith 82–3
Ireland 70–1, 171–2, 185
issues of the age 163–86
  bubble crises 170–6, *171*, *175*
  general principles 176–82, *179*, *181*
  paper vs gold crisis 182–6, *184*
  recoinage 165–70, *168*
Italy 103, 104
  See also Papal Mint, Rome

Jaucourt, Louis, chevalier de 27
Jefferson, Thomas 155
Jennings, Samuel 114
joint-stock companies 17–18
jokes about European commercial cunning 87, *87*

Kant, Immanuel 76
Kaplan, Steven 104
Keynes, John Maynard 73
Keys, Anne 110
King, Peter (Lord) 183
King, Rufus 155

Lahontan, Louis Armand, Baron de 87, 91
land 68, 95–6
land bank model 59, 164, 172–4, 180
Lange, Anne Françoise 126–7, *126*
Law, John
  Mississippi Scheme 174–5
  Money and Trade Considered 59, 173–4
Leonardo da Vinci 29
Levasseur, Thérèse 130
Linen Bank 103
Liotard, Jean-Etienne, *Still Life with a Lotto Game* 125
Lloyd, Edward 114
Locke, John 59–60, 61, 68, 79, 165–9
  Further Considerations Concerning Raising the Value of Money 165–6
  Second Treatise of Government 165
  Some Considerations of . . . Raising the Value of Money 165, 169
London, England
  minting of coins 31–3, 34, 37, 46
  personal use of money in 108–20, *109*, **116**, *117–18*, *120*
  political crises and coins 34, *35*

Low Countries 99
Lowndes, William, ... *an Essay for the Amendment of the Silver Coins* 165–6, 170
Luccasen, Jan 99

Madison, James 148
Malthus, Thomas 79
Mandeville, Bernard, *Fable of the Bees* 60
Marillac, Charles de 31
market, natural operation of 23–4
Marshall, Timothy 110–11
Mason, John 109
Massachusetts bills 140–1, 143, 146, 150, *150*, 156
Mather, Cotton 146, 157
McCulloch, J.R., *The Literature of Political Economy* 85
mechanical production of coins. *See* technologies of money
Melon, Jean-François 64
mercantile relations, conviviality of 69
mercantilism 5, 177
mercury and silver refining 40–1
Mestrelle, Eloi 31
Mexico, silver mines 39, 41
mill-money 31
Miller, Elizabeth 110
mines 39–40
mint marks 133
minting of coins 28–38, *30*, *34*, 41
Misselden, Edward 5, 81, 82
Mississippi Scheme 174–5
modern money 6–7, 12–16
money crops 147
money of account 97, 98
moneyers 29, 36–7, 38, 46
Montesquieu, Charles de Secondat, Baron de 62–4, *63*, 69, 70
morality of money 53–74
  benefits of money 67–73, *72*
  sociability of money 54–67, *56*, *61*, *63*, *65*
More, Thomas, *Utopia* 54
Morgan, Isabella 133
Morris, William 114
mortgages 95–6
Muldrew, Craig 57
multiple currencies 26, 109, 110, 112, 133

Mun, Thomas 85
Murray, Judith Sargent 152, 161
Muzzarelli, Maria Guiseppina 104

national debts 12, 23, 89, 159, 175
nature 84–6, 91
Neal, Larry 16
Netherlands 47, 100
Newman, Anne 112
Newton, Isaac 99
Newton, John 80
Northall, James 114
notaries and credit 104
notes of hand 97, 106, 113, 114, 115, **116**
novels about money 121, 128–9, 161

objects as currency 128–31, 140
Old Bailey Proceedings. *See* criminal trial records, money in
Olivier, Aubin 31
ontology of money 55

Pabst, Adrian 82
Pagden, Anthony 53, 78–9
Paine, Thomas 150
Pamstruck, Johan 47
Papal Mint, Rome 29, 30–1
paper money
  in art 127, *128*
  control of 164
  designs of 141–2, *142*, 149–50, *149–51*, 158, *158–9*
  development of 58–9, 60, 136–9, *138*, 140–2, *141–2*
  problems with 177–8, 180
  trust in 47–50, *49*, 57–8, 64, 66–7
  types of 102–7
  See also America, paper money in; Bank of England; banknotes (England)
Paper Money (character) 151–2, 153–4, 156, 157
Paris Mint 31, 32
pawnbrokers 104, 113, 114–15
Pennsylvania 48–50, *49*, 142, 152–3
penny (England) *34*, 45, 99, **116**, *117*
Pepys, Samuel 98
pickpocketing 109, *109*, 113
pieces of eight (Spain) 41, 135, *135*, 140
Pilkington, William Dawson 112–13

playing cards 48, 125–6
pockets 109
Pocock, J.G.A. 161
poems about money 147–8, 151–2, 154
political representation 160
poor people and money 100, 104
Pope, Alexander, *The Dunciad* 154–5
Pope, Elizabeth 95–6
Potosí, Bolivia 39–40, 42
Potter, William 57–8, 67–8
power in society, decentralization of 68–9
primitive mind and a secular economy 86–93, *87*
primitive money 135, 140
probate accounts, debts in 101–2, *101*
Protestant abstraction 91
prudence, discourse on 88–90
public bonds 8–9, *10*
public debt 6–7, 8–12, 16–17

quantity theory of money 174, 176, 177, 178, 179

Rammage, David 37
Ramsey, David, *History of the American Revolution* 158–9
Randolph, Peyton 146
reales (Spain) 41, 135, *135*, 140
recognition of coins 131
recoinage 33–4, 35, 38, 60, 68, 99, 165–70, *168*
refining technologies 40–1
representation, political 160
Revere, Paul 150, *150*
Revolutionary War 150–2, *150–1*, 157
Ricardo, David, *The High Price of Bullion* 183–4
rights of creditors 11–12
ritual and religion, secularization 75–94
  division between money and the religious 77–86, *81*, *84*
  primitive mind and a secular economy 86–93, *87*
Robert, Hubert 125
Robertson, John 73
Robertson, William 91–2
Rothschild, Emma 82
Rousseau, Jean-Jacques 71–3, *72*, 91, 130

Royal Bank of Scotland 138–9, *138*
Royal Mint, London 31–3, 34, 37, 46

satires of money 71, 153–5
Schumpeter, Joseph 172
Schwab, Marx 31
Scotland 32, 66, 90, 103, 138–9, *138*, 174
screw-press minting 29–30, *30*
scriveners 95, 96, 106, 114
secularization in the Enlightenment 77–86, *81*, *84*
self-interest 9, 17–18, 58, 64
Semer, John 95
sending money abroad 101
Shell, Marc 148–9
shilling (England) 116–17, **116**, *117–18*, 119, *120*, 131–2
shoplifting 109, *109*, 112
shopping 122–3
shortages of coinage 98–9
sign, money as a 62–6
silver coins 42
silver mines 39–41
Simmel, Georg 74, 148
slavery 18, 80
slaves, in mining 39–40
small change 42–7, *44*, 99, 101
Smith, Adam 66–7, 68, 69, 79, 81–3, 101
  Wealth of Nations 120, 149, 173, 181–2
Smith, Samuel 110
sociability of money 54–67, *56*, *61*, *63*, *65*
Sonenscher, Michael 104
South Sea Company 17, 18, *19*, 175
Spain 98, 103
  See also pieces of eight (Spain)
Speke, John Hanning 93
steam-powered coining 44–6, *45*
Stern, Julia 161
Steuart, Sir James, *Inquiry into the Principles of Political Oeconomy* 179–81
Stewart, Dugald 90
stolen money. *See* criminal trial records, money in
Stubbs, John 133
superstition 92
supply of money 98–9
Surinam 48
Sweden 47, 100

INDEX

Swift, Jonathan
    Drapier's Letters 171–2
    Gulliver's Travels 71
    A Modest Proposal 71
sympathy and financial independence 161

talking money in literature 121
    See also Paper Money (character)
Taylor, Charles 76, 83
technologies of money 25–52
    mechanical coining 28–38, *30*, *34*
    mines and mints in the Americas 38–42
    paper money and trust 47–50, *49*
    small change and industrial minting 42–7, *44–5*
thaler (Maria Theresa, Austria) 134–5, *134*
thefts from a specified place 109, *109*, 110–11, 112
theories of money 5–6
Thornton, Henry, *Enquiry into the . . . Paper Credit of Great Britain* 183
time, thought about 86, 88, 90
tobacco 140, 147
tobacco notes 140
token money 43
tokens 44, 100
Tower Hill mint, London 46
Tower of London mint 31–3, 34, 37
trade cards 123
trade coins 134
translation between religious and secular economies 83–4
trial records. *See* criminal trial records, money in
tricks played on American Indians 87, *87*

Trumbull, John
    The Anarchiad 154–5
    M'Fingal 151–2
Tucker, Josiah 79

usury 22

value of coins 133
value of money 26–7, 55, 59, 166, 168–9, 170–2
variety of money 128–31
Varin, Jean 32
Veblen, Thorstein 82
venality of money 73
Vigée-Lebrun, Elisabeth, *Marie Antoinette en chemise* 122
violent theft 109–10
visual culture of money. *See* art and representation

wages 39–40, 43–4, 100, 101–2
Watteau, Jean-Antoine, *Gersaint's Shopsign* 122–3, *123*
wealth in America 152
Weber, Max, *The Protestant Ethic and the Spirit of Capitalism* 78
Weiss Smith, Courtney 79
Wenham, Mary 109
Wennerlind, Carl 18
West, John 113
Whalan, John 112–13
Winstanley, Gerrard 54, 58
Wise, John 148, 156–7
Wood, Gordon S. 161
Wood, William 171